Rhetorical Philosophy and Theory
Series Editor, David Blakesley

Other Books in the Rhetorical Philosophy and Theory Series

Seduction, Sophistry, and the Woman with the Rhetorical Figure
Michelle Ballif

Kenneth Burke and the Conversation after Philosophy
Timothy W. Crusius

Breaking Up [at] Totality: A Rhetoric of Laughter
D. Diane Davis

Rhetoric as Philosophy: The Humanist Tradition
Ernesto Grassi

Unending Conversations: New Writings by and about Kenneth Burke
Edited by Greig Henderson and David Cratis Williams

Rhetoric on the Margins of Modernity: Vico, Condillac, Monboddo
Catherine L. Hobbs

Gorgias and the New Sophistic Rhetoric
Bruce McComiskey

Defining Reality: Definitions and the Politics of Meaning
Edward Schiappa

Where Writing Begins

Where Writing Begins

A Postmodern Reconstruction

Michael Carter

Southern Illinois
University
Press
Carbondale

Printed in the United States of America
06 05 04 03 4 3 2 1

Library of Congress Cataloging-in-Publication Data
Carter, Michael, 1950 Aug. 8–
Where writing begins : a postmodern reconstruction / Michael Carter.
p. cm. — (Rhetorical philosophy and theory)
Includes bibliographical references and index.
1. Rhetoric—Philosophy. 2. Rhetoric—Study and teaching. 3. Postmodernism.
I. Title. II. Series.
P301 .C29 2003
808'.001—dc21 2002151921
ISBN 0-8093-2520-9 (alk. paper)

Printed on recycled paper. ♻

The paper used in this publication meets the minimum requirements of American National Standard for Information Sciences—Permanence of Paper for Printed Library Materials, ANSI Z39.48-1992. ∞

For Janice M. Lauer,

who asked the question
to begin with

Contents

Preface

Sidney I. Dobrin poses a critical question for the field of composition, one that is central to the field but one that we have tended to ignore: "[W]hat is writing?" (9). He says that in ignoring this question we have neglected what it is that defines us as a field, "the 'thingness' of writing, as an object of study in need of serious conception and re-conception" (8). For the first half of the forty-year history of composition, he points out, our focus was on how to teach writing, not on writing itself. Then came the theoretical turn, with its emphasis on writing as social, political, and cultural (re)production and its agenda of student empowerment. But Dobrin argues that this move from pedagogy to theory was not about theorizing writing itself but theorizing writing as something else, as social, as political, as cultural (2–5). If we are to claim writing as the center of what we do, he says, we need to theorize writing itself, "not a unified, conclusive theory of writing, but theories of writing that consider writing as writing" (9).

That's what this book aims to do. But how do we theorize writing itself? What questions can we ask that could lead us toward an understanding of writing, not writing as something else but writing as writing? Such a question must somehow direct our gaze upon "the 'thingness' of writing." It must disrupt our ruling assumptions about writing, allow us to see writing anew.

The question I ask here is, Where does writing begin?

There is something compelling about beginnings. It may be that the first philosophical question any of us utters is "Mommy, where did I come from?" To a parent, this question may seem uncomfortably pragmatic, but there is a deeper, ontological sense at work here, an understanding that I am and therefore I must have a beginning. Perhaps it was at the same stage in the development of humankind that we began to wonder about our beginnings. Our distant ancestors would look at themselves, their family and tribe, their world, acutely conscious of their being, and ask, "Where did it all begin?" Among our earliest stories are those of beginnings. And we experience beginnings over and over in the form of certain rituals, the Fourth of July, the Jewish Seder, and the Christian Eucharist, for example, rituals of beginnings. What we claim and celebrate as a beginning says much about who we are, how we interpret the world, what our values are.

In this book, I apply that same consciousness of beginnings to writing. But I'm not asking, Where *did* writing begin? That's a historical and archaeological question that is better left to historians and archaeologists. Rather, because I am interested in writing as writing, I am asking a different question, Where *does* writing begin? This seemingly innocent question takes on greater significance because where we say writing begins has important implications for how we understand what writing is and what the good of writing is, issues of being and value. By its beginnings, writing is defined: the point at which it can be said to exist, can be identified, can be distinguished from not-writing. And by its beginnings writing is valued: a worth that is intrinsic to writing itself, not in any end it achieves outside the act of writing but in its beginnings, in and of itself.

My goal, then, is to apply the principle of beginnings to Dobrin's question, What is writing? As I explore what writing is, however, I also find myself wondering about teaching writing, not *how* to teach writing but what teaching writing is and what the good of it is, further questions of being and value. I think it is possible and even beneficial to understand writing outside the context of teaching writing. I also think it is more meaningful for those of us who profess writing to take the next step and seek to understand teaching writing itself as it is reconstructed on a fresh understanding of writing itself. Thus, I will look at both writing and teaching writing from the perspective of where writing begins.

There are three broad patterns—conceptual, structural, and methodological—woven together in this book. The conceptual pattern may be described as deconstruction and reconstruction, which I've taken from the reconstructive postmodern thought of David Ray Griffin and others who have been influenced by the process philosophy of Alfred North Whitehead. Briefly, these scholars believe that postmodernism is, for the most part, deconstructive, meaning both that it is heavily influenced by the Derridian critique of logocentrism and that it offers no possibility of a positive response to that critique. It stops at deconstruction. Constructive or reconstructive postmodernism has emerged from a frustration with both modernism and deconstructive postmodernism and offers itself as an alternative to both. It accepts the deconstruction of the modern but seeks to build on the ashes of that negative movement an affirmative philosophy that is between modernism and deconstructive postmodernism.

One of my aims for this book is to offer a reconstructed postmodern understanding of writing and of teaching writing. My focus on beginning is appropriate to this goal because beginnings are both deconstructive and reconstructive. They tend to destabilize things, to undermine structures of order. But beginnings also reconstruct new structures of order on the ruins of the old. Asking where writing begins deconstructs our usual conceptions of writing and then takes advantage of that deconstructive movement to reconstruct a new conception. I will proceed through three cycles of deconstruction and reconstruction in the three main parts of *Where Writing Begins:* Beginning, Writing, and Teaching Writing.

The structural pattern for this book is described by the dialectical interplay of the terms *writing* and *beginning.* Indeed, the question, Where does writing begin? invites such an interplay, each term set against and thus undefining and redefining the other. In part one, I set writing against beginning. Asking where writing begins deconstructs the whole idea of the beginning, our assumptions of beginning as a starting point of a process or the origin of an existence; writing destabilizes both assumptions and in the process is itself destabilized. In chapter 1, I show that there is no absolute starting point for writing, and in chapter 2, I demonstrate that there is no originating foundation for the existence of writing. Writing has no beginning.

If the question of where writing begins is to have any meaning at all, given the deconstruction of the beginning, it must be based on a reconstructed understanding of beginning. That is what I propose in the remaining chapters of part one. In chapter 3, I sketch out a radically different way of understanding beginnings, suggested by the ancient Greek philosophical concept of *archê:* the disruptive event that occurs at the intersection of two opposing forces and possesses the potential for new creation, beginnings. Chapter 4 is an investigation of this conception of beginnings in dialectical theory, a modern correlative of *archê,* and chapter 5 is an exploration of twentieth-century attempts to generate what I call an "archelogical" dialectic, a reconstructed understanding of beginnings.

Part two consists of the dialectical interplay of beginnings as set against writing. The question of where writing begins changes significantly when the beginning is refigured as *archê*. Beginnings are not innocent; they challenge the idea of a neutral starting point or a stabilizing principle of origin. Thus, pressing the question of where writing begins has the effect of deconstructing writing, challenging our assumptions of its being and value. In chapter 6, I take up the postmodern deconstruction of the definition of writing and offer a reconstructed postmodern definition based on beginnings, a shift from the stability and authority represented by visible language to writing as a destabilizing event with creative potential. And in chapter 7, I consider the concept of creativity as a way of arriving at a new sense of the good or worth of writing, a shift from the modernist locus of value as extrinsic to writing—in its ends, what it can accomplish—to a reconstructed postmodern locus of value as intrinsic to writing.

Part three takes up the issue of teaching writing. The dialectical movement that started by redefining the beginning in terms of writing, and then writing in terms of beginnings, now focuses on the interplay of both terms redefined. In this third section of the book, the issue of where writing begins shifts from the act to the institution, from writing to teaching writing. In chapter 8, I explore the definitional issues surrounding the teaching of writing by asking the question, Should writing be taught? Chapter 9 is an investigation of the problem of the ethics of teaching writing; I suggest a reconstructed theological sense of ethics that lies between the modern and the deconstructive postmodern.

This book is written, then, at the intersection of writing and beginning. Each challenges, frames, and refigures the other. In a complicated way, each acts as a mirror for the other, and in this pattern of mutual reflections, as each defines and is defined by the other, identities become unstable and start to shift. In this dialectic, I hope that readers come to see beginning differently and then through the lens of this new understanding of beginning come to see writing and teaching writing differently.

The methodological pattern is, I have to admit, a comic form. But comedy is appropriate for a theme of deconstruction and reconstruction and for the play of confused identities of beginning and writing. This comic methodology is best described by Stephen M. North, who divides the knowledge makers in the field of composition into three categories: Practitioners, Scholars, and Researchers (following North's capitalization). My work doesn't fit the first group, practical knowledge makers, nor the third, empirical knowledge makers. That leaves the Scholars, who comprise three subgroups: Historians, Philosophers, and Critics. In terms of this classification scheme, my methodology seems to correspond most closely to the second group, the Philosophers of Composition *(Making)*.

Now I must say that describing my efforts here as a philosophy sounds embarrassingly pretentious to me. When we think of a philosophy, we tend to think of grand systems built on firm foundations, typically billing themselves as *the* philosophy of something. Examples familiar to many of us are E. D. Hirsch's *The Philosophy of Composition* and George Campbell's *The Philosophy of Rhetoric.* This kind of philosophy is not what North—nor I—has in mind. Indeed, his none-too-flattering depiction of the philosophical method seems more like a caricature than a serious portrait. But it is, I think, an apt caricature: it certainly matches the key points of my own methodology and, more important, it keeps us from misinterpreting philosophy as the search for Truth. The philosophical method itself undercuts such philosophical pretensions.

North points to three characteristics of this method: establishing a problem, finding premises, and making conclusions.[1] As to the issue of where philosophers find problems to work with, North observes that most philosophizing about composition starts out by trying to answer practical questions but ends up instead considering the assumptions on which a practice is based. From an inquiry into what to do in teaching writing, the method shifts to an inquiry into the fundamental presuppositions of what we do in teaching writing (*Making* 100–101). As this description suggests, we could think of such researchers as accidental philosophers, like accidental tourists, waking up and finding themselves in a strange land. That's what happened to me.

Many years ago, when I first started looking into the beginnings of writing, my goal was to find effective methods for helping students begin to write. After spending a lot of time trying to solve what should have been a fairly simple problem, I realized that there must be a lot more to it than I had originally thought. I was making certain assumptions about beginnings: that a beginning was a discrete aspect of writing, separable somehow from other aspects of writing; that a beginning was a simple chronological necessity for any process and therefore also for writing; and that a beginning could be defined and categorized and judged for relative effectiveness. As I explored more deeply into beginnings, however, I discovered that all my assumptions were false, residing in a highly simplistic view of beginnings.

I also realized, much to my surprise, that inherent in this simplistic view of beginnings was an equally simplistic view of writing. An inquiry into where writing begins exposes certain key assumptions about writing, what it means to write and the good of writing. When I stumbled onto these assumptions about writing, my question shifted from the practical to the philosophical; I became an accidental philosopher. I realized that my larger question—Where does writing begin?—contained within it two other questions: what does it mean to write and what is the value of writing?

Even accidental philosophers need to find premises for their arguments. North, in his treatment of the next characteristic of philosophizing about composition, notes that philosophical premises in composition are usually found by "foraging" in other disciplines, a term whose disparaging connotations he admits (*Making* 102–5). *Foraging* means not only wandering in search of food but also plundering and looting. The latter activities seem more appropriate to me. North describes it this way:

> [T]he Composition Philosopher makes a foray into some field outside Composition itself, works to reach some expertise in it, then returns ready to work out an argument about the nature of doing, learning, or teaching writing on the basis of the foraged premises. (102)

I confess that I have foraged far and wide—and, it may sometimes seem, indiscriminately—for premises. Such extensive foraging was necessary because I had to philosophize not only about writing but also about beginning. I had assumed that my foraging would be rather limited, that I would find a ready-made understanding of beginning itself I could then apply to a reconstruction of writing itself. But I discovered that we in our culture have all but completely forgotten about beginnings, having a far greater interest in ends, bottom-line utility. So I took up my sword and sought booty of beginnings in many fields: theology, astrophysics, ancient Greek philosophy, dialectical theory, and scientific chaos theory, to name some of the more prominent ones.

Another feature of philosophizing about composition that North points to is the tendency to make the leap from dispassionate discourse about premises to advocacy of some sort of reform or action based on the premises. The problem comes when the philosopher stops philosophizing and goes to preaching; the premises take on an inappropriately moral character, and philosophy slides into polemic (111–15). Again I plead guilty. Though it is not my intention to advocate any particular teaching strategies in this book, I am interested in reforming the way we conceive of writing and the teaching of writing. I think there is a lot at stake here. The teaching of writing is not morally neutral; how we understand and justify what we do has important ethical consequences for our teaching. Indeed, it may be true that the best justification we have for teaching writing is moral. So there is no way I can remain disinterested and avoid stepping over that line between philosophy and preaching.

It's certainly not difficult to miss, in this depiction of philosophizing about composition, North's critique of it. He considers this brand of inquiry diffused and unpredictable and unfounded, a "second-order" form of knowledge making, meaning that its objects of study are the ideas and findings of other inquirers. Unlike historians, critics, or empirical researchers—with their historical documents, culturally significant texts, and reliable observations—Philosophers of Composition have only what they can haul in from chancier seas. And it's all so solipsistic: "the mind studying its own operations, the rational study of rational practices" (*Making* 60). It's just hard to take philosophizing all that seriously.

However unflattering it may be, I think North's critique is not only justified but also, for my purposes, useful: it emphasizes the comic nature of both philosophizing and beginnings. The accidental philosopher, the far-ranging forager, the polemicizing preacher—these are all comic characters, each one a little absurd, caught up in an unlikely common enterprise that gets the comedy going. But comedy, when it's done well, has the power to destabilize and subvert our usual way of looking at things and to reconfigure them afresh in a new relationship, a wedding. That's what beginnings are all about, the deconstruction—the disruption, the discontinuity, the comic turn—that leads to a reconstruction, something new. The method, in this case, is also the message.

Together, these three patterns—the conceptual, the structural, and the methodological—provide the framework for this book on writing and beginnings. However, I feel obliged to post a warning: "There is always the danger," Edward Said says, "of too much reflection upon beginnings" (76); "Once you start thinking this way about beginnings," Kenneth Burke adds, "you discover that they are to be found everywhere you turn" ("De Beginnibus" 31). The danger, as Said and Burke discovered, is that as we use beginnings as an instrument for undoing other things, beginnings may also, at some point, begin to undo us.

Acknowledgments

Many people deserve thanks for contributing in different ways to this book. They include

David E. Blakesley, editor of the Rhetorical Philosophy and Theory series at Southern Illinois University Press, for his faith in the project and his insightful comments on the manuscript

Karl Kageff, a senior sponsoring editor at SIU Press, who recognized the potential value of the manuscript and shepherded it through the publication process

Chris Anson, Deanna Dannels, Stan Dicks, Cindy Haller, Carl Herndl, Steve Katz, Susan Katz, Patricia LaCoste, Brad Mehlenbacher, Carolyn Miller, Nancy Penrose, Dave Rieder, Jason Swarts, and many other present and former colleagues at North Carolina State for the intellectual stimulation and warm friendships that have made it such a productive place to work

Carolyn Miller and Steve Katz, who read portions of the manuscript and helped me to understand where it was going, and Steve also for helping me with the Hebrew

members of the theological forum at White Memorial Presbyterian Church in Raleigh and its leaders, Alan Blatecky and Dan Durway, for providing an environment for open-minded and open-ended discussion of theological issues

countless others—friends, relatives, professional colleagues, complete strangers—who made the mistake of asking what I was working on and then were gracious enough to listen to me

and, of course, Jean.

Where Writing Begins

Introduction: Beginnings

> Beginnings are hardest: the beginning of a sentence, of a paragraph, of a section, of a stanza, of a whole piece. This is when you spend the most time not-writing: sitting, staring off into space, chewing the pencil, furrowing your brow, feeling stuck. How can you write the beginning of something till you know what it's the beginning of? Till you know what it's leading up to? But how can you know that till you get your beginnings?
>
> —Peter Elbow, *Writing Without Teachers*

Beginnings are hardest. That's one of the commonplaces of writing. Peter Elbow captures so well the familiar outward manifestations of beginning to write, being stuck in that uncomfortable space between not-writing and writing. I find it very interesting that so many of our cultural images of what it means to be a writer focus on this point of acute anxiety. The writer stares fixedly, frustration growing, at a blank page. The writer rips sheets of paper from a typewriter, the nearby wastebasket overflowing with crumpled wads of failed beginnings. An updated version of this image is the mocking wink of a cursor in the upper left-hand corner of the blank space of a blank computer screen. However we picture it, beginnings have played a prominent role in the lore of writers: writing is hard; beginnings are hardest.

When you stop to think about it, though, these cultural representations of beginning to write are odd. Why do we conceive of writing this way? I can think of no other act or skill in which beginnings are invested with such moment. In most other pursuits, beginning is understood as the commencement of learning, when you are a beginner. Beginning may be hard, but you typically pass out of the beginner's stage as you master the rudiments of the act. Beginning is associated with the initiate, the novice.

But writing is different. Freshman composition textbooks, for example, are full of advice and strategies for beginning writing, advice and strategies for people who have been writing for at least twelve years. And those cultural representations of beginning to write are not about beginning writ*ers* but experienced writers beginning writ*ing*. Beginnings are hardest even for many proficient writers.

When we think about where writing begins, we are no longer using the concept of beginning in the conventional sense of the beginning of a learning process, learning to write. Our usual understanding of beginning shifts from beginning to beginning*s*. Notice that what Elbow describes as hardest is beginning*s*. We are not talking about the beginning of the process of learning to write but a recurrent state associated with writing. Indeed, it's difficult even to say what it means to be truly a beginning writer except that all writers are, in a sense, beginners. Writing is marked by beginnings.

In his inaugural lecture at the Collège de France on 2 December 1970, Michel Foucault addressed the issue of beginnings:

> I wish I could have slipped surreptitiously into this discourse which I must present today, and into the ones I shall have to give here, perhaps for many years to come. I should have preferred to be enveloped by speech, and carried away well beyond all possible beginnings, rather than have to begin it myself. I should have preferred to become aware that a nameless voice was already speaking long before me, so that I should only have needed to join in, to continue the sentence it had started and lodge myself, without really being noticed, in its interstices, as if it had signaled to me by pausing, for an instant, in suspense. Thus there would be no beginning, and instead of being the one from whom discourse proceeded, I should be at the mercy of its chance unfolding, a slender gap, the point of its possible disappearance. (51)

These are the opening words of "The Order of Discourse." Though this piece has been much cited and much discussed, it takes on a different cast when placed in the context of beginnings.

What Foucault is acknowledging in this beginning is the strong desire to be able somehow to begin without beginning, the fantasy of sliding smoothly into the stream of discourse without so much as a ripple to call attention to oneself. "I think many people have a similar desire to be freed from the obligation to begin," he says, "a similar desire to be on the other side of discourse at the outset, without having to consider from the outside what might be strange, frightening, and perhaps maleficent about it" (51).

In opposition to this desire to escape all beginnings, Foucault points to the institution, which "solemnises beginnings, surrounds them with a circle of attention and silence, and imposes ritualised forms on them, as if to make them more easily recognizable from a distance" (51). The institution seeks to counteract the anxiety of beginnings by imposing an order that seems to domesticate discourse. It creates the illusion that any power that discourse possesses is actually derived from the institution (51–52). The institution, then, makes discourse safe for beginnings.

The irony of the institutional response, as Foucault acknowledges, is that the exquisite attention it pays to beginnings—the way it formalizes them, parades them in the open for all to see—is a response to the same anxiety of beginning that generates the desire to escape beginnings altogether. All that formalization of beginnings is actually a way of making us *less* aware of beginnings and thus feel more in control of discourse. And the irony is doubled, of course, because Foucault's own desire to slip unnoticed into this discourse is pronounced in an institutionalized ritual of beginnings that has been imposed by the ancient tradition of the European academy.

What is it about beginnings that provokes such anxiety? We can find hints of an answer in "The Order of Discourse." As I mentioned earlier, Foucault describes the longing to avoid beginnings as engendered by the desire to enter discourse "without having to consider from the outside what might be strange, frightening, and perhaps maleficent about it" (51). A beginning, then, places us, at least momentarily, outside discourse, between discourses, at a point both inside and outside discourse, both engaged and removed. Like Foucault, we find ourselves in that uncertain place between desire and institution, a place where the raw power of discourse is fully exposed. It is this position of doubleness and betweenness that generates the anxiety of beginnings: "anxiety at feeling beneath this activity (despite its greyness and ordinariness) powers and dangers that are hard to imagine" (52).

Desire and institution are, thus, reasonable responses to that anxiety, to what Foucault diagnoses as our culture's logophobia,

> a sort of mute terror against these events, against the mass of things said, against the surging-up of all these statements, against all that could be violent, discontinuous, pugnacious, disorderly as well, and perilous about them—against this great incessant and disordered buzzing of discourse. (66)

Desire represents the yearning for reprieve, to avoid the terror of beginnings. The institution represents the hope for safety, a way to suppress that terror. But that yearning and that hope only underscore the dread of beginning to write: to begin is to stand outside discourse, naked before its awful power.

Imagine yourself a member of the graduating class of 1962 at Bennington College, decked out in cap and gown, listening to a commencement speech by Kenneth Burke. Yes, Kenneth Burke. After a series of false starts, he finally gets to the business at hand:

> President Fels, Friends and Fellow-Students,
> With your permission, I should like to present a Commencement Address on the subject of Beginnings. (29)

You recognize in that subject the hackneyed grist of commencement speeches, but it's soon evident that Burke's "De Beginnibus" is no as-you-launch-your-ship-on-the-sea-of-life speech.

When you really look carefully at the subject of beginnings, he says, it ceases to be just about time.

> This is the point at which the purely temporal and the purely logical categories somehow merge. It's the point where we can suddenly surprise ourselves by discovering that we are not far from the realm of eschatology, thoughts on the nature of first and last things, thoughts that thus attain their most thoroughgoing form, perhaps, in theology, inasmuch as theology comes to a focus in the idea of God, and God may be thought of as both prime origin and ultimate end, both efficient and final cause. (31)

And this is the point at which you find yourself longing for that old sea-of-life analogy; at least that's something you can understand.

Burke's address to the class of 1962 is useful to us here and now because it captures so well the significance of beginnings and the way that concept fits into Burke's larger opus. As both temporal and logical, beginnings represent for Burke the terminological power residing in symbolic acts. Key terms, he says, are beginnings, for implicit in all terminology is a conclusion that is present from the beginning (31). Definitions are also beginnings, though Burke observes that "it is a somewhat ironic fact of history that often a writer does not clearly work out such 'beginnings' until quite late in his speculations or investigations" (32). Definitions, then, are principles that exist in beginnings but are not necessarily identified until much later—by the author or a critic—further emphasizing the paradoxical relations of temporal and logical priority.

And equations are beginnings, the deep structures embedded in all the constructions of human beings—works of art, political and philosophical theories, everything. These structures, which Burke also describes as "the automatisms of terminology," are the ideologies or warrants that ground our consciousness. "Such unobserved equations in our thinking set up the kind of 'beginnings,' or motivating principles, that can transform us into automata." His advice to the class of 1962 about the presence in their lives of such equations: "Don't expect to avoid it—but *watch* it" (32–33).

Beginnings, then, play an extremely important role in Burke's theories. They are the motives, the "motivating principles," upon which all symbolic action is presupposed. Another way of understanding the prominence of beginnings in Burke's philosophy is to imagine alternative titles to a couple of his works: "A Grammar of Beginnings," "A Rhetoric of Beginnings." As key words, definitions, and equations, beginnings occupy a central position in his understanding of the social nature of language and the linguistic nature of society; beginnings are the assumptions, the logical priorities, the ruling metaphors, the patterns of consciousness that ground all thought-action. Written into every beginning is a conclusion. Written into every beginning is a profound doubleness: both temporal and logical priority, the first and the last, Genesis and Revelation, origin and end.

Composition theorists have paid scant attention to where writing begins, probably because beginnings seem to belong only to the practical environment of textbooks. There are, however, a few notable exceptions. One is Kenneth Bruffee, whose article "Getting Started" opens with the commonplace of beginnings: "For years, I have noticed that for many students one of the hardest things about writing is getting started." But then he defines beginning more closely, not as sitting down and getting ready to write but as actually generating units of discourse (104). Bruffee is intrigued by the apparently universal difficulty of starting to write and sees in it the potential for a broader understanding of what it means to write. He uses Noam Chomsky's generative linguistic theories as a way of trying to get at that broader understanding.

Bruffee says that Chomsky's work is important because it portrays language as "nonlinear and discontinuous." Previous linguistic theories, he argues, had emphasized the linearity and continuity of language acts, always tying them to what came immediately before or to a sequential set of rules. Transformational grammar, however, is concerned with the *changes* that structure language. For Bruffee the implications of this understanding of language are powerful. Language is nonlinear and discontinuous in that, as he describes it, it both looks back at earlier units of language and looks ahead to units that have not yet been expressed. Transformational grammar, then, represents the special case of a more general explanation of the way language works: "[W]hat we say and the way we say it may be based in some way not only on what we have just said and what we said a few moments ago, but also on what we anticipate saying sometime later" (105–6).

Beginnings are so hard because they locate the writer at that point of discontinuity, between past meaning and future meaning. Bruffee points to the same problem that Elbow described: until we have some idea of the structure of what we are going to say, we cannot get started saying it. This observation holds true for all linguistic units, from starting a sentence to starting a book (106–7). It is at this point that the discontinuity and nonlinearity of language are most palpably revealed.

In a piece delightfully titled "It Was a Dark and Nasty Night It Was a Dark and You Would Not Believe How Dark It Was a Hard Beginning," Betsy S. Hilbert weaves together many different kinds of beginnings: beginning a school term, beginning writers, opening sentences, opening paragraphs, writers beginning to write. Beginning to write, she says, creates in the writer the sometimes debilitating self-consciousness of a public performance, a confusion between the person and the persona. The writer must put on the writer-mask but is at the same time very much aware that the *person* behind the persona is so exposed. It is little wonder, she observes, "that stage fright and writer's block bear remarkable similarities" (77).

Beginnings require "a psychic relinquishment of everyday existence" and "of emotional or ideological self." But few writers, especially basic writers, have had enough experience with "death and rebirths" to let go easily. Beginnings engender a "[f]ear of the unknown," a "fear of finding out what one really thinks" (77–78). Perhaps worst of all, beginning to write imposes on the writer the oppressive knowledge that the splendid fantasy of what a writer wants to say will always be thwarted by the messy materiality of words on a page. "For that reason, there is a strong tendency never to begin . . . not so much to avoid work but to avoid facing the truth of what happens to our ideas when they take real forms" (78).

In "Writing Assignments: Where Writing Begins," David Bartholomae takes yet another perspective on beginning to write. He starts out with the familiar paradox: "To begin to write is to 'know' what cannot be known" (300). He observes, however, that this view of beginning places knowledge inside the writer, that which must somehow be discovered in writing. What if, he asks, knowledge were thought of as existing outside the writer in the conventions and commonplaces of a discourse community? From this perspective, he says, "The struggle of the student writer is not the struggle to bring out that which is within; it is the struggle to carry out those ritual activities that grant one entrance into a closed society" (300).

This is, of course, an argument that is more fully worked out later in Bartholomae's well-known "Inventing the University."[1] In that latter piece, he observes that "the problem of a beginning is the problem of establishing authority" (157). What makes beginning to write so hard for students is that in order to establish authority for themselves as writers in an academic setting, they must pretend to be like us, to put on the mask (as Hilbert has it) of an academic. Such an approximation, however, places the writer in that difficult space marked off as a beginning:

> The movement toward a more specialized discourse begins (or, perhaps, best begins) both when a student can define a position of privilege, a position that sets him against a "common" discourse, and when he or she can work self-consciously, critically, against not only the "common" code but his or her own. (156)

Though Bruffee, Hilbert, and Bartholomae may disagree as to where it is that writing may be said to begin—generating units of language, opening sentences and paragraphs, assignments—all three acknowledge the difficulty of beginning to write, an anxiety that is generated at the point of disjunction. For Bruffee, that disjunction is represented in the discontinuity of linguistic acts, that awkward space between what the writer has said and what the writer is going to say. For Hilbert, it is represented in the dislocation of being both person and persona, of balancing one self with a contrived other. For Bartholomae, it is represented in the disruption that marks the invention of a writer's authority, between a privileged discourse and a "common" one. Beginnings are so hard because they define a space in which a writer is both and between opposing forces.

Edward Said's *Beginnings: Intention and Method* is a complex, challenging, and confusing work that reflects the complex, challenging, and confusing nature of beginnings. His primary interest in beginnings is in relation to literary criticism. For Said a beginning must be understood in terms of authorial intention, as "the first step in the intentional production of meaning" (5).[2] The literary critic finds that first step in much the same way as the literary author. Literature, Said suggests, should be thought of not as a sequential relationship of one work to previous works but as an adjacent relationship, discontinuous with what comes before (10–12). He argues that the critic shares a similar relationship with the previous tradition in criticism: in both modern literature and criticism, it is the repudiation of that tradition that becomes both intention and method of the critic (13).

Said's larger concern, which on the surface may seem somewhat outdated now (*Beginnings* was published in 1975), is an examination and defense of poststructuralist criticism. He uses the opposing concepts of beginnings and origins as a way of presenting the differences between poststructuralist and structuralist criticism. The idea of origins represents the preordained signifiers of structuralism, the assumption that we are written by, structured by, the discourses that surround us. Origins rule out any possibility of beginnings, the intentional act of meaning; Said refers to them as "theological." Beginnings are, in contrast, "eminently secular, or gentile, continuing activities. . . . [W]hereas an origin centrally dominates what derives from it, the beginning (especially the modern beginning) encourages nonlinear development" (372–73). The idea of beginnings represents a reversal, a discontinuity, an externality, and is thus emblematic of poststructuralist thought.[3]

Though Said's chief concern is literary criticism, his most interesting insights into beginnings come when he turns his attention to broader issues of writing. Beginnings, he says, have two aspects, which he labels transitive and intransitive. He describes the former as a "problem- or project-directed beginning," which assumes that "an individual mind wishes to intervene in a field of rational activity" (50). Said is aware that this idea of the transitive beginning, with its assumption of the intentional activity of the individual mind, runs counter to the structuralist position that we respond only to the impersonal orders of the discursive formations that surround us (50–52). He answers that argument by proposing the idea of "new beginning-as-construct" (56–65). In writing, beginnings occur in and through language; to begin is to enact a series of substitutions. "To use words," Said says,

> is to substitute them for something else—call it reality, historical truth, or a kernel of actuality. . . . [L]anguage is the beginning of *another* enterprise which, despite its seeming irrationality, has method. The difficulty of this method is that it does not imitate nature, but rather displaces it. This method does not center about a *cogito,* nor does it issue from the *cogito;* in fact, the individual subject has little more than a provisional authority to construct hypotheses (substitutions) bearing a perhaps distressing, perhaps seductive resemblance to delusions. Finally the logic of this method is not to be found in biological succession—that is, filiation—but as in the Oedipal complex, in departures and divergences from it or estrangements of it. (66)

Beginning to write, then, is marked by disjunction, the displacement by language of something else. The intention that is represented in writing is the beginning of something wholly other than what was. This is a very important argument because with it Said shows that beginnings are *in* writing, are the very method of writing. Writing is "an intentional structure signifying a series of displacements" (66). Intention, then, does not reside *outside* language, say, in the individual mind. Intention is the mind working in and with language, the potential that lies in language itself. Intention resides in the transitive form of beginnings—"new beginning-as-construct."

This transitive aspect of beginnings is the forward-looking dimension of writing. It is projective, aimed at an end, however vague and distant it be. The intransitive aspect of beginnings is the more occult, radical, conceptual sense of beginnings, which, Said says, "has no object but its own constant clarification" (72–73). Unlike the transitive dimension, which exists in the constructive quality of language, the intransitive is associated more with silence, that which is outside language, that which is "felt but not present." "The unknown," says Said, "is a metaphor for felt precedence that appears in glances backward, as an intimation of surrounding discomfort, as a threat of impending invasion, always ready to wreck our tenuously performed activity" (74).

Transitive and intransitive name two opposing natures of beginnings, two aspects that can be described separately but remain one in practice. One is a function of language, the other of silence; one fixes its gaze on a goal, while the other glances backward at what is perpetually lost; one "foresees a continuity that flows from it," as the other "challenges continuities that go cheerfully forward with *their* beginnings obediently fixed"; one is presence, the other absence; one is temporal, the other conceptual; one is "suited for work, for polemic, for discovery," the other "caught in a tautological circuit of beginnings about to begin" (76–77). Beginnings are both and between the transitive and the intransitive.

One of the most familiar profiles on ancient Roman coins is that of Janus, god of beginnings and thresholds, whose arresting image describes two faces peering in opposite directions. Actually, Janus long predates the Roman Empire. His shadowy origins lie in the animistic religions of the early residents of the Italic Peninsula. One of the most important gods of these peoples, Janus was associated with doorways or entrances of private houses or huts. Hence the double-faced head: on a threshold, you are neither in nor out but at once in and out, at once facing the past and the future, the known and unknown.

What's interesting, though, is evidence that this two-faced god was linked to the concept of beginnings before he came to be associated with thresholds. This link suggests that the ancient Italians thought of beginnings in terms of a paradoxical doubleness and betweenness, a condition ripe with mystery, fear, and auspice that required the doubly watchful countenances of this god. Thus the threshold itself could be understood as a later symbol of beginnings, an image that captured the complex and fearful idea of beginnings.

Janus was such a potent deity before the rise of Rome that he was later included in the pantheon of the Roman state religion, formally worshipped at a temple beside the Forum with, significantly, double doorways at either end. As the official god of doorways *(januae)* and archways *(jani)*, Janus was honored by a number of ceremonial archways in Rome, which were used as sacred points of departure for important enterprises, such as the ceremonial send-off of Roman legions. The beginnings of days, months, and years were reverenced to him; indeed, we still honor Janus's name in the first month of our year.[4]

Janus, with his attributes of doubleness and betweenness and association with thresholds, provides a powerful representation of beginnings as disjunction. The doorways of our own houses may have lost their awful mystery, but they still have symbolic value. A threshold marks a change, the end of one form of being and the beginning of another, both end and beginning. A threshold is not a junction, not a joining in the sense of a union of two entities to create a continuity. A threshold is, rather, a separation, a disjunction. As a condition of betweenness, it removes us from our normal sense of the continuity of time and space, quite literally a dislocation, a discontinuity. As doubleness, a threshold marks a space that is at once past and future, old and new, known and unknown. It is a disruption, a lacuna, an opening—to be both desired and feared.

Beginning to write is a threshold experience. It locates the writer in that disconcerting space defined by doubleness and betweenness. The ancient Italians seemed to understand well the source of the anxiety, even the terror, of beginnings and named it Janus. But the moderns I have looked at here have also called upon his image, even if they have not called upon his name.

Bruffee's language is particularly telling. Chomsky's notion of linguistic acts as nonlinear and discontinuous suggests to Bruffee "that if language units may 'look back' not only to immediately preceding units but also beyond those to earlier ones, they must also be capable of 'looking ahead' to language units yet to be uttered" ("Getting Started" 105). Hilbert describes beginning to write as that moment of awkward self-consciousness that comes with the realization of being both person and persona, between death and rebirth and between the fantasy of what the writer dreams of saying and the stubborn materiality of words. In Bartholomae it is that place between a privileged discourse and a "common" one, where writers must constantly negotiate authority. And Elbow describes beginning to write as that odd state of both writing and not-writing, where you can't begin until you have begun.

It is, as Said puts it, both the substitution of something wholly other and the fearful glance over the shoulder at what threatens to disrupt it; it is both constructive and deconstructive, both language and silence. For Burke, beginnings are fraught with anxiety because they bring us into the presence of the double nature of language, all symbolic acts bound to terminological ends in their prebeginnings.

Beginning to write is fearful because a beginning positions us, as Foucault suggests, on the threshold, at a point of disjuncture, between desire and institution, disjoined from discourse so that its terrible power is fully revealed. Yes, you would need a god both to embody and to palliate that terror.

Beginnings are hardest.

Part One
Beginning

1 At the Beginning: Starting Point

> The White Rabbit put on his spectacles. "Where shall I begin, please, your Majesty?" he asked.
>
> "Begin at the beginning," the King said gravely, "and go on till you come to the end; then stop."
>
> —Lewis Carroll, *Alice in Wonderland*

As the King does for the White Rabbit, we writing teachers find ourselves in the position of having to advise our students about where, and how, to begin. Beginning to write is, of course, notoriously difficult, especially for students, who must produce discourse on demand in artificial writing situations. They often suffer initial writer's block, continually stumbling over first sentences, finding nothing to write about, or returning obsessively to the assignment for inspiration or guidance. Alternatively, they may begin too easily, with shallow ideas that lead to shallow writing. It would be nice if we could simply say to them, "Begin at the beginning," but it's a lot more complicated than that.

A beginning may be understood as a starting point, the commencement of an act or process, the initiation of any discrete event, movement, or procedure that takes place in time. Because writing teachers work with students' writing in time, we have had to mark off starting points for writing and bring concrete strategies and helpful advice to those starting points. No matter what our theoretical or ideological bent is, few of us would deny that writing may be conceived, at least in part, as an event that takes place in time—and therefore must have a starting point.

So where does writing begin? Or rather, where do we *say* writing begins? Perhaps the best source for answering this latter question is writing textbooks, our richest repository of teaching techniques. Now, I recognize that few textbooks reside on the cutting edge of composition theory. Even Stephen North, who generally respects what he calls the Practitioners' lore, the collective wisdom of teachers, places textbooks on its outer edge because, he points out, they tend to obscure the experiential quality of that lore. They maintain a "catechetical function"; they are "talismanic," simplistic, propagandistic (*Making* 23–33).

For my purposes, however, textbooks are an ideal data base. They provide the best record I can find of what teachers over a wide expanse of time and theoretical inclination have said to students about beginning to write. Indeed, for better or worse, no other form of discourse in our field better represents the *institution* of composition than our textbooks. Thus, in addition to pointing out where writing begins, textbooks provide the opportunity to use those beginnings to assay the institution of writing and teaching writing.

A Survey of Textbooks

I surveyed seventy-five composition texts to find out what we've said about where writing begins. My search started out informally, just as a way to satisfy my curiosity about how writing teachers have dealt with beginnings. But once I got going, I had a hard time stopping. I picked up whatever textbooks came to hand in two academic libraries and in an office of freshman composition. Though I can't claim a rigorous sampling technique that would ensure any sort of proportional representation of textbooks, the sheer number ensured that I looked at a wide range of them. Almost all were designed as texts for freshman composition, though a couple of the older ones were intended for high school, and one or two more were designed for older adult learners for use outside the classroom. (The list of textbooks, with complete bibliographic information, is in the appendix.)

I skimmed each text, noting all references to a starting point for writing. Because my focus was on the beginning point for the writer, I ignored references to a beginning as an assignment, which typically comes from the teacher or other authority, not the writer; I wanted to know where we say the *writer* begins to write. I also paid particular attention to implicit as well as explicit chronologies of the writing process. Sometimes this focus required looking at what the author said the student should do "*before* writing." I interpreted that phrase as an indication that writing actually had its beginnings at the earlier point. I sometimes had to dismiss what authors explicitly said about beginnings in one place in the text because they set that point earlier elsewhere. In such cases, I accepted the earlier point in the process. For example, James M. McCrimmon, in the influential *Writing with a Purpose,* says that because good writing is always purposeful, the writer "must therefore always begin with a clear sense of purpose" (3). Later, however, he describes the choice of a subject as "a starting point" for writing in a process that goes like this: "choosing a subject, restricting it to a scope that can be treated with some thoroughness, selecting the material, and stating the purpose or dominant idea of the paper" (33). Choosing a subject, then, is chronologically prior, by several steps, to stating the purpose.

After collecting these writing chronologies, I reviewed them to identify certain repeated features that formed patterns for classification. I found that the books tended to fall into five groups: those that *(1)* had no reference to beginnings, *(2)* began with choosing and/or narrowing a subject, *(3)* began with finding a purpose, *(4)* began with recognizing a dissonance, and *(5)* began with observing experience.[1] I will describe these categories of starting points and present exemplary texts in each category.

1. *Textbooks that have no reference to beginnings.* It may seem strange to begin with a null set, but I think it is useful to look at what kinds of texts offer no guidance on beginnings. Generally speaking, such texts pay no attention to writing as an act in time. There are two kinds. One comprises highly formalistic texts that focus on descriptions of good writing, writing as an object to be gazed at and appreciated.[2] The second kind is made up of composition readers. Of the ten that I happened to review, eight have "writing" or "writer" in their titles, but it was clear that their focus instead tends to be on reading and reader. They all seek written responses regarding the reading, usually short answers, sometimes complex essays, but provide no concrete, chronological guidance for composing those responses.[3]
2. *Textbooks that begin with choosing and/or narrowing a subject.* This category is by far the largest, thirty-four texts, and seems to represent the most long-lived tradition of beginnings in composition. Some of the texts I looked at focused primarily on finding a subject (as distinct from narrowing one). A few texts describe writing as beginning with the choice of a subject but then provide only the criteria for recognizing a good one.[4] Other texts show students *where* they can look for subjects to write on, suggesting such sources as books, magazines, newspapers, dictionaries, encyclopedias, and personal experiences.[5] Generating lists of possible subjects is a strategy frequently recommended in texts. Other strategies include free association, keeping a journal, and unfocused freewriting.[6]

   After choosing a subject, the next step in the classic model of beginning to write is narrowing the subject. Many textbooks, however, assume a subject given in an assignment and portray the writing process as beginning with narrowing the subject. Either way, the texts I surveyed offer a number of strategies for narrowing or, as it is sometimes put, finding a topic within a broad subject, an act of moving the writer toward the specific. The student is variously advised to use tree diagrams, to make a list of her or his own characteristics that are particularly relevant to the topic, and to engage in brainstorming, focused freewriting, talking, and formulating relevant questions.[7]
3. *Textbooks that begin with finding a purpose.* A range of approaches is included under the aegis of purpose. One group of texts is clustered around the current-traditional standard of interpret-

ing purpose in terms of a thesis sentence.[8] Another approach, probably under the influence of McCrimmon, portrays purpose not just as a thesis sentence but as a more global concept that guides the writer in making other writing decisions. In McCrimmon, for instance, the writer's purpose is the controlling idea that directs planning, development, paragraphing, style, and revision. More typical, though, are texts that use purpose to guide the choice of an appropriate mode of discourse.[9]

A far different concept of purpose emerges in other texts: purpose as a function of goals that are derived from the rhetorical situation. Linda Flower's *Problem-Solving Strategies for Writing* exemplifies this concept of purpose. For the writer, she says, writing does not begin with a concern for the finished product. "Instead, your attention is focused on your goals as a writer, on what you want to do and say" (3). Writers begin to write by exploring a rhetorical problem, "a rather large, uncharted territory that contains you, your reader, your ideas, and all the things you could possibly do" (76). Strategies for exploring the rhetorical problem consist of creating an image of the problem and explaining the assignment to oneself (75–85).[10]

4. *Textbooks that begin with recognizing a dissonance.* This is the smallest group in my survey, consisting of only two texts and a brief mention in two others. This class hardly seems large enough to warrant a separate category, but it represents an important pedagogical departure from the others. The prototype of this approach in composition texts is Young, Becker, and Pike's *Rhetoric: Discovery and Change.* Writing is portrayed as a process of inquiry that begins with "a feeling of uneasiness" or with "tensions," such as

> a paradoxical "fact" that doesn't make sense, a situation that is incompatible with a person's values, an apparent opposition of two respected authorities on an important issue, the seeming inadequacy of a strongly held theory, a clash of two sets of values to which a person is deeply committed.[11] (72)

On the surface, this category may seem to be closely related to, perhaps even a variation of, the purpose category, but the differences are significant, highlighted in dissimilarities in the concept of problem. Whereas the previous category portrays a problem in terms of a goal or an end state, what the writer hopes to accomplish, the focus of the dissonance category is on the problem as an initiating state. And whereas purpose texts identify a problem as a function of a rhetorical situation, the dissonance approach analyzes a problem as an incongruity that sparks inquiry. As a procedure, the former directs writers' attention toward an end state, where they need to be; the latter directs writers' attention toward an initiating state.[12]

5. *Textbooks that begin with observing experience.* The texts in this category describe writing as beginning with a generalized encounter with the writer's experience. The previous group of texts portrays a more specific engagement, recognizing dissonances. The observation texts, though, are more indefinite, initiating writing by encouraging students to engage in both formal and informal observation of their experience. The most dramatic example I found of such a text is Paull and Klingerman's *Invention: A Course in Pre-Writing and Composition,* two-thirds of which is given over to heightening student writers' awareness of their experience through various kinds of informal writing: using a journal, reporting on a happening, engaging in written meditations, and generating written encounters with nonrepresentational art forms. This is not prewriting in the conventional sense; it is writing for the sake of enhancing observation. It is only in the last third of the book that students are encouraged to rework and expand their observations into formal essays.

   For Donald Murray in *Writing to Learn,* writing is an act of both collecting and recollecting, the former an engagement with experience and the latter the formal act of writing that does something with that experience. Collecting, he says, "may be done in response to living or in response to an assignment, but collecting information is the beginning of the writing process" (17–18). In a chapter on collecting, he offers students some strategies for collecting, such as brainstorming, mapping, freewriting, and making tree diagrams (15–48).[13]

What a Starting Point Says about Writing

There is nothing particularly new in this taxonomy of starting points or in the teaching strategies associated with them, no dramatic discoveries here. But the value of this survey is not so much in the starting points themselves but in what the starting points tell us about writing and teaching writing: what we teach as the starting point of writing has a profound effect on the way we and our students understand both what it means to write and what is important about writing. Each beginning marks off a temporal space that projects a representation of writing. In other words, by saying "this is where writing begins" we are also saying "this is what writing is" and "this is the value of writing." The starting point for writing is, quite literally, the defining moment in the larger act of writing. I will test this proposition by exploring the way each of the starting points identified in the survey implicitly defines and values writing.

That a starting point is the defining moment of writing holds true even in those textbooks that ignore beginnings. Some years ago we would have described these texts as portraying writing as a product: writing is a form and therefore must be approached formalistically. The most obviously formalistic of these textbooks are those that seek only to describe the characteristics of good writing, usually in terms of grammatical correctness, the abstract ideals of unity and coherence, or principles of arrangement (typically the modes of discourse). Having no beginning, then, defines writing in terms of an idealized end state, a static presence on the page. For students, the act of writing is valued primarily, using Robert Connors's apt description of it, as a way of demonstrating the ability to generate "error-free writing and the ability to follow directions" ("Rise" 446).

Beginning with choosing and/or narrowing a subject, the second category, suggests a relatively limited definition of writing and value for writing. Most textbooks that follow this method distinguish between assignments in which no subject, or perhaps only very loose parameters for a subject, is given and those in which an assigned subject must be narrowed. When we understand the defining moment of writing as the act of choosing a subject, writing itself becomes an act of saying something about *something*. The entire act is characterized by the initiating moment of coming up with something to write about, the emphasis on choosing *a* subject. Writing, then, is portrayed as emerging out of a need for something to write about.

We may seek to justify this approach to beginning writing by pointing out that it is a necessary function of the bare artificiality of the writing classroom, but the problem is that such justification does not reckon with the value of writing implied by this starting point. The reason for writing becomes no more than an exercise, a kind of fill-in-the-blank-paper activity; the only purpose for writing is that writing was assigned. Moreover, this approach to starting to write gives students the impression that subjects are simply out there somewhere waiting to be found and that finding subjects for writing can be a rather random process. The ludicrous image of students leafing through encyclopedias and dictionaries in search of subjects to write on says it all.

Texts that describe writing as beginning with narrowing a subject portray writing somewhat differently. It is still very much a subject-oriented view of the process: the focus remains on what to write about. The defining moment, however, is finding something of suitable *specificity* to write about. Richard M. Coe points to some of the problems associated with this concept of beginning. One is that this procedure, like the preceding one, ignores any rhetorical purpose for writing. Second, it tends to lead the writer to relatively trivial topics, a result of narrowing a broad subject to increasingly specific aspects of that subject. Third, narrowing, when taken too far, "comes close to being a muzzling": it has the effect of discouraging students from grappling with bigger ideas. And fourth, Coe says that the timing for narrowing is usually wrong. Textbooks typically ask students to narrow a subject before any thought of a purpose for writing; a particular focus, he says, ought properly to follow from purpose (273–74).

Coe's critique indicates some of the problems with narrowing as the defining point of writing, both practical and conceptual. Though it may be true that, to a certain extent, narrower subjects promote more focused writing, beginning by narrowing paints a picture of writing that is itself quite narrow. The reason for writing is, as Coe suggests, trivialized, the act of saying something about something *smaller.*[14]

The third category of beginnings, finding a guiding purpose, is marked by the initiating act of forming a thesis or analyzing a rhetorical situation. The more limited version of this type is the one associated with the thesis. As the defining moment of writing, this act invests writing with a sense of purpose that tends to get lost in subject-oriented beginnings; writing is not guided by what to write about but by what the point of writing is. The thesis, however, carries with it a constricted sense of purpose, which in turn limits the definition and value of writing. It is purpose as defined by a message to deliver to the reader, the rationalist ideal of writing as an act of transferring a message from one person to another.

The other form of purpose, a function of a rhetorical situation, suggests a richer conception of writing. The defining moment of writing given by the textbooks in this category is the identification and analysis of the rhetorical situation as a way of determining the goals of writing. Thus, the act of writing is defined by this wider sense of purpose as delineated by the situation. The subject- and message-oriented concepts of writing are, in contrast, relatively text-based; that is, they define writing primarily in terms of producing a text. When writing begins by turning outward toward the rhetorical situation, however, it is defined by that situation; no longer the relatively isolated act of simply producing a text, writing becomes a part of the dynamics of a larger environment. And the goal structures of this larger environment influence the goal structures of writing. Given this starting point, writing may be understood as a goal-driven act whose goals are derived from the situation.

The next group of textbooks in the survey portray the beginning of writing as a dissonance. In Coe's discussion of focusing writing, he offers as an alternative to the narrowing strategy something akin to finding a dissonance, citing as an example Young, Becker, and Pike. Coe says writing that begins with a contradiction has the advantage of complicating the writer's thinking, of encouraging the writer to see in the conflicting perspectives the complexity of the world. He describes this approach as more philosophical because it induces students to go beyond simply resolving the contradictions, leading them instead to explore the truth that lies within those contradictions (275–76).

When writing is defined by the initiating act of recognizing and analyzing a dissonance, it becomes, as its advocates claim, an act of inquiry. This definition of writing is significantly different from seeing writing as a goal-directed act. Writing that begins by identifying a purpose for the writing is circumscribed by that sense of purpose; though the purpose may shift during the writing, the act of writing is understood in terms of achieving a goal. Writing that begins with an "uneasy feeling," however, is not initially defined by a goal state; the dissonance becomes a motivating force for exploration, and writing itself becomes an act of active wondering. Its value is identified with an initiating dissonance and the inquiry that dissonance has sparked.[15]

The last category of textbooks portrays writing as beginning with a generalized engagement with experience. In his article "Write Before Writing," Donald Murray describes this initiating act of writing as a heightened form of perception. "The writer's perception apparatus," he says,

> finds significance in what the writer observes or overhears or reads or thinks or remembers. The writer becomes a magnet for specific details, insights, anecdotes, statistics, connecting thoughts, and references. The subject itself seems to take hold of the writer's experience, turning everything that happens to the writer into material. (376)

Writing whose initiating act is the perception or collection of experience is defined by that act. Its value lies in its ability to make the writer more deeply conscious of experience.

This perspective is different in important ways from the previous definition of writing as inquiry. Inquiry is born out of a particular kind of engagement with experience. It is much more focused; it begins with a recognition of conflicting interpretations and moves from there to questioning. Dissonance depends on the recognition of contradiction in the writer's experience, but observation of experience requires no such contradiction. It is, as Murray's terms of *collection* and *perception* imply, a relatively undifferentiated approach to experience. The concept of writing that emerges from this starting point is clearly the broadest of all the categories.

I've been exploring the proposition that where we say writing begins has significant influence on the way we and our students conceive of writing, what it is and why we write. To explore the validation of that proposition, I have discussed the various starting points from the survey as defining moments for writing. Each starting point projects its own conception of writing:

Beginning by	*Implies a conception of writing as*
• ignoring the starting point	• a noun, idealized object
• choosing a subject	• saying something about *something*
• narrowing a subject	• saying something about something *smaller*
• writing a thesis sentence	• delivering a message
• analyzing the rhetorical situation	• responding to a rhetorical goal

- discovering dissonance
- encouraging an awareness of experience
- inquiry
- heightened experience

It should be clear from this discussion that some of these conceptions of writing are more suitable for teaching than others. There are probably additional, theoretically interesting starting points that have eluded my taxonomy. However, the relative quality of these conceptions and the inclusiveness of this taxonomy are not as important as the idea behind it: the way we approach beginning to write sends a message to students about writing. Given the lack of attention to beginnings in composition scholarship, however, I suspect that most of us are unaware of the pedagogical consequences of where we say writing begins. Instead, beginnings seem to be taken as simply a fact of temporal life. The starting points we choose for our students are more likely to be a result of convenience, necessity, or habit than of a carefully considered understanding of what writing is and why we write.

The starting point for writing is not, I contend, an innocent conceit. Time is not merely a neutral passage to be negotiated any way we can. Our designation of where writing begins carries with it assumptions that reach far beyond the simple matter of just getting students started.

On the Borderline Between Writing and Not-Writing

This chapter is an investigation of beginning as a starting point in time. This chronological understanding of where writing begins naturally invites a pedagogical perspective: Given that writing takes place in time and therefore must have a starting point, how do we identify and manage that starting point for students? But now I'd like to shift perspectives, from the pedagogical to the philosophical. I must admit to grander ambitions for this study of where writing begins, not just where we say writing begins for the purpose of teaching but where writing really begins, an absolute beginning.

The idea is that a chronology of beginnings holds the possibility of an ontology of writing, an exploration of what writing essentially is. The starting point for writing is not just a pedagogical necessity; more broadly applied, it also marks off a temporal borderline that distinguishes "writing" from "not-writing." In other words, it is a line in time that allows us to say "this is where writing begins" and consequently "this is what writing is." When we say where writing begins, we are also making a claim for where writing begins to be *writing* or, to put it differently, where writing begins to *be*. We delineate the temporal territory of writing by differentiating it from the territories of not-writing. The idea of starting point gives us a way to make such a demarcation and thus allows us to say with more conceptual precision what writing is.

An interesting problem arises, however, when I attempt to establish an ontological starting point for writing, a problem that is illustrated in my taxonomy. Each category delineates a different boundary of writing; as we go down the list of categories, each one pushes the temporal borderline farther back in time, claiming more and more territory for writing. The smallest temporal territory is claimed by the choosing-and/or-narrowing approach. That implied boundary line places the locus of writing very close to the basic act of generating *a* text, for which the most elementary need is having *a* subject. The territory is widened when the starting point is a sense of purpose, from writing as generating a text to writing as achieving some purpose by writing. In the textbooks that define purpose according to the thesis statement, that widening is not very far, but in those that interpret purpose in terms of the rhetorical situation, the widening is dramatic. When beginnings are located in the rhetorical situation, the boundaries of writing include all the characters and actions in the scene of writing. The idea of writing as beginning with dissonance places the borderline back even farther, widening the boundary again to claim the broader territory of conflicting interpretations recognized in the writer's experience. The locus is at its widest when the beginning point is established in the writer's general experience. The temporal territory claimed by writing teachers keeps getting larger and larger with each of these starting points.

Now I don't want to give the impression that there is some kind of insidious Manifest Destiny at work here, the composition specialist's imperialist dream that writing should stretch across the entire continent of consciousness. The problem is not in the taxonomy itself, either. Rather, the taxonomy provides a ready illustration of something more powerful at work here, a principle of temporal displacement, which means that no matter where you draw the line for marking off the beginning of an event in time, something occurred in advance of that line that influenced the event and thus should be included in it. This principle dooms my hope of founding an ontology in chronology. The borderline that marks the essential being of writing becomes wider and wider, to the point that writing has no essential being at all. Indeed, my search for beginnings is haunted by the statements of two textbook authors I placed in the observation group. Nevin K. Laib:

> In some sense [writing] may be said to begin long before one ever decides to write about a particular subject. The preparation for writing includes your education, experiences, and observations, as well as the immediate work that goes into developing an essay. (8)

Donald Murray: "Writing begins with all that we have known since we were born, and perhaps with a lot of knowledge that was born in us" (*Writing* 3).

Most writers and writing teachers would agree, to some extent, with these statements. It seems, then, that wherever I draw a line as a beginning point, I am ruling out some experience that pertains to writing. Suppose, however, I take Murray's implied borderline and declare the beginning of each act of writing at the birth of the writer. Not only would that make for an extremely awkward point for establishing a viable pedagogical starting point for writing, but I would probably have people accusing me of ignoring certain vital prenatal experiences or the experiences of the writer's parents that may bear on the writing. Now I realize that I have probably crossed over into the absurd, but that's just the point. No matter where I establish the chronological frontiers of the act of writing, the boundary line is ultimately arbitrary.

Here's a third quotation, this one from Mikhail Bakhtin: "The process of speech, broadly understood as the process of inner and outer verbal life, goes on continuously. It knows neither beginning nor end" (940). Bakhtin serves as a reminder that the principle of temporal displacement concerns more than the writer's psychology. Instead, Bakhtin's denial of a beginning (and an end) of writing comes from his belief that no individual utterance can ever stand on its own because it can "not be isolated from the historical stream of utterances" that composes inner speech, the profoundly social "conversation" of our thinking (940). "Any *utterance,* no matter how weighty and complete in and of itself, *is only a moment in the continuous process of verbal communication.* But that continuous verbal communication is, in turn, itself only a moment in the continuous, all-inclusive, generative process of a given social collective" (939). What we have then is a double displacement of all utterances (including writing) into two historical streams, what Bakhtin calls the verbal milieu—"i.e., made up of other verbal utterances"—and the extraverbal milieu—i.e., the social, and especially ideological, context that allows for, defines, and is defined by the utterance. There can be no beginning point that is not completely arbitrary for any utterance because it is inevitably displaced into the historical streams of preceding utterances and ideological constraints.[16]

Establishing a firm temporal borderline for writing is, therefore, impossible, as is my ambition to establish an ontology of writing, where writing begins *to be.* But this effort has been useful for what it reveals about the problematic nature of all chronological beginnings. The problem lies in time itself, with its powerful implications of causation. There is no point in time at which we can claim an absolute beginning, at which we can say that nothing preceding that point had an effect on what comes after. Indeed, it may not be stretching the point too far to say that to be able to identify an absolute beginning of any act of writing we would have to go back to the beginning of time.

The problem of any beginning in time, however, lies much deeper than causation. As explained by Stephen W. Hawking in *A Brief History of Time,* before Newton, Western science and philosophy had conceived of time and space as separate forces, each absolute and stable. Newton challenged the idea of absolute space, demonstrating that all entities with mass exist in relation to other entities with mass through the force of gravity. The movement of any entity is affected by and affects other entities. In Newton's universe, though space was conceived as relative, time remained absolute, unaffected by anything. All that changed in 1905 with the publication of Einstein's special theory of relativity, which proved that time is relative to velocity. But the most dramatic breakthrough came in 1915 with the general theory of relativity. Before that, Einstein had to dismiss gravity from his calculations, unsure of the relationship among time, velocity, and space. His general theory posited that space and time were not only each relative but also relative to each other, composing a four-dimensional warped or curved universe. The implications of such a universe are unsettling. Before 1915, time and space were thought of as stable, fixed existences in which and through which events occurred. Events themselves could have no effect on time and space (18–34). The general theory of relativity revolutionized our understanding of that relationship. According to Hawking,

> [s]pace and time are now dynamic quantities: when a body moves, or a force acts, it affects the curvature of space and time—and in turn the structure of space-time affects the way in which bodies move and forces act. Space and time not only affect but are also affected by events that happen in the universe.[17] (33)

I don't pretend to grasp fully Einstein's general theory, but it seems to me that it does help us understand the elusive nature of a starting point for writing. The very idea of a starting point presupposes a fixed and stable quality of time: writing occurs in and through time; time is a neutral quantity, a fixed standard by which we can establish the temporal boundaries of any discrete act, like writing, that takes place in time. However, if time is a function of space-time and space-time is affected by and affects all events, then time is anything but fixed and stable. There are no temporal boundaries, no beginnings in time. Events don't occur in and through time; rather, events exist in a complex relationship with time-space, each having its existence in the other. The act of writing both defines and is defined by space-time, both affects and is affected by space-time. Thus, there can literally be no absolute starting point for writing or for anything else in the universe except, perhaps, in the starting point of the universe itself.

I began this chapter with the assumption that writing takes place in time and therefore must have beginnings in time. But when pressed by my search for an ontology of writing in chronological reality, that assumption has come unraveled. There is no point at which we can say writing begins that is not entirely arbitrary. If we take the common definition of beginning as a starting point in time, then asking where writing begins deconstructs beginning.

The main problem, it seems, is the radically unstable nature of time. The idea of starting point presupposes a fixed and determined understanding of time, time as out there, unaffected by events that occur in time. There is, however, no standard time. Nothing happens *in* time; time is not an abstract, externalized environment in which and through which we pass our existence. Indeed, it is as true to say that events have a starting point in time as it is to say that time has a starting point in events. Time is relative. It is this undoing of time that undoes beginnings in time.

The undoing of time also creates troublesome implications for writing. In assuming time as fixed and stable, we also assume writing as a fixed and stable act in time. As my search for an ontological boundary for writing has suggested, however, writing is just as relative as time. Where we say writing begins is utterly discretionary because there is no absolute starting point for any act of writing. The implications of this statement are troubling for me. It suggests that what we do when we teach writing is invent writing. We believe that writing exists as a discrete and separable event in time and is therefore teachable. But when we look at writing in terms of the problematic nature of time, we realize that we have it backwards: it's not that the act of writing exists and thus lends itself to teaching; instead, it's that in teaching writing we arbitrarily declare a temporal existence for writing. It is the teaching that defines what it is that is taught.

This is not to say, of course, that people don't write, that people have not been writing for thousands of years. The act of writing, though, has a fluid temporal existence. We cannot define it, isolate it, mark it off from not-writing. That, however, is precisely what we've tried to do in teaching it, making a discipline of it. And in doing so, we may have, ironically, made writing more difficult for our students. By making the act of writing the special object of the writer's attention, removed from the normal motivations, constraints, and rewards of writing outside the writing classroom, we may have invested it with a daunting hyperreality, turning it into an overly complicated performance that exists for itself.

Not only does writing deconstruct beginning but beginning also deconstructs writing and the teaching of writing. It's clear, then, that if I am going to pursue the question of where writing begins, I am going to have to establish a different understanding of what it means to begin—and what it means to write. In the next chapter, I will take up the concept of beginning as origin.

2 In the "Pre-beginning": Origin

In the beginning was the pre-beginning, already enigmatically containing within itself the principle of the count-down:

6 5 4 3 2 1 — BLAST-OFF
Roger—go go- ga-ga
OVER—and over

—Kenneth Burke, "De Beginnibus"

My dictionary provides two main senses of what it means to begin. One is captured in the term *starting point,* "to set about . . . to perform the first steps or stages of; do or perform the first actions of." This is the sense of beginning that I explored in the previous chapter: where writing begins as the first stage of the act of writing. The other sense is rendered in the term *origin,* "to found or call into being: . . . establish an origin for."[1] In this case, where writing begins refers to the deep structure of writing, a structure that preexists and thus founds writing.

This is the understanding of beginning that Kenneth Burke was trying to get across to the graduates of Bennington College in his commencement address (see Introduction). A beginning in this sense is that which exists before—typically implicit, unnoticed—and has a profound effect on what comes after. Beginnings, he says, may be understood as "key terms," the terminological screens that predetermine the conceptions we build; as "definitions," principles that preexist and inform conclusions we draw; and as "equations," the motivating principles that underlie all the symbolic actions we construct. In the epigraph to this chapter, Burke images the drama and mystery of beginnings as origin in the metaphorical mix of Genesis and a rocket launch, which would have resonated deeply with his audience in 1962: the starting point of the blastoff is already grounded in the prebeginning of the countdown.

Both starting point and origin are temporal, but they represent quite different conceptions of temporality. The first depends on chronological time, time as a sequence of events; a beginning in chronological time is the first of a self-contained series of acts or events. A beginning as origin projects the temporal not in chronology but in the principle of precedence, that which precedes and, as Said puts it, "centrally dominates what derives from it" (373; emphasis removed).[2] It is not the first step in a process but a founding concept that exists before we think and act and is instrumental in shaping the way we think and act.

Another way of understanding origin is as *premise,* which comes from the Latin for "to place ahead, send ahead." In formal deductive logic, the major premise is made explicit and founds the minor premise and conclusion to follow. In informal reasoning, however, the major premise is typically left unstated, the presupposition or warrant or assumption that is simply understood and thus represents an even greater force on the conclusions that are derived from it.[3] Such premises act as prebeginnings, foundations that shape and support the structure of thought, though they remain largely hidden. Conceiving of beginning in terms of a premise helps us understand what Burke means when he describes a beginning as "the point at which the purely temporal and the purely logical categories somehow merge" (31).

In this chapter, then, the question of where writing begins shifts from starting point to origin, from beginning as a chronological event to beginning as that which goes before, a founding premise. Of course that was Burke's focus in his own search for prebeginnings, those structures in thought and language that preexist and heavily influence all symbolic action. The idea was that if he could understand the structures of these beginnings, then he would be able to understand symbolic action itself: in the prebeginning are the motives that shape symbolic action. It is a similar idea that drives my search for the beginning of writing in its prebeginnings—prewriting, as it were—what it is that precedes and warrants writing and what it is that allows us to teach writing. I will explore these beginnings—and the challenge that demands we rethink them.

Origins in Writing

What if the experience of writing were utterly new every time we wrote? What if we had to invent writing afresh at every writing? What if every writing event were completely isolated from every other writing event that preceded it? No matter how I put it, it's difficult for me to imagine it. We would write with absolutely no founding premises, no guiding concepts whatsoever, completely new, removed from all origins. That is, of course, not the way writing seems to work; evidently, quite a lot precedes our writing and allows us to write at all.

The same can be said about teaching writing. If we accepted the idea that the writing experiences of our students were categorically singular, independent of all other writing experiences, we would not be able to teach writing, at least not in a way that resembles the way we teach it now. For writing to be teachable, something must precede and thus shape and structure the understanding of writing that we bring to the classroom. Every syllabus we construct represents a set of preconceptions about writing. Every comment we make to a student about his or her writing is a reflection of a model of writing that preexists that instance of writing. Every grade we give symbolizes standards we bring to writing. Teaching depends on the assumption that we can systemize and formalize writing and thus present it in meaningful terms, that there exists something beyond each individual act of writing that allows us to generalize about writing, that there is something we can say about writing in a writing class that has anything to do with writing in another setting. These assumptions are grounded in origins, the premises each of us brings to our teaching of writing, shaped by our own experience and by the discipline in which we work.

Indeed, it is because we believe there are certain premises that ground the study and teaching of writing that composition is a discipline at all. I'm sure there are many such premises, but I will focus here on those that are represented in the two themes I introduced earlier—definition and value. Definition directs our attention toward what it means to write. I am using *to define* here in the sense of making something finite or definite, of delineating it or rendering it distinct and clear. This is the act of de-finition. As writing teachers, we bring to our classes an understanding of what writing is; that understanding structures and guides our teaching, whether we are aware of it or not.

It would seem, however, that definition provides an unstable presupposition for composition; instead of being a site of unity in the field, it is a site of division. Perhaps the best way to spot the definitional fissures in composition is to look at some of the better-known taxonomies of the discipline. Composition has been divided into Aristotelian rhetoric, positivist or current-traditional rhetoric, Platonic rhetoric, and new or epistemic rhetoric (according to epistemology); into an expressive view, a cognitive view, and a social view (according to theories of the composing process); and into cognitive rhetoric, expressionist rhetoric, and social-epistemic rhetoric (according to ideological orientation).[4] Each of these categories—and there are many more—defines writing in a particular way, and the taxonomies themselves describe the field of composition by its various definitions. We tend to understand the field as a complex of competing theories or paradigms, each offering a different vision of what it means to write. Each of these visions is a way of making writing finite and thus teachable. The taxonomies, then, offer a collection of definitions of writing, a way of understanding the assortment of premises that influence how we teach writing.

From an outsider's perspective, this variety must look odd indeed: how can we call ourselves a discipline of writing and not even be able to agree on what it means to write? The same may be asked about value. Just look at some of the many ways we have described the good that comes of writing: writing as a means of self-actualization (e.g., Rohman), of learning (e.g., Emig), of discovery (e.g., Flower and Hayes), of meaning making (e.g., Berthoff), of knowing (e.g., Reither), of social construction of knowledge (e.g., Bruffee, "Social"), of participating in discourse communities (e.g., Bizzell, "Cognition"), of resisting dominant ideologies (e.g., Berlin, "Rhetoric"), of resisting patriarchy (e.g., Juncker). Where is there a premise to underlie and unify the field of composition in these contending claims for value?

This quick overview of the variety of responses in our field to definition and value of writing indicates that they are sites of contestation in composition. From an insider's perspective, however, these are surface-level disagreements that actually point to a deep-level agreement. Yes, our discipline has been characterized by vigorous and often vituperative debate over what it means to write. The warrant for that debate, however, is the concurrence on the broader issue that writing *can* be defined, that writing can be made definite and explicable for the purposes of teaching and research.

Yes, the disputes over the value of writing have sometimes turned bitter, but beneath those disputes lies the assumption that writing has value and—going even farther—that writing has value in and of itself. Beyond the field of composition, writing is typically valued as instrumental; that is, the good of writing is located in values outside writing itself, for what it can accomplish, not in the act itself. One of the key assumptions in composition, however, is that writing possesses intrinsic value; indeed, it could be argued that we became a field when we came to understand collectively that writing has intrinsic value and that teaching itself is valued according to that intrinsic value. All those values I mentioned earlier—self-actualization, learning, discovery, et cetera—are attempts to describe the value of writing in and of itself, a notable source of agreement that grounds the discipline. Now we may still speak of instrumental values—such as the success that effective writing can bring at school and at work—when we talk to our students on the first day of class or to college administrators or to parents or to faculty in other departments. But these values are not, by and large, those that drive us as teachers and researchers of writing, that make us passionate about what we do, that have led many of us to endure the low pay and lack of prestige often associated with teaching of writing.

A Postmodern Challenge to Origins in Writing

This rather rosy picture of the discipline of composition as grounded in certain key assumptions does, I believe, capture the sense of most teachers and scholars of writing. This conception of the field, however, has been shaken to its very foundations by some postmodern compositionists who radically challenge the premises of definition and value, and all other premises besides.

Of course, the postmodern in composition is by no means monolithic, as Elizabeth A. Flynn's "Rescuing Postmodernism" shows. Flynn argues that much of the misunderstanding surrounding the postmodern in composition stems from a confusion of the relationships among postmodernism, modernism, and antimodernism and from the inclination of postmodernism to problematize itself while also problematizing modernism and antimodernism. There is also the tendency among postmodern compositionists to "misrepresent postmodernism, seeing it as the binary opposite of modernism despite postmodernism's problematizing of binary oppositions" (544–45). Flynn cites as examples Lester Faigley's *Fragments of Rationality* and David Bartholomae's position in his public debate with Peter Elbow. Both, she says, unfairly portray postmodernism in strict opposition to modernism, conflating it with antimodernism (544–46).[5]

Another way of understanding the complexity of the postmodern in composition is the division between "resistance" and "ludic" postmodernism. These terms are most closely associated with the work of Theresa L. Ebert, who uses them in regard to academic feminism. Heavily influenced by Marxist and neo-Marxist thought, resistance postmodernism has as its end a transformative politics, the emancipation that comes from opposition to and freedom from systems of exploitation founded in gender, race, class, and sexual orientation. Ludic postmodernism, on the contrary, is perpetually disruptive and destabilizing. It engages in what Ebert calls a discursive politics, the radical dismantling of any assumed correspondence between signifier and signified. "Briefly, ludic postmodernists address reality as a theatre for the free-floating play (hence the term 'ludic') of images, disembodied signifiers and difference, as in the works of Lyotard, Baudrillard, and Derrida" ("'Difference'" 887). Ludic postmodernism is characterized by its thoroughgoing suspicion of all totalizing metanarratives, including in its suspicions the metanarrative of transformative politics or any other hoped-for social transformation. In lieu of the metanarrative, ludic postmodernists prefer the local, the plural, the specific, the concrete. Ludic postmodernism is, as Ebert has it, postpolitical.[6]

Ebert's work is an extended critique of ludic postmodernism, particularly its tendency to disallow the materialist critique that highlights social contradictions and thus may lead to social transformation. Some composition scholars have used the resistance-ludic dichotomy as the basis for a critique of the ludic position (e.g., Addison and Hilligoss; Reynolds). The reverse, however, is also true. For example, arch-ludic Victor J. Vitanza accuses resistance postmodernists of being "social-consensual theory-hopeful rationalists, who through social reengineering and instrumental reason . . . want to cure society and make the world into a great, good place." The problem is that though resistance postmodernists claim an antifoundationalist position, they "are not antifoundationalist," as Vitanza points out, "but only incipient foundationalists" (157). They are not sufficiently suspicious of the metanarratives that found the idea of ideological resistance itself. The wrongheaded idealism of this political stance, he says, "is strong and steadily growing . . . and, therefore, must be resisted strongly" (143).

Even this distinction between resistance and ludic postmodernism has been complicated somewhat. Albert Rouzie, for instance, sees it more as a continuum whose extremes are exemplified by the work of James A. Berlin and Vitanza but whose middle is occupied by those who apply the play of the ludic to the serious task of social transformation. D. Diane Davis questions Ebert's dichotomy, particularly the implication that the ludic is apolitical. Davis points out that while the pragmatic approach of outwardly political feminisms has effectively challenged some gender inequalities, "stopping there leaves feminism trapped within the 'masculinist' theoretical framework against which it labors" (139).[7] To add to the confusion, some scholars who seem on the surface to be ludics are not. For example, Thomas Kent argues against any sort of preexistent grounding for language acts, dismissing all governing theories for writing and speaking. But though his position is similar to the ludics', his rejection of Big Theory is stated simply as a linguistic fact of life, not as a basis for destabilizing playfulness.[8]

My point here is neither to defend nor to question the resistance-ludic dichotomy but to establish the place of the ludic in composition in order to further explore the idea of beginning as origin. Ludic postmodernism, in its suspicion of totalizing metanarratives, represents a radical challenge to origins, which are, in essence, metanarratives, structures that precede and largely determine how we know and what we do. If I am to understand where writing begins as origins, and particularly if I am to understand the problems with the very idea of origins in writing and teaching writing, then I must examine the ludic skepticism toward origins. To do that, I will focus on the work of three scholars who represent the ludic postmodern in composition: Lynn Worsham, Vitanza, and Davis.[9]

Worsham's 1987 article "The Question Concerning Invention: Hermeneutics and the Genesis of Writing" is one of the earliest ludic challenges in composition. Though its focus on invention and inventional strategies makes it seem a little dated, its indictment of the way composition has technologized writing to make it teachable gives its insights far wider scope. As the term "genesis of writing" in the title suggests, this article is about origins in writing. Worsham's argument is that by imposing the totalizing premise of inventional technologies on writing, we have given in to the will-to-mastery of writing, the illusion that there are origins that render writing systemizable and controllable. Thus founded in technology, writing becomes an answer, not, as she thinks it ought to be, "a radical form of questioning" (210).

Worsham identifies two kinds of writing, one residing in a question of being, the other in a Heideggerean question of Being. The former of these she identifies with any attempt to found writing in a method or technology, the illusion that what comes before offers the potential for mastery over language. Writing as a question of Being, however, is "a hermeneutical understanding of writing, one in which no method will guarantee that process yields product, one that will recognize neither truth nor knowledge apart from an endless process of concealing and revealing" (218). Technology grounds writing in a method or procedure that preexists an act of writing and turns that act into an anemic search for answers. Hermeneutics, writing as "a radical form of questioning," challenges all origins in its questioning, subverts all notions of mastery derived from anything that precedes writing.

In a later article, "Writing Against Writing: The Predicament of *Ecriture Féminine* in Composition Studies," Worsham makes a similar argument, but this time putting it in the terms of French feminist thought. She begins by posing two discourses that exist in seeming opposition, one the discipline of composition, which has traditionally been defined by an "epistemological attitude" and valued as preparing students to enter academic discourses, and the other *écriture féminine,* "a language event that, in its more accessible moments, unleashes a damning critique and denunciation of academic discourse as the instrument par excellence of phallocentrism" (82). The problem as Worsham sees it is that the epistemological attitude seeks to domesticate *écriture féminine.* She advocates instead a postmodern "refusal of the epistemological attitude" (92) that exposes it as premised on a web of modernist assumptions that the world is ordered, reasonable, explicable.

The postmodern refusal of the epistemological attitude cannot be transported into the academy as it now exists and certainly not into the composition class, with its goals of positioning students for mastery of academic discourses. Given these goals and the pedagogical imperative that dominates composition, *écriture féminine* has become merely another teaching strategy, another form of origin that provides the illusion of a preexisting order or reason to support the mastery of writing (98). A postmodern reading of *écriture féminine,* however, interprets language as always and ultimately revolutionary. Thus, trying to apply *écriture féminine* to the composition class, Worsham says, will have one of two results: *écriture féminine* will either be neutralized, losing its radical possibilities, or will weave such a powerful web of doubt around the whole academic enterprise that "composition would cease to exist as we know it, and by implication the university, along with its constituent discourses, would come tumbling down" (94).

Vitanza refers to his "Three Countertheses: Or, A Critical In(ter)-vention into Composition Theories and Pedagogies" as a "perverse comedy" that places in doubt what we believe writing is all about, "places in doubt especially the revealed wisdom of even teaching students to write" (140). Vitanza nails these countertheses to the door of our profession as a way of exposing what he sees as its chief flaws: "(1) the will to systemize (the) language (of composing), (2) the will to be its author(ity), and (3) the will to teach students" (144). First is the idea that language can be explained according to an order or system that precedes and grounds it. Using Lyotard and Deleuze and Guatteri, Vitanza argues against this will by pointing to the very nature of language itself, which resists any foundational principle because it works against all grand narratives, all theories and models. Language is paralogical; it drifts, shifting us off every foundation (146–48).

The second counterthesis concerns the drive to locate authority over language in something external to language itself, traditionally in the author. This traditional locus of authority has been displaced by social rhetoricians who vest authority in the "social bond"—the foundations of context, situation, or interpretive communities. Vitanza says that though this theoretical shift has been valuable in supplanting the hegemony of the subject, it is only a trade-off, one metanarrative for another (157). The third counterthesis is about the will to teach. Vitanza counters this "pedagogy hope" with what he calls "a pedagogy other(wise)." Such a (non)pedagogy resists all the temptations of grand narratives, becoming instead a nondiscipline (de)centered on the use of "counterstrategies" which "would attempt to lessen the oppressive forces of discursive language; would be discontinuous, random, and filled with fragmented thoughts and digressions; would attempt to call each previous statement into (rhetorical) question; and would attempt to use sophistic ruse and counterruse" (165). A pedagogy other(wise) would, in other words, be founded in no precepts at all, nothing that grounds writing in anything that comes before it.

Davis's *Breaking Up [at] Totality: A Rhetoric of Laughter* is the most extensive and ambitious treatment of the ludic postmodern in composition that I am aware of, and thus the most difficult to summarize quickly. Laughter is the master trope here, a laughter that shatters all origins. But it is also an affirmative laughter, not an empty laughter at nothingness but an unsuppressed laughter at the comic, the overflow, the excess. It is a laughter "that leaps out of the binary, calling hopelessness into question without positing a new god/foundation/philosophy" (64). Davis says that we are laughed by language: though language typically masks itself as the signifier of certainty, knowledge, meaning, reason, subjectivity, it is actually laughter, disrupting all that it apparently signifies.

Davis extends this rhetoric of laughter to make a distinction between writing and composition. The problem is that "writing gets codified, disciplined, domesticated in the typical composition course; indeed, writing is often sacrificed *in the name of 'composition,'* in the name of this 'discipline's' service-oriented and pre-established requirements" (6). Composition has perpetuated the myth of common-being, that writing should begin in commonplaces, those areas of commonality that define and are defined by our communities (12–13). Davis prefers writing that "takes off from *anywhere* but 'common ground'" (14). She calls for a pedagogy of laughter that will be "a critical unworking of pedagogical violence, a perpetual unraveling of what is called composition" (213). This pedagogy of laughter would focus on writing itself, writing for the sake of writing. It would break up [at] knowledge, totality, truth, ego, definition, myths of common being, and any preexistent idea of "good writing" (235–47).

The Ludic Challenge to Origins in Composition

Earlier in this chapter, I ventured what I took to be an extreme hypothetical, what writing would be like if it were utterly new with each experience. But that's the kind of writing that Worsham, Vitanza, and Davis call for. It is writing that launches itself without any prebeginnings in a countdown, writing removed from all origins. What these three renderings of the ludic postmodern have in common is a resistance to origins based on *différance,* the Derridean notion of deferral, that is, one concept grounded in another concept, which is grounded in another into infinity. There can be no ultimate origin for writing, nothing that comes before and defines it.

It is significant that these three ludic postmodernists all refer to writing in contrast to composition, which is a key source of origins in writing. The power—and the threat—of ludic postmodernism is that it demonstrates clearly that our ability to teach writing is based on the assumption that something goes before writing, premises that ground writing and make it teachable—logical, orderly, systematic—and then it casts doubt on that assumption as *mere* assumption. I find this argument persuasive; at the very least, it casts substantial doubt on the concept of beginning as origin. In this section I look at the argument more closely to try to understand what makes it persuasive. I use the themes of definition and value I focused on before: we are a discipline because we agree that writing can be defined and that writing has intrinsic value. As I see it, however, the ludic critique of composition may be summed up this way: the assumptions of definition and value in composition are based on teleology, and all teleological arguments are fallacies. I'll consider the teleological fallacy of definition first.

Teleology is derived, of course, from *telos,* the "end" or "goal" or "purpose." A teleological argument is, as Daniel C. Dennett puts it, "one that explains the existence or occurrence of something by citing a goal or purpose that is served by the thing" (24; emphasis removed). It would perhaps be helpful to explore this concept of definition by teleology by looking at a prime example of it, the teleological argument for the existence of God or, as it is better known, the Argument from Design.

At its most basic, the Argument from Design holds that the world possesses a design and therefore must have been generated by an intelligent designer. The roots of the modern version of the Argument go back very far, with important precedents in the classical and medieval periods. In the modern era, however, the Argument formed the basis of what became known as natural theology. Sir Isaac Newton, for example, claimed that the order he discerned in the universe must reveal the hand of God as both creator and sustainer. Later, William Paley in *Natural Theology* (1802) used the complexity of the human eye and its adaptation for sight as proof of a divine Artificer. He offered the analogy of finding a watch on a desert island and, of necessity, reasoning from the design of that artifact to a human designer and creator. But under the skeptical scrutiny of John Locke and David Hume and counterexplanations of Charles Darwin, natural theology lost its sway.[10]

Natural theology may have faded, but not the explanatory power of teleology. When Darwin looked at the order inherent in natural adaptation and explained that order according to the shaping purpose of natural selection, he also was engaging in a kind of teleological argument. Such an argument, then, consists of two steps, first discerning an order in a phenomenon and then explaining that order in terms of a shaping purpose or design that is external to and preexists the phenomenon. It is delimited and made explicable by that purpose or design.

What we've been doing in the field of composition is engaging in our own argument by design, looking at the order that is writing and describing it in terms of a preexistent shaping purpose or design, for example, expressionistic, cognitive, or social-epistemic. This kind of argument is so natural to human thinking that, except in some extreme instances, it may not seem like an argument at all, just the way things are.

The ludic postmodernists, however, take the teleological argument and expose it not only *as* an argument but as a *fallacious* argument. Their critique is initially revealed in their explicit dismissals of all the ways writing has been defined in composition theory. Worsham rejects writing as defined by problem solving and the linguistic turn ("The Question" 214–15, 217) and by social theories ("Writing" 100). Vitanza also runs down the list of accepted definitions and casts suspicion on them all: including the foundational—which "is composed variously of current traditional rhetoric, of expressionistic rhetoric, and of scientistic, cognitive rhetoric"—and the supposedly antifoundational, social-epistemic rhetoric (143; see also 148). And Davis cites current-tradition, cognitive, expressive, feminist, and social-epistemic rhetorics as all part of the same insidious system designed to provide just enough of unruly language to students to produce the desired subject-citizen (233).

It is the suspicion of metanarratives that makes the idea of a preexistent shaping design suspect, what Worsham refers to as the epistemological attitude, Vitanza the will to systemize, and Davis the myth of common-being. It's not that any one of these definitions itself is necessarily inaccurate or inadequate but that *all* definitions of writing are necessarily inaccurate and inadequate. The ludic critique demands that we understand our attempts to define writing, to limit and control it, as imposing a design or shaping purpose on writing that is always and inevitably false.

The ludics take their challenge to definition one critical step further. Yes, we could admit that all definitions are false but continue to argue, for the good of the discipline, that one definition is *better* at defining the order that is writing. The postmodern critique, however, counters that there *is* no order that is writing. In other words, all attempts at defining writing are condemned from the outset not just because all definitions are inadequate in reflecting an underlying order but because *there is no underlying order.*

Vitanza uses paralogy in his counterthesis against the will to systemize language (146–48). It is significant, I think, that each of his countertheses is based on Gorgias's three claims from "On Nature." The first is, in Vitanza's rendering, "Nothing [of essence] exists" (145).[11] There is, in other words, no founding order that would even allow the inference from design to a preexisting shaping purpose. Paralogy, he says, "bear[s] witness to the unintelligible," to the radical dissolution of all essences (146). For Worsham the epistemological attitude is driven by the powerful desire to know, which is itself "rooted in our need for meaning when confronted by meaninglessness. . . . When the epistemological attitude encounters the unknown," she points out, "it becomes resourceful." It encircles the unknowable in a comfortable sameness, making the unknowable appear to be knowable ("Writing" 83–84). It is laughter for Davis that unravels any sense of an underlying order. Laughter shatters common ground, system, codes, anything that seeks to impose an order on language.

This critique of composition is so unsettling because it radically questions our basic disciplinary assumption that writing is a definable act, that it possesses an order that submits to a preexisting shaping purpose or design. The critique is difficult to comprehend and even more difficult to accept because, as a part of our modernist heritage, the idea that we can define writing seems so natural to us, unquestionable. But that's exactly what the ludic postmodern does: it questions that idea by presenting it as a teleological argument and then exposing the teleological argument as a fallacy. All attempts at a shaping purpose or design are false, first because they impose on a phenomenon a shape that inevitably misrepresents it and second (and more damning) because there is no order in it to represent. Saying that writing cannot be defined changes everything about the way we describe and theorize it, about the way we conceive of what it means to be a discipline of writing.

The postmodern critique also exposes our understanding of the *value* of writing as teleological—the "why" question related to value—though supported by a somewhat different sort of argument. I mentioned in my earlier discussion of value the concepts of instrumental and intrinsic value.

I took these concepts from axiology, the study of value, which has for a long time been interested in the source of value, that is, whether value is, generally speaking, intrinsic—located in the act, person, event, or object itself—or instrumental—located outside the phenomenon in its consequences or in its relationship to other phenomena.[12] A similar distinction exists in ethics, the debate over whether the good of an act is deontological, that is, determined by the concept of duty or right conduct or moral obligation—all intrinsic to the act itself—or is teleological, determined by its ends (Nozick 494; Olsson 88). The question, then, is how do we talk about value: is the good or worth of something to be found somehow in its own being or in its outward effects, intrinsic or teleological?

I have argued that one of the most important moments in our profession was when we began to think of writing as possessing intrinsic value. The ludic critique, however, casts doubt on the values we have associated with writing. One of the major themes of Worsham's "The Question Concerning Invention" is her condemnation of composition for turning writing into a technology, "a study of systems of methods as means to various ends, which include self-realization or expression, the creation and discovery of knowledge, the promotion of the democratic process and economic prosperity" (210). Vitanza also criticizes our usual ideas of the value of writing, among which he identifies the "establishment and maintenance of social bonds" (141), economic success (142), making the world a better place (145), writing as discovery (150), "rational consensus" (151), the "alleged 'empowerment' of students" (161), and knowledge (164). Davis is the most pointed in her critique. She says that in most composition courses the aim of teaching lies in some goal beyond writing itself (6). All pedagogies, whether on the left or right, fall into the trap of "pedagogical tyranny: using the pedagogical position to foster particular kinds of subjects or student-citizens, either to take their place in the economic/political system or in the Grand March against it" (224). Either way, composition teachers "prostitute" themselves for values that lie outside writing (230–31).

Underlying these critiques is the insistent question of the source of the value of writing. The accusation: even though we revolutionized composition by conceiving of writing in terms of the values inherent in the act itself, we persist in thinking of those values as teleological or instrumental. According to this critique, all the values of writing that have dominated our profession continue to be sited *outside* the act of writing; they are described as an *effect* of writing, what writing can do or accomplish or achieve. We continue to think of writing in terms of ends or purposes that precede and lie outside it.

Once again, this seems like a perfectly natural way of understanding value, but the postmodern critique exposes it for what it really is: a teleological fallacy based on the illusion of Cartesian subject-object duality. The problem, in general, is that in a subject-object relationship, writing becomes an object and thus a tool of the writing subject. Worsham, Vitanza, and Davis all address the issue of subject-object duality. Worsham uses Heidegger's critique of science and technology as a way of undercutting the subject-object duality in composition and its characteristic will-to-mastery, "an aggressive kind of thinking that renders everything, including Being, representable, calculable, and usable" ("The Question" 209). According to Heidegger, science and technology are a result of the human sense of a universal subjectivity that gives rise to a complementary universal objectivity in the Other. This objectivity turns everything into an object of knowledge and thus "subject" to procedure or methodology. Methodology, then, has a way of objectifying everything it is turned toward and thus transforming all relationships into instrumental, means-ends relationships (205–9).

Vitanza deals with this teleological fallacy in his second counterthesis, concerning authority over language. The illusion of authority is vested in the idea of the writing subject as the author and controller of language, which is itself the object of this authority. Vitanza disrupts these assumptions by using Lyotard's contrast between our usual way of conceiving of language, as a "spoken game," and the postmodern way of conceiving of language, as a "listening game": it functions like an addressee without an addressor; in other words, we are spoken by language (152–55). This deconstruction of the "natural" authority of the author radically disrupts the equally "natural" view of language as a tool of the writing subject. Davis makes a similar argument, starting with Descartes' understanding of the writer as the master of language and language as "a tool to communicate and commune with others." She displaces this humanist view of language as a tool with her ludic conception of the writer as being laughed by language. No longer the object, it is laughter in language that possesses and calls into Being the writer (69–72).

The ludic postmodern critique of composition identifies all of our stated values as instrumental and then challenges the very concept of subject-object that supports the instrumental. When we say that the act of writing may be valued as an act of discovery or of knowing or of resistance to patriarchy we are imposing an instrumental value on writing, turning it into a tool, an object of the subject-writer. These values are not intrinsic at all but teleological, derived from ends or purposes that go before and are outside writing itself. As a discipline, then, we have persisted in the teleological error of seeing writing as an object, subject to the writer and the writing teacher, subject to the will-to-mastery. The ludic challenge to this subject-object duality is also a challenge to our conception of the value of writing founded in that duality.

Putting the ludic postmodern critique of composition within the context of our disciplinary argument from teleology helps to explain why I find that critique persuasive. First, it exposes the otherwise hidden argument from teleology and then dismisses it as a fallacy. It's little wonder, then, that Worsham, Vitanza, and Davis take care to differentiate writing from composition. Composition lies in origins, in teleology, a shaping purpose and instrumental value that enable writing teachers to control and systemize writing. Writing, however, destabilizes all presuppositions. Writing disrupts the subject-object duality, disrupts authority, disrupts the will-to-mastery. Writing, the ludics say, is undisciplined and may therefore not be subject to a discipline.

Perhaps Kenneth Burke was wrong: there is no beginning in the prebeginning. Perhaps we cannot understand symbolic action by searching out the motives that precede and thus ground and structure that action. Vitanza, in fact, refers to this approach as characteristic of "the modernist, nostalgic Burke" who, in *A Grammar of Motives,* sought "to systemize ambiguity" (163). Perhaps that is what all of us writing teachers and researchers are guilty of doing. It may very well be that, as the ludic postmodernists claim, writing is paralogical and thus by its nature resists all attempts to systemize it.

The ludic critique of origins of writing undermines my efforts to discern where writing begins as origin. It is doubtful, then, that writing can be said to have a starting point in time or an origin in precedence. Thus, asking where writing begins has the effect of deconstructing both beginning and writing. But this deconstruction opens a space for a reconstruction of beginning and writing. In the next chapter I will start the reconstruction of beginning.

3 In the Beginning

At first there was only darkness wrapped in darkness.
All this was only unillumined water.
That One which came to be, enclosed in nothing,
arose at last, born of the power of heat.

In the beginning desire descended on it—
that was the primal seed, born of the mind.
The sages who have searched their hearts with wisdom
know that which is is kin to that which is not

—"Hymn of Creation," from the *Rig-Veda*

Toward the end of chapter 1, in what must have seemed like a fit of hyperbole, I stated that to find an absolute beginning in time for any act of writing we would have to go all the way back to the beginning of time. This was my response to the apparent impossibility of locating with any certainty a starting point we could identify as where writing begins. But maybe going back to the beginning of time is not such a bad idea in this search for beginning. That's what I'm going to do in this chapter. The goal, however, is not to establish a beginning of writing but to understand more generally what it means to begin.

As I have pointed out, asking where writing begins has the effect of problematizing both beginning and writing. We bring certain temporal preconceptions to our understanding of beginning. One is that a beginning is a starting point in time. But when this preconception is scrutinized through the lens of writing, we find that all starting points are ultimately arbitrary, temporal boundaries of convenience that allow us to make sense of a process, though at the inevitable cost of misrepresenting it. This insight into chronological time also affects our understanding of writing. If where we say writing begins is completely arbitrary, then what we say writing *is* is just as arbitrary. The implication is that in teaching writing we *invent* writing as a separable, definable, and—most important—teachable act, which casts doubt on the teaching of writing.

The second preconception we bring to beginning is origin, that which precedes and structures an existence or process that comes after. However, the concept of origin has been effectively challenged by ludic postmodernists in their general suspicion of metanarratives. This challenge places into question even the most basic assumptions we bring to writing and teaching writing, assumptions that provide a conceptual grounding for both. The ways that we have defined and valued writing and teaching writing are exposed as founded on false premises based on teleology.

Thus asking where writing begins deconstructs our assumptions about beginning and has an equally deconstructive lateral effect on writing. To a certain extent, then, the way we think about writing is linked by a set of shared assumptions to the way we think about beginning. Thus a reconstructed understanding of beginning has the potential for leading to a reconstructed understanding of writing.

In this chapter, I will step back and look at beginning itself, not from the perspective of writing but from the perspective of *the* beginning, that is, the beginning of everything. *The* beginning, which embodies both starting point and origin, provides a crucial paradigm for conceptualizing beginning; that is, the way we think about the beginning of everything acts as an archetype or principle for thinking about what it means to begin. Moreover, the beginning may hold the key to a reconstruction of beginning: a fresh set of assumptions that provide a new way of understanding beginning.

There are two broader purposes at work in this exploration of the beginning. One is that the act of reconstructing beginning may provide a model for reconstructing writing. The other is that a reconstructed conception of beginning holds out the possibility of changing the basic sense of my initiating question, Where does writing begin? A radically different concept of beginning will engender a completely new question, which should allow for a new approach to finding an answer.

I will frame this discussion of the beginning with references to the shared opening words of Genesis and the Gospel of John, the most dramatic and sweeping opening I know of anywhere: "In the beginning." Though they are the same words in English, translated from the Hebrew and the Greek, they refer, I argue, to different conceptions of the beginning. It is this difference that sets the stage for my reconstruction of beginning.

בְּרֵאשִׁית בָּרָא אֱלֹהִים אֵת הַשָּׁמַיִם וְאֵת הָאָרֶץ׃

"In the beginning God created the heavens and the earth"

This stunning statement, austere and matter-of-fact, is the opening of what is surely one of the best-known texts in our culture, the creation account in Genesis 1. *Genesis,* based on the Greek word for origins, actually comes from a Greek translation of the Hebrew Bible, or Old Testament, known as the Septuagint. In Hebrew, this first book of the Torah is called *Bereshit,* the first word in the book, a Hebrew compound form for "In-the beginning" (*Torah* 3). *Reshit* (or *reshith*) is the word for "the beginning" used elsewhere in the Torah in the usual sense of the beginning of a process or existence (*Ramban* 20). At the beginning of the Torah, however, it takes on a more profound meaning, the beginning of everything. For me, *reshit* is emblematic of *the* beginning. Ramban, a thirteenth-century commentator on the Torah, puts it this way: "Now listen to the correct and clear explanation of the verse in its simplicity. The Holy One, blessed be He, created all things from absolute non-existence" (*Ramban* 23).[1] That is the concept of the beginning I will pursue here.

The power of this concept of beginning may be understood in the context of beginnings in other cultures. Indeed, the very idea of the universe as having a beginning is not itself universal. In *The Creators,* Daniel J. Boorstin describes various beginningless worldviews that are portrayed in other religions and philosophies. For Hindus, creation has nothing of the sense of our bringing into being that which did not exist. It is, rather, the opposite, a disintegration, a fall from oneness. Creation is represented in the countless cycles of birth and death and the hoped-for return to unity. In Chinese tradition also, the idea of the beginning of everything is completely foreign. Confucius could not have been bothered by such trivial, other-worldly concerns. Taoists conceive of a universe in which there is no beginning, only the eternal yin and yang. The Buddha was also indifferent to questions of the beginning, primarily because his goal was to escape the world, to cast off its illusions. The physical origin of the world was simply not relevant. Ancient Greek mythology was also little concerned with the beginning. Homer was much more interested in the heroic human struggle that was reflected in the portrayal of very human gods. And Hesiod's *Theogony* was the saga of genealogy as seen in innumerable acts of procreation (Boorstin 35).

The radical nature of the creation narrative in Genesis may also be contrasted with other Near Eastern narratives. Even though Genesis is liberally sprinkled with borrowings from many sources of that time and region, the story of the six days of creation that culminated in man and woman is apparently unprecedented. A God that simply exists without predecessors and without explanation, a God that is the only God, a God that is utterly omnipotent creating a consummately ordered world without struggle and without dirtying its hands, a God that preexists and is separated from Creation, a God that gives a principal place and role in creation to humankind—this is a portrayal of the act of creation by a Creator God that is unique to that time and place (Armstrong 10–12). This is truly *reshit.*

But there is a second creation story, in Genesis 2.4b–25, immediately following the first. This latter narrative describes a different order of creation: God made the man, Adam, first and then vegetation, animals, and finally the woman, Eve. Biblical scholars tell us that these two stories were collected and written down in two different historical eras and for different purposes. The Adam and Eve story is the older of the two. Scholars use what they call the documentary hypothesis as a way of mapping the complex relationships among the various sources that comprise the Torah or Pentateuch, the first five books of the Hebrew Bible (Humphreys 73–78). The oldest of these sources was a collector and editor known as the Yahwist, a reference to the tendency to use the word *Yahweh* when referring to God. The Yahwist gathered the tales and histories of the Hebrew people sometime in the tenth century BCE at or near the height of the David-Solomon empire (Borg 63; Humphreys 74–76).

This historically earlier creation story is concerned less with *reshit* than with what it means to be human. It is widely interpreted as a theodicy, an explanation of the origin of evil. The first command God gives to Adam after putting him in the garden is the prohibition from eating the fruit from the tree of the knowledge of good and evil. With the initial act of human disobedience, the original harmony of Eden crumbles and all humankind is cursed, denied access to the tree of life, which was in the middle of the garden with the other tree. The narrative is a justification for a moral order, at the center of which is Yahweh's demand for obedience and the human struggle with this demand, a theme that runs throughout the Hebrew Bible (Humphreys 80).[2]

The other story, the one in Genesis 1, is truly and most dramatically about *reshit*. It was one of the latest texts to be included in the Torah and was probably collected by a group of Hebrew priests about four hundred years after the earlier story. Genesis 1 is part of a larger body of material referred to as P, or the priestly source, because it concerns the matter of formal, cultic observance and laws, most of which is found in the last part of Exodus and all of Leviticus ("Creation Account" 941; Humphreys 242).

This historically later version offers a completely different vision of creation. For the Yahwist, creation itself is of secondary importance to the human considerations. In the priestly source, however, creation is the central focus of the account. The styles are also different. The Adam and Eve narrative possesses the quaintness of a folktale and ease of an oft-told family story. But the creation story of Genesis 1, with the terse phrasing and stately rhythms and repetitions in the Hebrew (Armstrong 9; *Torah* 3) has a distinctly liturgical, even doctrinal, character. In fact, most scholars believe that it was originally a separate document that was recited at rituals of worship (Humphreys 242). There is nothing folkloric about the serene majesty of this account of creation.

The different portrayals of God are also telling. In the older work, God is highly anthropomorphic, walking in the garden in the cool of the day and conversing directly with the man and woman. In the priestly tradition, God is the Supreme Creator; it is the immense power of the act of creation that is emphasized. The overwhelming sovereignty of this Creator God is underscored by the *way* God creates—by the fiat of the word, calling forth existence out of nothing: "'Let there be light,' and there was light." In the Genesis 2 narrative, God creates like a potter (2.7, 19), an image that may also be found in Egyptian and Mesopotamian literature ("Creation Account" 942). But in the priestly account, creation is removed from any analogy to the creative acts of humans or other gods.

Genesis 1 is a recounting of the origin of the universe that underscores the incomprehensible power of God. It is clear that this awesome power is directly related to *reshit:* the very word of God is the cause of all that is. Indeed, Boorstin points out that the ancient Hebrew name for God, the unutterable *Yahweh,* was probably derived from the Hebrew verb for "to be" or "to bring into being": "the One who brings into being" (40). There is no more dramatic image of God in our culture than this one. The idea of *reshit,* then, plays a crucial role in this understanding of God.

There is in our culture another important *bereshit:* In the beginning was the big bang, which generated the universe and all that is in it. And the universe was without comprehensible form; all the matter and energy that presently exists was contained in something of about zero size but of infinite mass and heat. About a microsecond after the big bang, the universe consisted of a radiation soup of quarks and leptons undergoing supercooling in the dramatic inflation of the explosion. At about the one second mark, the temperature had cooled to about ten billion degrees and the cosmic soup had coalesced into photons, electrons, and neutrinos, as well as some protons and neutrons. About a minute and a half after the big bang, the universe was one billion degrees and protons and neutrons started to combine to form the nuclei of heavy hydrogen. Soon the production of helium began. As the universe continued to cool, the denser irregularities began to pull together through gravitational force, eventually collecting as galaxies at about one billion years after the big bang. Smaller clouds of matter in these galaxies collapsed under their own gravity and became hot enough to initiate nuclear fusion, which converted the helium into heavier elements such as carbon and oxygen, thus providing the raw materials for life. Our own planet was formed of matter blown off in a stellar explosion some 10.5 billion years after the big bang. And now, about fifteen billion years after the beginning of the universe, we human beings, you and I, contemplate the beginning of the universe (Hawking 116–21; Odenwald 27–29; Powell 18–19).

Most of us, if we were asked by a child how the universe "really" began, would tell a story something like this one, a scientific explanation. It may be surprising, then, that the idea of the universe as having a beginning point in time and space is relatively new to science. Aristotle argued that the universe must be eternal, thus having no beginning in time (*Physics* VIII, 1: 251a8–252a3), and his authority was followed by most natural philosophers and, later, scientists, including Isaac Newton: there was simply no empirical evidence that the universe was anything but eternal and unchanging.

This was the state of scientific thought at the beginning of the twentieth century. In 1917 when Einstein applied his general theory of relativity to the workings of the universe, he found that his theory posited an unstable universe that would either expand forever or collapse under its own weight. He thus included in his equations a "cosmological constant" so that his conclusions would agree with the accepted notion of a static universe (Odenwald 26). In 1922, however, Soviet physicist Alexander Friedmann recognized the potential in Einstein's equations for alternative models of the universe, two of which had an absolute beginning (Odenwald 26; Hawking 40).

The first piece of empirical evidence to support Friedmann's theory was the stunning discovery by Edwin Hubble that all the stars and galaxies in the universe are moving away from each other and that the farther away a celestial body is from us the faster it is moving away. There seemed to be just one conclusion from this observation: that the universe is expanding in all directions. Two competing theories emerged to explain this expanding universe. To many scientists, the fact that galaxies were sailing farther and farther apart could only mean one thing: that once the distance between them was zero, that at the beginning of space-time, all the matter in the universe had existed in one extraordinary cosmic mote. Thus the universe did indeed have a beginning (Hawking 38–39).

An alternative explanation for the expanding universe was offered by Fred Hoyle and his colleagues, Hermann Bondi and Thomas Gold. In the late 1940s, they hypothesized a universe that had no beginning and thus no likely end. It came to be known as steady state theory, a misnomer in a way because the universe they portrayed was dynamic, eternally expanding, and continuously creating new matter. Hoyle had previously demonstrated that higher elements can be formed from helium in the nuclear fusion that takes place at the core of stars. Steady state theory, then, describes a universe in which the galaxies are moving away from each other, but instead of matter thinning out, more matter is constantly being generated in the stars. The result of this continuous creation is a universe that maintains a consistent density of matter, new stars eventually forming new galaxies so that the universe will look generally the same from any point in it (Brush 63–68).

The term *big bang* had been used as a sarcastic label by Fred Hoyle, ridiculing the childish idea that the universe began with fireworks. Unfortunately for Hoyle and company, that label stuck but their own theory didn't. The scales of scientific evidence tipped dramatically in favor of big bang theory in the mid-1960s when Arno A. Penzias and Robert W. Wilson of Bell Laboratories stumbled onto a Nobel prize with the discovery that microwave radiation occurs consistently throughout the universe. What's important about this discovery is that microwave radiation serves as an indirect measurement of the temperature of the universe, and their measurements placed that temperature at about 2.8 degrees Celsius above absolute zero. Steady state theory had postulated that in a beginningless universe the temperature would be zero. But the level and consistency of the numbers generated by Penzias and Wilson showed that the universe, though apparently cooling down, still seemed to contain some of the heat from an originating cosmic blast (Albright 712).

So there is also a *reshit* supported by science. The two dominant creation stories of our time, Genesis and big bang theory, are astonishingly similar; indeed, they are both essentially the same story, the story of a universe that has a beginning point in time and of time. This similarity has not been lost on some theists. Pope Pius XII, addressing the Pontifical Academy of Science in 1951, said about "a mind enlightened and enriched with modern scientific knowledge":

> With the same clear and critical look with which it examines and passes judgment on facts, it perceives and recognizes the work of creative omnipotence, whose power, set in motion by the mighty "Fiat" pronounced billions of years ago by the Creating Spirit, spread out over the universe, calling into existence with a gesture of generous love matter bursting with energy. In fact, it would seem that present-day science, with one sweeping step back across millions of centuries, has succeeded in bearing witness to that primordial "Fiat lux." (qtd. in W. Carroll 59)

"True Science," he added, "to an ever increasing degree discovers God as though God were waiting behind each door opened by science" (qtd. in Q. Smith 217). Now religious fundamentalists may disagree that there is a similarity between Genesis and classical big bang theory, preferring a literal understanding of the former. Given the long tradition of scientific assumptions of an eternal universe, however, classical big bang theory appears to offer scientific evidence for a God-like creation out of nothing.[3]

If the beginning acts as a paradigm for beginning, then this understanding of *reshit,* the radical beginning of the universe, would seem to support our understanding of beginning as starting point and origin. The beginning is temporal. There is an absolute starting point in time and of time. There is also in the beginning a potent projection of origins: origins in the power of God; origins of evil in the human disobedience of God's commands; origins of the complete dependence of the universe on God; origins of the laws of physics that structure the universe and provide for scientific predictability within that universe. These origins precede and shape our understanding of the divine, of human beings, and of the physical universe. Thus the story of *the* beginning precedes and shapes the concept of beginning.

As one might expect, however, it's not really that clear-cut. *Reshit* in science and theology is more complicated than these accounts of the beginning suggest, and this fact also complicates our understanding of beginning.

Scientific Questions about the Beginning

Pope Pius's confidence that theology and science were speaking with one voice about the beginning was based on an understanding of scientific theories before quantum physics. So far, in this discussion I have been referring to *classical* big bang theory, which is based largely on Einstein's general theory of relativity. Most of the recent work in astrophysics, however, has been based on quantum theories that have led many scientists to take an entirely different perspective on the beginning. These quantum theories have allowed physicists to address the supposedly unknowable—the *singularity,* a term used to describe the physical and mathematical properties of the initiating point of the big bang itself.

According to Stephen Hawking, who has done some of the best work in this area of physics, "[a] singularity is a place where the classical concepts of space and time break down as do all the known laws of physics because they are all formulated on a classical space-time background" (qtd. in Q. Smith 222). The result of this breakdown of the laws of physics is that mathematics is no longer applicable and thus all predictability is lost. It is not simply a matter of not having the *correct* theory to work with; rather, a singularity indicates a point at which no theories in physics *can* apply. It is, by definition, completely beyond the comprehension of physics and mathematics. Hawking says, therefore, that it makes no sense even to speculate what could have come before a singularity because the singularity itself would make it so that what came before could have no effect on what came after (46).

But the idea of the singularity has come under intense scrutiny of late. Physicist Sten F. Odenwald says, "Actually, it was recognized rather early that the singularity state was an artifact of a theory, general relativity, that was pushed into a domain in which it could not be expected to make meaningful predictions" (35). John Maddox, former editor of *Nature,* says of big bang theory with its singularity: "In all respects save that of convenience, this view of the origin of the Universe is thoroughly unsatisfactory" because it suggests that "the origin of the Big Bang itself is not susceptible to discussion." He predicts, therefore, that such an inadequate theory will soon fall. And Stephen Hawking, whose research has done perhaps the most to make a case for a singularity at the beginning of space-time, now finds himself in the uncomfortable position of making the opposite argument: "It is perhaps ironic that, having changed my mind, I am now trying to convince physicists that there was in fact no singularity at the beginning of the universe" (50).

The shift from general relativity to quantum mechanics has enabled physicists to extricate themselves from the theoretical embarrassment of the singularity. As a result, the whole idea of a beginning of the universe is now under some strain. In fact, the standard understanding of the beginning of time, a definite starting point from which the universe originates, is completely lost in many recent cosmologies, as a few examples will show.

One is the theory of the oscillating universe, that is, a universe in which the pattern of expansion and contraction is repeated over and over again. Russian cosmologist I. L. Rozental proposed such a "big bounce" theory, saying that "the origin of the Metagalaxy (or the world around us) out of nothing is nonsense; this was always the opinion of the great philosophers and physicists" (112). Rozental worked out a theory in which each cycle collapses into and emerges from a vacuum, which allows him to avoid the problems of the singularity (97–129).[4]

In a book provocatively titled *The Big Bang Never Happened,* physicist Eric J. Lerner advocates a plasma cosmology, an alternative theory founded on the pioneering work of Swedish Nobel laureate Hannes Alfvén. Plasma physics, the study of gases that conduct electricity, has been around for quite a long time, but when wedded to astrophysics it supports a revolutionary view of the cosmos. Alfvén and his followers, applying the concepts formed in the laboratory to the larger scale features of the universe, have theorized a universe that is controlled not by the relatively weak force of gravity, as posited by classical physics, but by the strong forces of electricity and magnetism.[5] This theory presents a radical challenge to big bang theory, especially its idea of the beginning. Lerner puts it this way:

> Instead of working forward from a theoretically conceived beginning of time, plasma cosmology works backward from the present universe, and outward from the earth. It arrives at a universe without a Big Bang, without any beginning at all, a universe that has always existed, is always evolving, and will always evolve, with no limits of any sort. (14)

Andrei Linde also dismisses big bang cosmology and proposes instead a fundamentally different vision of the topology of the universe. In Linde's theory, the universe is a kind of infinitely large space-time foam out of which a multitude of mini-universes—ours is just one of them—have inflated into existence and into which they revert (65–67). Linde, then, rejects the possibility that the part of the universe that we observe around us could have been created as a whole at some moment before which there was nothing. "If the universe is infinitely large . . . then it cannot have had a single beginning; a simultaneous creation of infinitely many causally disconnected regions is totally improbable" (67).

Finally, in his best-selling (if not necessarily widely read) *A Brief History of Time,* Stephen Hawking ventures yet another solution to the problem of the singularity at the beginning of the universe. Though it is likely to be counterintuitive to those of us unused to the abstractions of theoretical mathematics, this proposal represents the logic that is possible in the shift from classical to quantum physics. Briefly put, Hawking's theory depends on the mathematical concept of imaginary numbers, which must be used to calculate the possible movements of quantum particles, and on the idea of Euclidean space-time, in which time itself must be understood as imaginary. This dazzling trick of quantum mechanics allows for a third alternative to the mystery of time and the universe: instead of having a beginning and an end or having no beginning and no end, "it is possible for space-time to be finite in extent yet to have no singularities that formed a boundary or edge" (136). The universe would start as a single point, expand, and then contract to a single point in the elapse of imaginary time, but it would do so without any boundaries of time (133–41). "There would be no singularity at which the laws of science broke down. . . . The universe would be completely self-contained and not affected by anything outside itself. It would neither be created nor destroyed. It would just BE" (136).

It is important for nonscientists to understand that these theories of the universe are not coming out of science fiction; rather, they are products of the scientific observation and mathematical modeling of credible physicists. And these are only a sample of the many scientific challenges to big bang theory.[6] All are responses to the apparent physical impossibility of the beginning as represented in the initial singularity as well as to the difficulties in the empirical evidence supporting the theory. Even steady state theory, which had been all but embalmed, has found new life recently as the questions related to the big bang have begun to mount (Arp; Arp et al.).[7]

The problem, I believe, lies in *reshit* itself, in the overwhelming challenge of making scientific sense of an absolute beginning of the universe. The difficulty created by an initial boundary of the universe takes us to the boundaries of science. This conundrum is the reason so many astrophysicists propose possible scenarios for a beginningless universe. It is much more reasonable to say that the universe has no beginning than to say that the beginning is scientifically incomprehensible. This response is not merely a result of scientific vanity; rather, it is a result of the intractable nature of the beginning in scientific terms. Aristotle may have been right all along: there may simply be no beginning of the universe. That possibility certainly complicates my search for a paradigm for beginning located in the beginning.

Theological Questions about the Beginning

There is something about the beginning that encourages even a physicist like Stephen Hawking to wax metaphysical: "So long as the universe had a beginning, we could suppose a creator. But if the universe is really completely self-contained, having no boundary or edge, it would have neither beginning nor end: it would simply be. What place, then, for a creator?" (141).

What place, indeed. The difficulties in astrophysics with the beginning raise questions about what had appeared to be a rather tidy relationship between Genesis 1 and big bang theory. Hawking suggests that a universe without a beginning is a universe without a creator. How, then, can the awesome power of God be represented in a universe that is eternal and thus has no Creator God, and perhaps no God at all? Of course, the Genesis story need not depend on science for its veracity or for its message about the beginning. There are, however, many questions about the story itself, or at least the way it has been interpreted, that cast doubt on the biblical idea of a radical *reshit*. I will look at two of these questions generated by theologians and philosophers of religion who have studied Genesis in its historical context. The issue here is not whether the account is literally true but whether there is an underlying basis of support for the concept of the beginning in time.

The first question concerns one of the most dramatic features of the Genesis 1 narrative, God's creation of the universe out of nothing. Known as *creatio ex nihilo*, this true and absolute beginning serves as a sign of the power and dominance of God. But is creation out of nothing really biblical? Genesis 1 itself is intriguingly ambiguous about it:

> [1] In the beginning God created the heavens and the earth. [2]
> Now the earth was formless and empty, darkness was over the
> surface of the deep, and the Spirit of God was hovering over
> the waters. [3] And God said, "Let there be light," and there
> was light.[8]

When did creation actually begin? Did it begin out of nothing in verse 1, or is that verse a summary of the whole creation process detailed afterward? Did it begin in verse 2, and if so, had God already created the chaotic matter described in that verse? Or did creation actually begin in verse 3 and all the chaotic matter preexist that act, uncreated by God?[9]

In translations that start with "In the beginning," the answer to these questions remains indeterminate, though one could certainly make the case that this rendering of *bereshit* implies an absolute beginning of everything out of nothing. Other translations divert attention from the beginning itself and thus deemphasize, or even dismiss, the issue of *creatio ex nihilo*. For example, Robert Alter's recent rendition of Genesis: "When God began to create heaven and earth, and the earth then was welter and waste and darkness over the deep and God's breath hovering over the waters, God said, 'Let there be light'" (3). The authoritative English translation by the Jewish Publication Society makes it even clearer that something existed before creation: "When God began to create the heaven and the earth—the earth being unformed and void, with darkness over the surface of the deep and a wind from God sweeping over the water—God said, 'Let there be light'" (qtd. in L. Ford, "Contrasting" 97–98).[10]

If Genesis itself is unclear about creation out of nothing, then where did the idea come from? History suggests that its source is more political than biblical. Of the many accounts of creation throughout the Old Testament (e.g., in Job, Psalms, and Isaiah), none can be put up as clear support for the *ex nihilo* argument. The first definite reference to creation out of nothing comes in 2 Maccabees 7.28, an intertestamental book dating from the second century BCE. This reference is not connected to religious doctrine; it is a plea to a vicious ruler by a woman whose sons he had killed. She praises the awesome powers of God by saying that God created the universe out of nothing (Drees 261–62). But even this text is ambiguous about *creatio ex nihilo* (Towner 18).

There is a good reason that the formal doctrine of creation out of nothing is most closely associated with the monotheistic religions of the Near East—Judaism, Christianity, and Islam (Long 94). Each rests on a single, omnipotent God. In Christianity, the doctrine emerged mainly out of the confrontations in the early church with other philosophies and theological interpretations, especially in the second century (Drees 34–35). Among many competing models of creation, each with its own implications for a relationship with the divine, mainstream Christianity staked out its own claims to legitimacy with an *ex nihilo* argument.

The challenges came from two main sources, classical philosophy and early Christian dualism. The two most influential classical philosophies offered different cosmologies, Plato describing a demiurge that formed the world out of preexistent matter according to the ideal Forms, and Aristotle positing a universe that was eternal, having no beginning. Against the former, Christian leaders argued that the eternal God could not coexist with an eternal matter out of which the world was formed. Against the latter, they argued that a beginningless universe would diminish the power of God represented in the act of absolute creation (Hepburn 253; Reese 111).

Many Christian groups also offered alternative views of creation, views that were branded by the early church hierarchy as heretical. Followers of Gnosticism, Marcionism, and Manichaeism, for example, believed in a dualistic universe in which Creation, i.e., the material world, was allied with evil forces against the immaterial and spiritual forces of the divine.[11] Such radical dualism was seen by moderates as usurping the place of God the Creator of heaven *and Earth* and thus severely diminishing the divine power associated with creation. In response to these threats from Greek philosophy and heretical Christian theologies, early Christian leaders made an equally radical claim for God the Creator, a God that created the universe and all that is in it out of nothing. There is no thing that is coequal or coexistent with God. The material world is essentially good because it was made by God; it is from human disobedience that evil originates. *Ex nihilo* is a fundamental statement about the act of creation and God's relationship with the created world: God's absolute supremacy and omnipotence are represented in the profoundly powerful act of creating the universe out of absolutely nothing.

Creation out of nothing, then, may be understood as a political construction that became religious doctrine, not only in Christianity but also in Judaism and Islam (Vollert 7–13). Thus, it tells us little about *reshit* itself. So the doctrine of *creatio ex nihilo,* when looked at in its historical context, does little to support the concept of an absolute beginning in time and thus a principle of beginning.[12]

Another question that raises doubts about *reshit* revolves around the historical and rhetorical background of Genesis 1. Unlike the Yahwist's tale of Adam and Eve in the Garden, which was one of the texts gathered together during the heady times of the Solomonic empire, scholars think that the priestly story of creation was part of a group of texts collected during or soon after Babylonian Captivity in the sixth century BCE, which followed the destruction of the temple in Jerusalem and the wholesale removal of the Israelites to Babylon (Borg 66). This creation story may be seen as both a borrowing from and a reaction against the Babylonian epic of creation, the *Enuma Elish*. In that story Marduk, the chief god of the Babylonians, engages in a titanic struggle with Tiamat, the watery chaos that symbolized death. After defeating Tiamat, Marduk then created the universe as an assemblage of various lower deities, each with its own domain within the natural world. This was a myth of the basic cycles of the seasons and was ritually reenacted during the new year's festival in Babylon (Humphreys 234–44; "Creation Epic" 942).

The Genesis 1 story is indebted in some ways to the *Enuma Elish*. They both open with a watery chaos from which the universe is formed; indeed, the Hebrew word for this state is *tehom,* a holdover from the Babylonian Tiamat (Von Rad 47; *Torah* 18). And the sequence of creation is roughly the same. It is in the differences between the two, however, that the rhetorical significance of the Genesis story is revealed. In Babylon, the Hebrews were a defeated people, living in the land of their victors and worshipping a God whose power had seemingly been overwhelmed by that of Marduk. This helps to explain why Yahweh in Genesis 1 is portrayed as beating Marduk at his own game. Whereas Marduk must anthropomorphically struggle in a great battle with chaos, Yahweh majestically creates simply by calling the universe into existence. Whereas Marduk creates lesser gods, Yahweh alone is divine; the manifestations of the universe are not gods. And, very important for the Hebrews, whereas Marduk created people only as an afterthought and only then because the gods needed help in their labors, Yahweh created people—Yahweh's people—in Yahweh's image to "fill the earth and subdue it" (Gen. 1.28; Humphreys 244). "To despairing exiles," says Walter Brueggeman, "it is declared that the God of Israel is the Lord of all life" (25).

The priests of the Hebrews in exile needed an all-powerful Creator God that could successfully challenge the apparently victorious Marduk. This was a dramatic one-upsmanship: creation as an act of majesty, of complete dominance, a Creator God that was above the fray, whose mere words called forth all that is. The issue, of course, is power. The Hebrew people, defeated and humiliated and exiled, craved a God that was all-powerful. Their priests composed a liturgy that expressed Yahweh's power in the most compelling way they knew, a Creator God whose sovereignty and dominion made their God far superior to Marduk and all other deities of the region. As theologian Karen Armstrong puts it, "P [the priestly source] seems to be embarked on a polemic against the dominant religious ideas of his time" (12).

The creation account in Genesis 1 is so much a part of our cultural fabric that it may seem strange to think of it as rhetorical. It is certainly not my intention to diminish its power by doing so. Indeed, it is the very power of the passage that makes it worthy of such an investigation. *Reshit* does have power, but that power does not lie in the beginning of everything. In fact, Genesis 1 does not really seem to be about the beginning of everything after all. This is probably why the priestly source is so obscure about the physical nature of absolute beginning: that simply wasn't the point. The cosmological origins act as but a backdrop for a play about God and God's relationship with a chosen people. This is the way Rashi, the medieval commentator of the Torah, interprets it (Ramban 20–23; *Torah* 18). And this has been the position of many of the most influential Christian theologians of the twentieth century, a general shift to what has been called "a strictly ontological, ahistorical interpretation of creation explicitly independent of *any* scientific meaning." (Russell 25). The biblical idea of creation is a parable of the relationship between God and Creation; thus, it is theologically significant not for what it says about the physical matter that surrounds us but for what it says about the radical nature of this relationship.[13]

Bereshit, the opening word of the Torah, is the inspiration for this investigation of the beginning of everything, starting point and origin. The purpose of this study of *reshit* is to find principles that can be applied to understanding the concept of beginning defined by the temporal. The surprising consonance of *reshit* presented in Genesis and big bang theory certainly seemed to support hope for such principles. However, the whole idea of *reshit* has been rendered doubtful. In astrophysics that doubt is due to the problem of the singularity that marks *reshit* in big bang theory. And a closer scrutiny of the doctrine of *creatio ex nihilo* and the creation story of Genesis 1 itself challenges our assumptions that Genesis 1 is truly about *reshit,* at least as I have been using the term, the beginning of everything.

The problem lies in the beginning itself, particularly as it is vested in the temporal. The idea of the beginning in time and of time raises troubling questions about beginning as a temporal concept. This problem has been revealed in my apparently naive question of where writing begins. It has been revealed further in my investigation of beginning as it is modeled on scientific and theological *reshit.* When examined closely, beginning as a temporal phenomenon collapses, unable to support the interrogation of beginning and writing.

What I need, then, is a whole new beginning.

Εν αρχη ην ο λογος: "In the beginning was the Word"

The other biblical source I am using to frame this treatment of the beginning is John 1.1. Most readers of the opening phrase of this gospel hear echoes of Genesis 1.1, the cosmological context that links Jesus, the Word, to the beginning of everything. But in *archê,* "the beginning," there is a much richer, more complex point of reference. And it is the richness and complexity of *archê* that provides passage to a whole new beginning.

To understand the way *archê* is used in John, it is helpful to look at that gospel in the light of the two most important rhetorical challenges faced by the author. First, he had to reach a largely Greek audience, one that did not share the worldview of the Jews, the primary audience of the earlier gospels. The Gospel of John was probably written in Greek at about 100 CE in Ephesus, one of the leading cities of the Greek world. By that time, Christianity was no longer a Jewish sect; indeed, it had become overwhelmingly Greek, a religion of gentiles who would have had little or no familiarity with Jewish history and sacred texts.[14] The difficulty facing John, then, was how to take this very Jewish religion and translate it into terms that would be both comprehensible and persuasive to a Greek audience (Barclay xxi–xxii).

The second rhetorical challenge was to address the theologically delicate issue of the humanity and divinity of Jesus, particularly given the strong influence of Gnosticism at that time. Gnosticism, one of the radical dualistic heresies I mentioned earlier, held that Jesus could not have been human and divine at the same time. God, the Gnostics said, was completely removed from material existence, occupying an entirely different realm, perfect and pure. They argued that there could be no possible intersection of the divine and the human and that Jesus, therefore, must have been immaterial, even to the point of claiming that when he walked on Earth he left no footprints. This is why John takes such pains to portray Jesus as somehow both fully human and fully divine, rendering this dual existence most graphically in 1.14: "The Word became Flesh and made his dwelling among us" (Barclay xxvi–xxxi).

John met both of these rhetorical challenges in his use of *archê,* prominently positioned at the beginning of the gospel. Most commentators on this opening phrase, *en archê,* miss the implications of *archê,* either simply noting the allusion to Genesis or ignoring it altogether in their rush to essay upon what appears to be the far more weighty *logos.*[15] However, Arnold Ehrhardt, a German theologian who escaped to England during World War II and spent the rest of his life there, makes a strong case that the full significance of *archê* has been overlooked. In his book, *The Be-*

ginning, he argues that if John had intended a simple adverbial phrase he would have used *ap arches.* There is, he points out, no example in the New Testament or in the Greek Septuagint of *en archê* used adverbially (192).[16] More important, he asks, what could those opening words have meant to its intended Greek audience? First, they would not have had the same associations with the first words of the Torah as would a Jewish audience. More to the point, however, the Greeks would not have understood the concept of the universe as having a beginning at all. So *en archê* would have made no sense to them either as a reference to Genesis 1.1 or to a cosmological beginning. Instead, Ehrhardt says, those Greek readers would have understood "the beginning" in a completely different way, grounded in a centuries-old debate in Greek philosophical and religious circles centering around the concept of *archê.*

Ehrhardt argues that John knew exactly what he was doing with his use of *archê.* No mere adverbial phrase, *en archê* serves to locate the gospel within the broader philosophical context of *archê,* which Ehrhardt defines as "the point where the infinite enters the finite, and the eternal the temporal" (20). That concept of the beginning is far removed from a beginning in time, a starting point or origin. In this one word, then, John finds a way of meeting both of his rhetorical challenges. *Archê*—a thoroughly Greek concept with, as I will show, a long and well-known Greek philosophical provenance—provides a way of addressing the issue of the intersection of the divine and human in a manner that John's Greek audience would readily understand. *En archê* creates a context that enables John to make his challenging theological argument about Jesus accessible to his readers.

Archê is crucial for this study of beginning and writing. In this chapter I am seeking an understanding of the beginning that can serve as a paradigm for beginning. The temporal conception of the beginning of everything projects a paradigm for beginning in time, as starting point or origin. But my investigation of beginning so far has fully illustrated the problems that accompany beginning in time, both chronology and precedence. This is a difficulty Ehrhardt notices as well. "It appears," he says, "that the problem of 'the beginning' is itself an ontological problem. . . . For it is time which engenders the concepts of 'beginning' and 'ending', whilst equally time makes it impossible to think of an absolute beginning 'in time'" (18). Time itself is the issue. As Ehrhardt points out, it is time that supports our assumptions of beginning in time, but it is also time that renders those assumptions unsupportable. What *archê* offers, then, is an alternative paradigm for beginning that is not encumbered by time, a shift from the temporal to the ontological: the beginning is a state of being defined by the productive intersection of contradictory forces. To understand this alternative paradigm for beginning, it is necessary to follow its development in Greek philosophical thought, which is what Ehrhardt does in *The Beginning.*

The first thing Ehrhardt does is dismiss the traditional usage of *archê* as applied to the sixth-century BCE monists whose main contribution to Greek philosophy was their search for the fundamental matter of the universe, usually fire, air, earth, or water. This matter has been traditionally referred to as *archê*. But Ehrhardt points out that there is no evidence that the monists themselves used that term. It was applied to monistic philosophy much later by Theophrastus, a pupil of Aristotle (21–22).

In its proper philosophical usage, *archê* is, in fact, the exact opposite of this monistic principle. After the early monists, ancient Greek philosophical thought was dominated by dualism, the belief in the existence of opposing worlds, one static, pure, and infinite; the other mutable, corrupt, and finite. One of the commanding philosophical questions, then, was what is the relationship, if any, between these two worlds? At stake in this question was how people conceive of their temporal world and the degree to which that world may be affected by or even reflected in the world of the eternal.

The first documented philosophical use of *archê* was in a fragment by Anaximander: "The beginning *[archê]* of all that exists is the infinite *[apeiron]*" (23). In Ehrhardt's reading of this fragment, "the infinite" was not just a vague reference to the unknown. Anaximander recognized that the infinite could only be understood as existing dialectically with the finite. "Without an existing finite the infinite could not 'exist' any more than the cosmos could 'exist' without an existing infinite" (29). It is important to understand that this was not a causal relationship, as in causing the cosmos to come into existence. Rather, the intersection of the infinite and the finite makes the former an *active* principle, bringing order to that which was generated "accidentally." "It follows from all this," Ehrhardt concludes, "that *archê*, the beginning or principle, is the point at which the infinite and the finite meet with each other, and correspondingly is identical for both" (30).

The early Pythagoreans used the ideas of *archê* and *apeiron* as crucial components of their idealistic philosophy. Ehrhardt even hypothesizes a direct connection between Anaximander and Pythagoras (39). Infinity, in the case of the Pythagoreans, became the pure and ideal world of number, the primary ordering principle that defines the world we know. The obvious examples, because they are so closely associated with Pythagoras, are the numerical patterns that may be discerned in the relationship among the sides of the right triangle and among musical tones in harmonic chords: to the Pythagoreans, these patterns were not merely descriptive but instead revealed the profound influence of a normative and static world of number on the visible and changing empirical world that surrounds us.

This relationship between the infinite and the finite was enunciated in the Pythagorean idea of the world of numbers as represented in the One or monad—the divine and the good as well as Nous, the highest nature of the mind itself—and the empirical world as represented in the dyad—the demon, evil, and the lower nature of humankind (41). It was the monad that possessed the active and form-giving power that determines the existence of the passive and material dyad (47). This intersection of the determining monad and the determinable dyad was the *archê,* the point at which the form-giving power of the infinite world impressed itself on the matter of the empirical world. For the Pythagoreans, however, this was not a single causative event of creation but a continuous activity, the evidence of which could be discerned in the mathematical patterns that continue to define the temporal world.

The concept of *archê* also played a significant role in the philosophies of Plato and Aristotle. "Plato's theory of the 'beginning,'" Ehrhardt observes, "is consistently a theory of a 'beginning of motion'" (87). Plato was working within the context of a great philosophical debate over motion and its implications for understanding the cosmos. Many natural philosophers had claimed that movement and change were the dominant characteristics of the empirical world and therefore had challenged the idealistic position that posited a primary world of stasis and permanence. Even if such a world did exist, they argued, there could be no connection between it and the empirical world, for how could motion be generated by a static world (144–45)? So the question of *archê* was of great import for Platonic idealism: "how, if at all, the finite could spring from the infinite or, inversely, the infinite could even touch the finite" (88).

Under the influence of Pythagoreanism, Plato envisioned two opposing worlds, the noetic world of Ideas and the empirical world that surrounds us. His philosophy, however, demanded some interaction between the two, a way for human beings to know the Truth. In *Phaedrus,* for instance, he describes the individual soul as the point of intersection between the two worlds. According to Ehrhardt, the solution in this case was the soul as self-moving mover, "being a beginning rather than having a beginning, yet not absolute motion, but controlled motion" (95). The movement and change of the empirical was not directly caused by the world of Ideas but by the soul, the self-moving mover that acted as *archê,* the link between the two worlds (148).

This solution was not satisfactory either, because Plato needed to build an ontology on something more stable than the individual soul. In *Timaeus* he advances the idea of the *cosmic* soul or world-soul, which is superior to all individual souls. It possesses a gyratory motion, like a top, and penetrates and envelops the empirical world (Ehrhardt 97). Most important, this soul acts as the *archê* of the empirical world "in the sense that it mediates between the world of ideas, the things of the eternal Nous, and creation" (98). The cosmic soul itself was created by the demiurge, which aligned the soul with the eternal and unchanging. Yet by acting as the link between the infinite and the finite, it was not only the cause of motion and change in the latter but also brought with it the possibility of finding the unchanging Truth associated with the former (98). The cosmic soul, the universal self-moving mover, was the *archê:* "The entry of the infinite into the finite world was in the eyes of Plato that 'beginning' which set the cosmos in motion" (102).

Archê was also an important concept in Aristotle's work, particularly in *Metaphysics* (Ehrhardt 115–16). His understanding of *archê,* however, differs dramatically from the mystical treatments by Anaximander, the Pythagoreans, and Plato, whose skepticism concerning the empirical world led them to seek a source of Truth beyond it. Aristotle, materialist that he was, conceived of *archê* less as a cosmological problem than as a physical problem, primarily one of causation (133–34; 151). Aristotle questioned Plato's world of ideas, focusing his attention instead on the empirical world as the source of truth. Yet in doing so, he posited a realm of empirical truth that depended on *archê,* which he represented as the unmoved mover.

For Aristotle, Ehrhardt says, "the ultimate 'beginning' must be closely related to ultimate truth" (132). Aristotle's key insight was that in nature, observations were repeatable and therefore must be true. Thus, he reasoned, the agreement among the subjective truths of many observers must point to an objective truth at the foundation of the empirical world. "This conception of truth, therefore, introduced a static element into the empirical world, that static element for which all the other philosophers had been clamouring" (152)—and seeking outside the empirical world. Yet this truth was not itself in and of the empirical, not itself subject to the senses. Once again, the problem was change and motion in the empirical world. Objective truth was static, unchanging, but the doctrine of physical causality was grounded in motion. Aristotle needed to find a link between the two (152–53). "This solution was found by Aristotle in the figure of the unmoved mover. He had to be unmoved because he was infinite truth; and he had to be the mover because the very existence of the incessantly moving world was brought about by him" (153).

In his consideration of the relationship between the infinite and the finite, Aristotle ended up in a place similar to that of most of his predecessors, but his route was far different. His starting point was the possibility of discerning the infinite in the data gathered in the finite world. Yet *archê* still played an important role as the intermediary between the static state of objective truth and the observable world, the intermediary through which critical observers could discover objective truths by accumulating data through the senses.[17]

It was this philosophical context that John chose to emphasize in the opening phrase of his gospel. For his Greek audience, *en archê* probably would have evoked the issue of opposing worlds and the potential intersection between them. John's argument against the Gnostics would have made sense in this context. *Archê* represented an ancient tradition of the mysterious interpenetration of the infinite and the finite, the divine and the human, the spiritual and the material. John could counter the radical dualism of the Gnostics by alluding to the concept of a powerful and productive interrelationship between seemingly contradictory worlds. In the context of *archê* it was possible, then, to imagine God not as absolutely removed from this world but entering into it. It was possible to imagine Jesus as both fully divine and fully human, leaving footprints as he walked. By using *archê,* Ehrhardt says, John does more than simply establish a connection to the creation event; more significant, he achieves a special messianic emphasis on newness, a new beginning, a new order, a new creation. The import of the gospel is that Jesus, both God and human, was the link between the infinite and the finite, the disruption of an old order and the embodiment of the new (194).[18] Jesus is manifested in and symbolized by *archê,* enabling John to made a case for the possibility of a whole new beginning, a whole new world.

I have framed this chapter by the two instances of "In the beginning" from Genesis and John as a way of dramatizing the differences between two ways of understanding "the beginning" as represented in *reshit* and *archê*. *Archê* offers a fresh paradigm for beginning, moving from the temporal to the ontological. This concept provides the groundwork for a reconstructed understanding of beginning and thus where writing begins. I must admit, however, that thinking of beginning as somehow divorced from time runs counter to all the connotations we bring to the word. The next two chapters will seek to clarify this nontemporal beginning by exploring *archê* as it is manifested in modern dialectical theory and in twentieth-century philosophy.

Then there is the problem of how to distinguish in print this "archelogical" concept of beginning from the more common temporal one. Ehrhardt indicates that archelogical usage by putting the word in quotations—"the beginning." I think there is still a problem with this solution because the singular *beginning* persists in giving the sense of *the* beginning. I prefer to denote archelogical beginning with a plural ending, beginning*s*, capturing the sense of an ongoing and continuous potential for newness in beginnings. Beginning is tied to time, starting point or origin; beginnings, however, is a principle that indicates a relationship between opposing forces that could occur at any point in time, the disjunctive event of new beginnings.[19] To make that point, I would translate the opening of John differently: "In beginnings is the Word"; or "In the principle of beginnings is the Word."[20]

Beginnings still has kinship to the beginning in that they both imply a creative potential, the generation of something new. In beginnings, however, that potential is perpetual and unlimited, in contrast to the singular beginning associated with the cosmic event of the beginning of everything—much like the difference between steady state theory and big bang theory. *Archê,* as I've said, is a state of being marked by the intersection of opposing or contradictory forces and thus carries the potential for newness. Thus, it harkens back to the concept of beginnings I sketched out in the Introduction, providing a label for the power that marks the disjunction of contradictory forces described in that chapter. The image of Janus could very well be the visage of *archê:* two faces looking in opposite directions, indicating the dual existence of contradictory elements; the threshold emblematic of the intersection of these contradictory elements; the creative potential of a new endeavor.

In this chapter, then, I move from the beginning as reflected in *reshit* to beginnings portrayed in *archê*. The sages referred to in the epigraph, an excerpt from the Hindu "Hymn of Creation," seemed to understand well that beginnings lie not in the darkness and watery waste of unknown cosmological origins but in desire, generated in the intersection of contradictions, the kinship of is and is not. The darkness and waste may very well have been at first, as the poem says, but in beginnings is "the primal seed, born of the mind." Thus, creativity is not external, spent in one great heave in the beginning. Rather, creativity is "born of the mind," which generated creation itself, both scientific and theological, but then placed creation outside itself. The "Hymn of Creation" reminds us of this power of beginnings in its wonderfully skeptical glance at the beginning:

> Whence all creation had its origin,
> he, whether he fashioned it or whether he did not,
> he, who surveys it all from highest heaven,
> he knows—or maybe even he does not know.[21]

4 Dialectical Beginnings

> The beginning is not pure nothing, but a nothing from which something is to proceed; therefore being, too, is already contained in the beginning. The beginning, therefore, contains both, being and nothing, is the unity of being and nothing; or is non-being which is at the same time being, and being which is at the same time non-being.
>
> —G. W. F. Hegel, *Science of Logic*

In the previous chapter, I initiated a reconstruction of beginning by establishing a nontemporal beginnings in the classical principle of *archê*. *Archê* is crucial to this study because it provides a means to conceptualize beginning without the burden of time and thus to recast the question of where writing begins, making it a question not about the temporality of writing but about the ontology (and, as I will show, the axiology) of writing. But *archê* carries with it its own burdens: it is an arcane term, weighted by its mystical, idealistic, and theological heritage. Also, it doesn't exactly resonate in the modern consciousness. I have established a principle of beginnings but have not developed it into a workable concept that can be applied to writing. In this chapter, I will advance that cause, and the broader reconstruction of beginning, by searching out the archelogical themes in dialectic.

"Dialectic," says Ian Hunt, "involves the claim that reality is in some way contradictory" (15). This contemporary definition suggests a couple of interesting parallels between dialectic and *archê*. Both are means of labeling the sense that human existence is marked by the potential for contradictory experiences. The classic archelogical experience is the interpenetration of opposing and otherwise separate worlds, the infinite and finite, the eternal and the temporal, the static and the mutable. This otherworldly connection is not necessarily the kind of contradictory experience Hunt is talking about in his portrayal of the contradictions that inhere in the deep structures of reality. But the two are linked by the idea of contradiction itself and a worldview that embraces the mutual existence of opposing forces.

The other parallel is the issue of reality, what is it that we call the real world. For classical idealists such as Pythagoras and Plato, reality existed apart from this corrupt and material world of illusion, a pure and immaterial world of Number or Eternal Forms. *Archê* acted as the critical principle for a possible connection between that reality and this empirical world, the possibility for knowing the real world, experiencing the Truth. For classical materialists such as Aristotle, reality was located in this empirical world, and *archê* was the principle, the unmoved mover, that allowed for knowledge of eternal truths about this reality. Of course, contemporary dialectical theory accepts none of this talk of distant worlds or eternal truths, but, as I will show, the modern history of dialectic is constructed around strongly contested claims about reality, the ideal versus the material.

Now, I am not claiming that there is a direct historical relationship between the two; such an argument would be speculative at best. I do think, however, that there is a substantial conceptual relationship between *archê* and dialectic. Modern dialectic is, in many ways, a conceptual heir to *archê*. It is this relationship that enables me to take *archê* from its obscure classical roots into the modern era.

I must admit, however, that defining a term by associating it with dialectic brings its own risks. The problem is that *dialectic* itself has become semantically promiscuous. Ronald Hall in *The Encyclopedia of Philosophy* lists eight definitions of dialectic and concludes that any one definition that tries to encompass them all would be completely meaningless (385). In *A Grammar of Motives,* Kenneth Burke identifies twelve different definitions, the last of which, he points out, could be taken as either the opposite of or a prime example of dialectic.[1] Those of us without philosophical training tend to use dialectic casually as a way of referring to any sense of give and take, to a relationship between somewhat dissimilar ideas, to some indistinct notion of a middle ground between two extremes, or to anything having to do with Marxism. How can such a vague and polysemous term offer any hope for defining *archê?*

The irony is that in using dialectic as a way of understanding *archê,* we will find that *archê* at the same time helps us to understand dialectic. In a way, the dialectical pairing of these terms permits each one to illuminate the other. What I will do in this chapter is trace modern dialectic back to its source, focusing especially on Kant, Hegel, and Marx and the conceptual shift from contradiction in thought to contradiction in reality, an archelogical understanding of reality.

Dialectic as Contradiction in Thought

Let me start by returning to the modern dialectical claim that "reality is in some way contradictory." In the long history of the philosophical usage of dialectic, it has typically been associated with contradiction. For most of that history, however, it has been contradiction in thought or logic, not contradiction in reality. Aristotle called Zeno of Elea the inventor of dialectic because he pioneered the argumentative method of taking an opposing proposition and proving it illogical by deriving two contradictory conclusions from it (Freeman 47; Guthrie 2: 82).

It was in this sense of the term that dialectic became a potent philosophical method. Hall, for example, describes the Socratic method as "a prolonged cross-examination which refutes the opponent's original thesis by getting him to draw from it, by means of a series of questions and answers, a consequence that contradicts it" (386). And dialectic, of course, played a crucial role in the philosophical methods of Plato and Aristotle, a form of argument that had as its immediate goal either to lead an opponent into contradiction or to avoid falling into self-contradiction (403).[2]

The main reason dialectic provided such a potent form of philosophical argument was that it rested on the assumption that there were no contradictions in reality. *Archê* represented the contradictory experience of the intersection of opposing worlds, but for classical philosophers, the result of this contradictory experience was the knowledge of a reality that was itself not contradictory. Whether material or immaterial, this was the true reality, unified, self-consistent, eternal. Only by penetrating into this reality could one know eternal Truth. Thus, in this sense, reality could not be contradictory. This was precisely why dialectic played such an important role in the logic of the time: true reasoning could not be contradictory because reality itself was not contradictory.

In *Metaphysics,* Aristotle set forth his dictum on the issue: "For the same to hold good and not to hold good simultaneously of the same thing and in the same respect is impossible. . . . This, then, is the firmest of principles" (qtd. in Wilde, "Logic" 277). From this statement emerged three laws of logic related to contradiction: the Law of Noncontradiction, that A and not-A cannot be maintained together; the Law of Excluded Middle, that any well-defined thesis is either true or false, that there can be no middle ground; and the Law of Identity, that everything is identical with itself, that A always equals A and therefore can never equal not-A.[3]

Any contradiction in thought, then, was by its very nature false because it countered assumptions of an absolutely noncontradictory reality. So dialectic, at its most general, was a method of testing a proposition for its adherence to that reality. Any evidence of contradiction in thought failed to meet the test.

Dialectic fell into disrepute, however, when it lost its role as the premier method for uncovering logical inconsistencies and came to be identified, ironically, with the intentional use of these inconsistencies for insidious purposes. And Aristotle was largely to blame. Though his *Topics* established the formal procedures of dialectic, it was superseded by *Analytics,* with its more rigorous method of scientific demonstration, the source of what was for him true scientific knowledge. Aristotle distinguished between the dialectical and analytical methods by their premises: whereas dialectic began with premises that were generally accepted by most people, analytic began with premises that were self-evidently true (Hall 387).

And it was Aristotle who was most influential in the conception of dialectic in the Middle Ages and Renaissance, at first the positive view in the *Topics* and later, when it was rediscovered, the negative view of the *Analytics*. By the eighteenth century, dialectic was considered a thoroughly unsavory enterprise. In his *Logic,* for example, Immanuel Kant describes dialectic as:

> a *logic of semblance (ars sophistica disputatoria),* arising out of an abuse of the analytic, inasmuch as by the mere logical form there is contrived the semblance of true knowledge, the characters of which must, on the contrary, be derived from agreement with objects, and therefore from the *content*. (qtd. in N. Smith, 173)

Kant makes a clear distinction between the false logic of dialectic, the sophistical reasoning that dupes the listener by creating the illusion of truth in the guise of logic, and the true logic of the analytic, which reveals the truth because it is a logic that reflects true reality. Dialectic is only to be disdained.

A dramatic rehabilitation of dialectic in the late eighteenth and early nineteenth centuries, however, was initiated by Kant's reconsideration of dialectic in his later *Critique of Pure Reason*. For most of his career, Kant had worked within the rationalist paradigm founded in Aristotle and exemplified for him most immediately by Leibniz. Late in life, though, Kant began to question the foundations of rationalism, reporting that he noticed certain irreconcilable problems within rationalist metaphysics. The most important cause of his questioning, however, was his discovery of David Hume's empiricism. The issue for Kant came down to two conflicting views of human knowledge. In one, knowledge was based on *a priori* understanding, the rationalist view that the structures inherent in the mind are able to reveal fully the real structures of the world around us; in the other, knowledge was based on experimentation, the empiricist view that our understanding depends on sense perceptions that accumulate in the memory and become knowledge. The former is deductive and relies on what Kant called concepts, the latter inductive and depends on intuitions, Kant's term for sense perceptions.[4]

In *Critique of Pure Reason,* Kant investigates this epistemological dilemma by studying the knowledge structures of three disciplines—mathematics, physics, and metaphysics. The first two qualify as real sciences because they incorporate both concepts and intuitions; deductive reasoning may be legitimated by proofs of evidence. The critique of pure reason, however, does not begin until Kant turns his attention to metaphysics. His broad purpose here is to expose metaphysics as inherently fallacious because it exists in a realm in which there is no empirical basis for testing ideas against empirical perceptions. He makes this purpose abundantly clear:

> There has always existed in the world, and there will always continue to exist, some kind of metaphysics, and with it the dialectic that is natural to pure reason. It is therefore the first and most important task of philosophy to deprive metaphysics, once and for all, of its injurious influence, by attacking its errors at their very source. (29–30)[5]

That "very source" is, as Kant indicated, dialectic, "a *logic of illusion [Schein]*" (297). What is significant about Kant's use of dialectic, though, is that he extends the concept of dialectic beyond its usual parameters of logical error. In the earlier *Logic,* from which I quoted above, dialectic was presented as the province of sophists and other shysters who dressed their falsehoods in the respectable clothing of analytic logic. Such dialectical reasoning was considered relatively inconsequential because it was founded on logical error that could be eliminated simply through more careful attention to true logic (N. Smith 173–74). In *Critique of Pure Reason,* however, Kant sets forth quite a different understanding of dialectic: a form of reasoning that creates an illusion that is impossible to expunge because it is based only on pure reason.

> There exists, then, a natural and unavoidable dialectic of pure reason—*not* one in which a bungler might entangle himself through lack of knowledge, or one which some sophist has artificially invented to confuse thinking people, but one inseparable from human reason, and which, even after its deceptiveness has been exposed, will not cease to play tricks with reason and continually entrap it into momentary aberrations ever again calling for correction. (300; my emphasis)

This "transcendental" dialectic represents a major shift from the dialectic of the rationalist tradition. In its strictly logical form, dialectic had been an error in thought, a relatively superficial problem caused by a lack of adherence to the rules of analytic logic, which, when applied, would expose the error through its contradictory conclusions. But as transcendental, dialectic becomes a necessary result of a certain way of thinking about the world, which for Kant was the pure reasoning of metaphysics. Dialectic was no longer a contradiction in thought but a contradiction in the very fabric of deductive reasoning. Kant illustrates this transcendental dialectic with what he calls the antinomies of pure reason, four sets of contradictory arguments concerning the great metaphysical issues of all time, the first of which is, perhaps not coincidentally, the subject of the previous chapter: that the world has a beginning in time and is limited in space and that it has no beginning and no limitations. The theses and antitheses of the antinomies face each other in opposing columns on the pages, graphically representing Kant's point that they can never be resolved because they are subject only to pure reason, without the validating possibilities of empirical knowledge.[6]

Thus, transcendental dialectic signifies for Kant the contradictory deep structure of deductive thought and provides him with his most persuasive argument for the critique of pure reason. As such, his transcendental dialectic represents a much more profound understanding of dialectic than the merely logical dialectic of the rationalist tradition. The emphasis is still on contradictions, but these contradictions are now considered inherent in pure reason. Kant, then, does not represent the revolution in dialectical theory that defined dialectic as contradictions in reality, but he prepared the way for that revolution, which came full force in Hegel.

Dialectical Beginnings in Hegel

In 1812, thirty-one years after Kant first published *Critique of Pure Reason,* Hegel surveyed the philosophical scene in the preface to the first edition of his *Science of Logic*. What he found in the aftermath of the Kantian revolution did not please him.

> That which, prior to this period, was called metaphysics has been, so to speak, extirpated root and branch and has vanished from the ranks of the sciences. The ontology, rational psychology, cosmology, yes even natural theology, of former times—where is now to be heard any mention of them, or who would venture to mention them? (25)

He lays all blame at the feet of Kant whose philosophy, he says, teaches that the use of pure reason "generates nothing but fantasies of the brain" (25).

Hegel's philosophy, in contrast to Kant's, may be described as a *defense* of pure reason. However, instead of simply a challenge to Kant, Hegel's work may also be seen as building on the foundation laid by Kant, particularly that part of it that was the dialectic. In *Science of Logic* Hegel points appreciatively to Kant's elevation of dialectic from its earlier status as mere illogical trickery to "a *necessary function of reason*" (56).

Hegel, then, builds on Kant's idea of dialectic as a necessary part of the structure of reason, but he reverses the conclusions Kant reached on the basis of that premise. This reversal is evident in the terms of Hegel's definition of dialectic as "the grasping of opposites in their unity or of the positive in the negative" (56). In this definition Hegel takes a dramatic step away from Kant, for whom the dialectical antinomies existed forever in mutual negation. Hegel, then, redefines dialectic in a radical way—according to the mutual identity innate to contradictory forces. In doing so he not only challenges Kant but also the age-old prohibition against contradictions in reality. It is no accident, therefore, that Hegel specifically rejects all three laws of contradiction: the Law of Noncontradiction, the Law of the Excluded Middle, and the Law of Identity (Kainz 15; Wilde, *Marx* 17–18). Kant may have raised dialectic to "a *necessary function of reason,*" but he kept the opposing forces apart—static, sterile, and unproductive. Hegel revolutionized the concept of dialectic by declaring the incompatibility of contradictions as illusion, thus offering a more complex understanding of the world and the potential for a productive relationship between contradictions. Dialectic, in his hands, became a necessary function of reality.

For Hegel, reality itself is contradictory, and the power of dialectic comes from its ability to reveal that fundamental nature of reality. It is unfortunate, then, that most people's understanding of Hegel's dialectical theory may be summed up—and then summarily dismissed—by reference to thesis-antithesis-synthesis. This is a gross distortion of what is a complex, subtle, and powerful understanding of dialectic. Indeed, that three-part structure was never used explicitly by Hegel; it was from the earlier theory of the philosopher Johann Gottlieb Fichte (Hall 387–88; Wilde, *Marx* 13). In fact, Hegel says that Fichte's theses and antitheses were contradictory only in the old sense, unconditional absolutes that opposed each other categorically (*Science* 95). For Hegel, on the contrary, the opposing principles were ontologically related to each other.

Hegel radically altered the concept of dialectic from contradiction of thought to contradiction in reality, an alteration that goes far beyond thesis-antithesis-synthesis. What makes Hegel particularly interesting for this study, however, is that he draws an explicit connection between dialectical contradictions in reality and the concept of beginnings, a connection that provides a link between dialectic and *archê.*

After the introductory section of *Science of Logic,* Hegel opens the monumental work with a section entitled "With What Must the Science Begin?" He is asking a question much like my own guiding question about writing; his question is, where does philosophy begin, or more accurately, where does philosophical *thinking* begin? He observes that in the philosophical tradition, this question of beginnings has typically been a question of the absolute ground upon which to build a philosophy. In their search for such a ground, philosophers tended to lean either toward *objective* principles—"water, the one, *nous,* idea, substance, monad, etc."—or toward *subjective* principles—"thought, intuition, sensation, ego, subjectivity itself" (67). None of these principles has provided the sought-for ground, says Hegel, because all of them were already mediated by thought, already existing as concepts. To get at a true beginning, he says, one must rid oneself of all preconceptions and simply observe reality. What one sees is pure being, a *"simple immediacy,"* abstract and indeterminate (69).

Hegel's idea of pure being as a beginning point for philosophical thinking is important because pure being is dialectical, a composition of contradictory elements. The epigraph to this chapter is a sample of Hegel's attempt to work out this difficult idea of dialectical beginnings. For him, dialectical beginnings is the interpenetration of contradictory principles, of being and nothing, of sameness and difference, existing together in a complex relationship. On the one hand, he says, a beginning is nonbeing because that which begins doesn't yet exist. But it is a nonbeing that carries within itself a reference to being, the other, that which begins. On the other hand, a beginning already is because if it is a beginning it is no longer nonbeing. A beginning, then, is a state marked by the contradictory relationship between being and nothing (74–75).

This effort by Hegel to understand where philosophical thinking begins represents a significant shift in *archê,* the principle of beginnings. For the classical philosophers in Ehrhardt's discussion of the beginning, *archê* was conceived as a way of accounting for the contradictory experience that allowed them to found their thought in a noncontradictory reality. As Hegel points out, all philosophers since then have done that as well, seeking absolute grounding in either the objective or subjective reality, solid and unified first principles for beginning their philosophical thinking. Hegel's insight, as I see it, is that the contradictory experience of *archê* is itself the principle of beginnings in philosophy because reality is, at its root, contradictory. First principles or beginnings for Hegel are contradictory because reality is contradictory. Dialectic, which was always concerned with contradiction, became the primary method for Hegel's philosophy.

Hegel further explores the dialectical beginnings of being and nothing in the wider compass of *becoming,* "a movement in which both are distinguished, but by a difference which has equally immediately resolved itself" (83). *Movement* is the key term here because, as Hegel explains it, the apparent contradiction of being and nonbeing may be resolved when we see them together as becoming. Being is not static but is always passing into nothing, or ceasing to be. Nothing, likewise, is always passing into being, or coming to be. They are becoming and, as such, are both identical and nonidentical—being and nothing (106). Pure being and pure nothing are both distinct and the same, separated and unseparated. This relationship can only be explained as becoming, which, Hegel says, is more than simply a unity of being and nothing; it defines the ontology of both being and nothing.

Hegel's idea of becoming, thus, runs directly counter to the traditional Western approach to contradiction, particularly the Law of the Excluded Middle, which states that all things either are or are not, that there is nothing that is not either A or not-A. "But against this," he says, "it has been shown that being and nothing are, in fact, the same [and] . . . that *there is nothing which is not an intermediate state between being and nothing*" (104–5).

The structure of *Science of Logic,* like the structure of most of Hegel's works, reflects the principle of dialectical beginnings writ large. Every chapter (considering the last two as one) reflects the dialectical relationship of being, nothing, and becoming; together all the chapters form an interlocking set of dialectical relationships, starting with being and nothing and ending up with (actually circling back to) the Absolute Idea. In each case, an initial negative movement is countered by a second negative movement—"the negation of the negation"—which results in a new essence or immediacy only to be mediated by further dialectical movements. This circular movement from immediacy to immediacy is, Hegel says, "universal, and in this universality, the *negativity* that constituted its dialectic and mediation has also collapsed into *simple determinateness* which can be a beginning" (838).

Thus, Hegel's dialectical system may be described as a complex interweaving of beginnings. The contradictory relationship of being and nothing acts as a ruling principle for his dialectical philosophy, representing a much larger play of dialectical beginnings. Hegel describes this process as

> a *circle* returning upon itself, the end being wound back into the beginning, the simple ground, by the mediation; this circle is moreover a *circle of circles,* for each individual member as ensouled by the method is reflected into itself, so that in returning into the beginning it is at the same time the beginning of a new member. (842)

Hegel's dialectical philosophy, then, is also a philosophy of beginnings. The principle of beginnings itself, as embracing both being and nothing in becoming, is a principle of change, of the possibility for something new located in the openness that occurs in the tension of contradictions.

Dialectic is archelogical, at least the way dialectic is used by Hegel in the relatively early *Science of Logic.* This is not, however, the way the term is used in much of Hegel's later work. As Hegel became more and more conservative, he began treating dialectic not as an open system but as a closed one—deterministic. For example, in *The Philosophy of History* he portrays all of history as a narrative plot, the enactment of God's purpose in the gradual realization of human freedom. The dialectical structure originates in ancient Greek society, which revolved around communal needs at the expense of individual liberty, moves through the individualistic challenges of Socrates and Christianity to the violent excesses of the French Revolution, and finds its ultimate integration in the German society of Hegel's time, a harmony of freedom and communal order (Singer 78). It is obviously an argument for the status quo. Other books, such as *The Philosophy of Right* and *Encyclopedia of Philosophy,* also define dialectic more in terms of necessity and inevitability than the eternal openness of the *Science of Logic.*

For Hegel, then, dialectic became a tool for bourgeois conservatism. But there was still within dialectic itself a revolutionary potential. Karl Marx recognized that revolutionary potential and spent much of his life trying to harness it.

Dialectical Beginnings in Marx

"Nothing in Marxist philosophy," says Chris Arthur, "is more obscure than the precise relation of Marx to Hegel on the question of the dialectic" (87). Just as Hegel did with Kant, Marx both challenged and built on Hegel's dialectical theory. My purpose here, however, is not to unravel the intricate web of this relationship but to discern in Marx's use of dialectic the archelogical nature of reality postulated by Hegel. To do this, I will frame my discussion with a consideration of two passages from the afterword to the second German edition of *Capital* in which Marx addresses his use of Hegel's dialectical method. In the first passage, he describes his concept of dialectic in contrast to Hegel's. In the second, he shows how they are similar.

Here is the first passage:

> My dialectic method is not only different from the Hegelian, but is its direct opposite. To Hegel, the life-process of the human brain, i.e., the process of thinking, which, under the name of 'the Idea', he even transforms into an independent subject, is the demiurgos of the real world, and the real world is only the external, phenomenal form of 'the Idea'. With me, on the contrary, the ideal is nothing else than the material world reflected by the human mind, and translated into forms of thought. (*Karl Marx* 420)[7]

At issue in this excerpt is the ancient archelogical problem of the locus of reality: is it the external, immaterial world of Hegel (the Idea) or the very present, material world of Marx? That is the crucial difference between the two philosophers, as Marx sees it. Perhaps the clearest elaboration by Marx of this difference is presented in a set of manuscripts written in 1844 but not published until 1932. Marx takes as his source Hegel's earliest major work, *Phenomenology of Spirit,* in which Hegel describes the dialectical movement as originating in alienation. Men and women become alienated from the world when they believe that the objects of the world are other than themselves, alienated or externalized from themselves. Such alienation, says Hegel, is an illusion because these objects are actually projections of the mind. This is the alienation of the object from the subject, an illusion that is overcome in the understanding that there is no separation of the material object from the spiritual subject, that indeed everything is spirit, everything is mind (*Karl Marx* 100).

Marx says that the problem with Hegel's dialectic is that it begins and ends with abstract idealism. Marx, though, proposes the opposite movement. Whereas Hegel begins with the self-alienation of the mind—the illusion of objects as externalized from the subject—and overcomes that externalization in the self-possession of the mind, Marx begins with the self-alienation of the material reality—the illusion of production or goodness as externalized in private property or religion—and overcomes that externalization with a movement back to the material (*Karl Marx* 97–100).[8] The real for Hegel resides in the ideal, for Marx in the material. For Hegel, then, the problem is how to fully experience the ideal in the material; for Marx, it is how to fully experience the material in the ideal. This is the archelogical movement that each describes, though in opposite directions, as dialectic. Each requires the interpenetration of contradictory forces to move from illusion to reality.

Now for the second passage, which comes one paragraph after the first. In the intervening paragraph, Marx says that he had been highly critical of Hegel thirty years before when Hegel was still the dominant figure in German philosophy. But now that Hegel's philosophy has been given up for dead, Marx has come to its defense by pointing out that though Hegel's dialectic may have been used in the service of the Ideal, Hegel was still the first to incorporate it as a comprehensive critical method, a distinction between what he calls the mystified form of dialectic and the rational form.

> In its mystified form, dialectic became the fashion in Germany, because it seemed to transfigure and to glorify the existing state of things. In its rational form it is a scandal and abomination to bourgeoisdom and its doctrinaire professors, because it includes in its comprehension an affirmative recognition of the existing state of things at the same time also the recognition of the negation of that state, of its inevitable breaking-up; because it regards every historically developed social form as in fluid movement, and therefore takes into account its transient nature not less than its momentary existence; because it lets nothing impose upon it, and is in its essence critical and revolutionary. (*Karl Marx* 421)

What Marx sees in Hegel's dialectic, despite its tendency toward idealism, is its revolutionary potential, the powerful opportunity for—indeed, necessity of—change, the possibility for something new. As early as 1844, Marx observed that there was in Hegel the kernel of productive criticism. Indeed, he says, it's possible to see in the *Phenomenology* two Hegels, both defender of the status quo and critic of it. The first of these is the caricature of Hegel as the archconservative using his theory as a justification for the present state as the necessary product of previous contradictory movements. The latter, though, is Hegel as dialectical critic, who "conceives of the alienation of man's self and his being, the loss of his object and his reality, as self-discovery, manifestation of being, objectification, realization" (*Karl Marx* 108). At the core of this critical dialectic is the recognition of the fact that reality is contradictory and of the revolutionary potential generated by contradiction.

One place where Marx explores this relationship between contradictions and criticism is in *The Poverty of Philosophy,* an attack on Pierre Joseph Proudhon's *System of Economic Contradictions: The Philosophy of Poverty.* In it, Marx condemns Proudhon for many wrongs against economic theory, but especially his misuse of dialectic, both relying too much on and deviating too much from Hegel.

The first accusation concerns Proudhon's embrace of Hegel's idealism, an idealism that purposely abstracts itself from real history, choosing not the sequence of *history* but "the sequence of *ideas*" (*Karl Marx* 199; my emphasis). The second accusation interests me more because it provides a better understanding of the revolutionary potential Marx found in Hegel's dialectic. Marx condemns Proudhon for misconceiving dialectic as a static concept. *Contradictions* in Proudhon's title is a clear reference to Hegel, but, Marx points out, "M. Proudhon has nothing of Hegel's dialectics but the language" (204). Proudhon's idea of contradiction is that every economic concept has two sides, good and bad. Slavery, for example, is a moral evil but is also good because it is beneficial to world trade. What Proudhon seeks to do, then, is to eliminate the bad while keeping the good. Thus he has reduced Hegel's dialectic, Marx observes, to a problem of good versus bad, which completely misses the point of that dialectic. "What constitutes dialectical movement is the coexistence of two contradictory sides, their conflict and their fusion into a new category. The very setting of the problem of eliminating the bad side cuts short the dialectical movement" (204). The problem is that without contradiction there is no opportunity for movement, no possibility for beginnings; Proudhon's one-sided dialectic is not contradictory at all and thus ignores the real movement of history and offers no opportunity for change (206).

What Marx sees in Hegel's dialectical method is the necessity and value of the experience of contradictory reality. It is in the productive nature of contradiction, I believe, that Marx finds the principle of beginnings within his own philosophy. In *The Poverty of Philosophy,* for example, Marx identifies revolutionary beginnings in the contradiction of class antagonisms: "An oppressed class is the vital condition for every society founded on the antagonism of classes. The emancipation of the oppressed class thus implies the creation of a new society" (*Karl Marx* 14). And in *The German Ideology,* Marx (with Friedrich Engels) says that the critical point of contradiction is the division of labor. When this contradiction becomes intolerable, a new stage of history will be ushered in, one in which labor will no longer be forcibly divided against the interest of the individual but will allow each individual to do whatever labor he or she wishes (*Karl Marx* 169).

Nowhere is Marx's debt to Hegel's dialectical beginnings more clearly exhibited than in *Capital,* with its masterful representation of the contradictory nature of political economy. Just as Hegel finds his beginnings in the contradictory nature of pure being, Marx finds his beginnings in the contradictory nature of commodity, "the economic cell-form" of capitalism (*Karl Marx* 415–16). Commodity is composed of the opposing elements use-value and exchange-value, the *quality* of a thing and the *quantity* of a thing (421–25). Use-value itself is composed of matter and labor (426), and it is because of this material quality that use-value "is the very opposite" of exchange-value, which has no material existence at all, "a purely social reality" (429). Exchange-value is also composed of two forms, the equivalent and the relative values, which Marx describes as "two intimately connected, mutually dependent and inseparable elements of the expression of value; but at the same time, are mutually exclusive, antagonistic extremes—i.e., poles of the same expression" (430). Marx points out that the internal "opposition or contrast" within a commodity is at its clearest when one commodity is placed beside another for the sake of determining value (*Capital* 71).

Much like Hegel's being and nonbeing, the dialectical nature of commodity forms a pattern that defines other economic entities, money, labor, circulation of commodities, and on and on. *Capital* exposes a web of contradictory relationships painstakingly historicized. For what purpose? To show that capitalism was not, as many of its "doctrinaire professors" had suggested, an economic monolith that could survive indefinitely but rather a collection of contradictions that would soon collapse upon itself in its "inevitable breaking-up" (421). And it is dialectic, in its rational form, that allows Marx to demonstrate this potential for material change, the recognition that all social forms are indeed fluid. The source for this opportunity for newness lies in the intersection of contradictions, the knowledge that every state of being holds within itself its opposite.

For Hegel, the contradiction at the root of pure being radiated throughout the *Science of Logic;* for Marx, the same may be said for the contradiction at the root of commodity in *Capital*. Similar to Hegel, then, Marx sought his beginnings not in some noncontradictory reality but in the contradictory experience of reality itself as represented in *archê*. The archelogical method, as developed in Hegel's dialectic, provided Marx an effective way of describing a material reality that in its very core is contradictory. That reality, *because* it is contradictory, is forever in motion and thus bears with it a creative potential, the possibility for change, for beginnings.

Conclusion

In this chapter I've sought to establish conceptual links between *archê* and dialectic as a way of developing the principle of beginnings as a relevant, working concept. The key to understanding those links is the shift in dialectic from its focus on contradiction in thought to contradiction in reality. As a method of reasoning, dialectic was used by Plato and Aristotle and others to root out contradiction in thought in order to identify the Truth, which by its very nature must be noncontradictory because true reality was itself noncontradictory. As I suggested in the previous chapter, the principle of *archê* played a prominent role in Greek philosophy as a way of representing an intersection between the opposing worlds of the infinite and finite, an intersection that allowed philosophers to make claims for a unified and self-consistent Truth based on a knowable static reality.

The revolutionary shift in dialectic from contradiction in thought to contradiction in reality was prepared by Kant and fully instated by Hegel and Marx. I see in this shift also a critical refocusing of *archê*, from the experience of contradiction that allows for knowledge of a noncontradictory reality to the experience of contradiction *as* reality. Though I certainly cannot claim that Hegel and Marx consciously applied the ancient principle of beginnings to their work, I discern critical themes of *archê* played out in their revision of dialectic. Hegel, for example, is obviously concerned with beginnings in philosophy and sees the value of his own work as providing a new source of beginnings, not in the originary foundation of noncontradictory substance but in contradiction itself, as represented in the immediate experience of pure being. Marx incorporated the same principle of beginnings variously instantiated as class antagonism, the division of labor, and commodity, each a contradiction in reality. For both Hegel and Marx, the principle of beginnings was not simply a starting point for their philosophies but rather permeated their philosophies at every level.

Another archelogical theme in dialectic is found in the disagreement between Hegel and Marx as to the source of reality. Reminiscent of the disagreement between Plato and Aristotle, Hegel placed the real in the ideal, Marx in the material. There is also the theme of the beginning of motion in the relationship between the static world and the mutable world. For Hegel, inherent in pure being is also the principle of becoming, because written into the contradictory nature of pure being is nonbeing, which is always a state of becoming being just as being is a state of becoming nonbeing. It was this dialectical motion innate to contradiction that Marx seized on as the source of revolutionary potential in Hegelian dialectic: that which may appear to be monolithic and thus static is, in reality, internally contradictory and thus the source of newness—beginnings. Hegel's dialectic, then, allowed Marx to portray *social realities* as changeable also. James Farr notes that it is important to understand the Marxian concept of motion not just as quantitative or spatial but also as qualitative, which he describes as "experienced internally by an entity, as its very identity changes and unfolds." Just as in

Hegel, the contradictory forces in Marx "have 'inner connections' and 'hidden potentialities' to develop into the other. . . . They are negated as they pass out of existence and emerge into newer and usually higher forms" (Farr 112). Thus, it is not that contradiction simply *allows* for newness but that contradiction is the *source* for newness.

This potential for newness ties in to the last archelogical theme I will mention, the creative potential in the experience of contradiction. According to Milton Fisk, the contradiction at the heart of every entity creates a basic instability that functions as a kind of promise as well as an impetus for change. Fisk concludes that "change is inseparable from contradiction" (128–29). Of course, there are different visions of the kinds of changes Marx was talking about. Wilde, for example, says that human beings are alienated from their true creative essence by the capitalist system and that our creativity can be liberated only through a revolution in the mode of production (*Marx* 94–95). Erica Sherover-Marcuse, however, describes creativity in terms of an emancipatory consciousness that results in the "transformation of subjectivity" (4). Whatever the change, Marx recognized in Hegel's dialectic the creative potential for something new and thus the revolutionary hope for a change in the human condition.

The archelogical themes in dialectic help us to understand more clearly a nontemporal conception of beginnings. Dialectic, then, provides an important extension of my reconstruction of beginnings. In *Science of Logic,* Hegel conceived of his philosophy as a series of beginnings, each marked by contradictory terms and each circling back to a new beginning. Though Marx doesn't refer explicitly to beginnings as Hegel does, that same pattern characterizes *Capital*. This is not beginnings in time and certainly not of time. Rather, it is beginnings as a state of being marked by the intersection of contradictory forces and the potential for newness generated in that contradiction. Beginnings is a way of understanding reality as contradictory and thus as possessing that potential.

5 Archelogical Dialectic

> Without Contraries is no progression. Attraction and Repulsion, Reason and Energy, Love and Hate, are necessary to Human existence.
>
> —William Blake, *The Marriage of Heaven and Hell*

In the previous chapter, I used dialectic as a way of defining more clearly the ancient principle of *archê*. The point was to take this remote Greek concept and bring it into the modern era by searching out a kinship between it and dialectic, one of the most widely used and evocative concepts in modern thought. The kinship between *archê* and dialectic is located in contradiction, particularly the idea that reality is contradictory. Looking at *archê* as dialectical helped me to define more clearly the principle of beginnings, not only by focusing on the shared theme of contradiction but also by exposing certain patterns of beginnings in the dialectical methodologies of Hegel and Marx.

In this chapter, I will shift from the perspective of *archê* as dialectical to one of dialectic as archelogical. This shift invites a more refined conception of the relationship between dialectic and *archê*. The problem, as I showed in the introduction to the previous chapter, is that dialectic itself is so diversely defined that it severely limits its value as a conceptual correlate. Delineating an archelogical dialectic within other forms of dialectic not only will make the archelogical more definite but also will help to make more sense of the diversity within dialectic.

The two chief goals for my investigation of archelogical dialectic are to establish the viability of *archê* for this study of beginnings and where writing begins and to construct a model of beginnings that I can use later in my consideration of writing and teaching writing. To achieve those goals, I will pluck out the archelogical thread from the dialectical methods of Hegel and Marx and follow that thread as it runs through the dialectical tradition of the twentieth century—existentialism, post-Marxism, and William Desmond's philosophy of the middle—and beyond that tradition—chaos theory and process philosophy. In addition to generating a greater appreciation of the role of *archê* in contemporary thought, this treatment of dialectic as archelogical will lay the groundwork for understanding writing as archelogical.

An Archelogical Dialectic

The first step is to establish more precisely what *archê* means in dialectical terms. To do that, I will return for a moment to John's use of the concept in the fourth gospel. As I've suggested, John called upon this rich Greek philosophical term to evoke the experience of the interpenetration of contradictory worlds. *Archê* was a way of expressing the mutual relationship of contradictions, opposing principles caught in creative tension, each existing both within and apart from the other, at once identical and different. Thus, *archê* provided John a powerful concept with which to mount his argument that Jesus was the *archê,* both fully human and fully divine. It was a double argument against the idea that Jesus was merely human and not God at all as well as against the idea that Jesus was absolutely God and not human at all. It was not, then, an idealist's rejection of the material for the sake of the pure reality of another world; John was, after all, contesting the claims of the Gnostics, who believed that this world was essentially evil and thus completely removed from God. The principle of beginnings in the first two words of John's gospel established an opening, the possibility for newness in the universe created by the reciprocal intersection of human and divine. As fully God and fully human, Jesus was emblematic of the interrelationship of these contradictory worlds.

Thus, Jesus was a manifestation of contradiction, the promise of a new reality founded in the productive tension of opposing worlds. As *archê,* Jesus represented the reality of contradiction. Now this is not the same as saying that reality is contradictory, but it is close enough to enable me to project an archelogical dialectic. It is a form of dialectic in which the contradictory terms coexist in an exquisite tension, marking the creative potential in contradictory reality. This form emerged in my discussion of Hegel and Marx in the previous chapter, but I have already admitted to a highly selective approach there. It may be helpful, then, to place archelogical dialectic in the context of two other forms that dominate our sense of the dialectical.

One reason that it is useful to look at Kant, Hegel, and Marx together is that they provide a model for a dialectical way of understanding dialectic. That is, dialectic may be interpreted in either of two opposing positions or in a way that is defined by the tension between those extremes. This middle position is an archelogical dialectic, the one that best captures the sense of beginnings. On one extreme is Kant's dialectic of difference or of doubt, with its rigid separation of contradictions as represented in the antinomies of pure reason. This is a dialectic of doubt related to the oldest philosophical application of the term, a way of using contradiction to cast doubt on a thesis. Kant was an important figure in the rehabilitation of dialectic, showing that it was a necessary result of engaging in pure reason. But for Kant, dialectic remained a negative concept, still about contradictions in thought (i.e., contradictions inherent in metaphysical thinking), not reality, still about contradictions as logical incompatibilities. The contradictory arguments of the antinomies remain apart, a dialectic of static reality, offering no opportunity for creative interaction.

Opposed to the dialectic of difference or doubt is the other extreme position, the dialectic of identity or certainty. This latter dialectic represents a deterministic vision of the world in which the contradictory elements of reality are resolved, resulting in an absolute certainty that the world is locked into large patterns of reality, moving toward a predetermined end. It is this teleological dialectic that dominates popular conceptions of dialectic, with the pseudo-Hegelian concept of thesis-antithesis-synthesis and the supposedly Marxian idea of the inevitable end of history. My understanding of the dialectical theories of Hegel and Marx are obviously much more complex than that. I must admit, though, that there is a decided tendency toward dialectical determinism in both. This is the teleological Hegel for whom history, aesthetics, political science, and practically everything else is guided by a Spirit to its ineluctable end. This is the teleological Marx whose writings were used to support the dogmatisms of "historical materialism" and "dialectical materialism" and to provide the theoretical framework for Marxist-Leninist Communism.[1]

These two dialectics represent the extreme positions in the broader dialectic I am proposing. Each may be defined by the way it views contradictions. The static dialectic of difference emphasizes the distinctions in contradictions and thus keeps them apart, isolated from each other in their differences, a sterile relation. The teleological dialectic of identity emphasizes the sameness in contradictions and thus the necessity of their unity, a deterministic relation. The first is a radical separation marking impossibility, the second a radical closure marking necessity. Neither of these dialectics possesses the power of *archê*. An archelogical dialectic must be defined in terms of both difference and identity, doubt and certainty, separation and closure, impossibility and necessity; thus, between the extremes, offering a both-and relationship, is this dialectic of productive tension and hope.

Now, I have already suggested that portrayals of Hegel and Marx as monolithic teleologists are exaggerated. Hegel's *Science of Logic* expresses the open-ended, productive potential of an archelogical dialectic, which he moved away from in many subsequent writings. Marx, however, is a more complicated case. Indeed, there has been a tendency in recent studies to identify two Marxes, one the determinist, pointing toward the preordained end of history; the other the humanist, supporting individual and communal liberation in the day-to-day struggle with oppressive ideologies.[2]

Perhaps the most radical statement of an archelogical dialectic by Marx is in his *Critique of Hegel's Philosophy of Right*. In the context of a larger review of Hegel's political thinking, particularly the idea that a monarch occupies the necessary middle position between the extremes of a legislative and an "estates element," Marx addresses the idea of a middle or broader term. "Real extremes," he says,

> cannot be mediated precisely because they are real extremes. Nor do they require mediating, for they are opposed in essence. They have nothing in common, they do not need each other, they do not supplement each other. The one does not have in its own bosom the longing for, the need for, the anticipation for the other. (Marx and Engels 88)

As an illustration of this principle, Marx uses the pairs north and south and male and female as examples of oppositions that are not real extremes, those that attract each other and indeed define each other. He says that such oppositions are not true contradictions because they are of the same *essence*. "*True actual* extremes would be pole and *non*-pole, human and *non*-human species" (88). Only in these cases would there be an actual contradiction of essences. "Hegel's chief error is to conceive the *contradiction of appearances* as *unity in essence, in the idea,* while in fact it has something more profound for its essence, namely, an *essential contradiction*" (91).

In this passage, Marx is arguing against what he sees as Hegel's dialectic of necessity by pointing out that Hegel's contradictions are not really contradictory at all. They are contradictory only in appearance, not in essence. Essential contradictions cannot be subsumed into any larger category. Though it could be argued, as Colletti has done, that Marx's insistence on essential contradictions places the very concept of dialectic in question, it seems to me that Marx's argument against the contradiction of appearances is a way of positioning himself apart from the teleological Hegel, not casting doubt on dialectic but proffering a dialectic of the middle, a relationship defined in the tension inherent in the contradiction of essences.

This is the sort of dialectic we find in *Capital,* the meticulous investigation of the essential contradictions at the root of capitalism. This criticism is founded on neither difference nor identity but on both. Marx brings the contradictory forces together but steadfastly avoids unifying them: use-value and exchange-value are not resolved in commodity nor in money nor in the circulation of commodities nor in any other component of the economy but are maintained in their unsettling discontinuity throughout. By bringing essential contradictions into a productive tension, Marx established a way of understanding the world that goes beyond both destructive doubt and blind necessity to offer a hope for something new in the inevitability of change.

I also think, however, that Marx is unfairly generalizing in his criticism of Hegel as trading only in contradictions of appearances. I have argued that there is also in Hegel ample evidence of essential contradictions. Indeed, this interpretation is borne out by much of the recent scholarship on Hegel. Howard P. Kainz, for example, treats the Hegelian dialectic as producing not synthesis but paradox in which contradictions are maintained in a perpetual tension. Terry Pinkard describes a "nonfoundational" view of Hegel, whose method, unlike Kant's, avoided *unique* solutions to questions of philosophy by offering merely tentative, speculative solutions that were never intended to be absolute but simply possessed, for the moment, a more powerful explanatory value (7). And Menahem Rosen proposes an argument against the teleological interpretation of Hegel's method, "namely, to grasp human experience through a double dialectical movement, both *a priori* and *a posteriori,* respecting the ambiguities and paradoxes encountered, and avoiding suppressing them univocally" (xviii). What is emphasized in these views of Hegel is the perpetual tension in the relationship between contradictions, a tension that cannot exist in a dialectic of difference and is lost in the rush for closure in the dialectic of identity.

It is *this* Marx and *this* Hegel that define an archelogical dialectic. In contrast to the Kantian form, an archelogical dialectic entails the interpenetration of contradictory forces, not just negation but the negation of negation, a dialectical form that is not sterile but creative. And in contrast to the teleological form, those contradictory forces resist resolution in the closed universe of necessary ends; instead, they maintain a creative tension and an open universe. It is this productive tension that is the key to an archelogical dialectic, a way of representing the opening that is created between impossibility and necessity. It is this archelogical openness that has captured the imaginations of many twentieth-century thinkers who have followed in the dialectical tradition.

An Archelogical Dialectic of Existence

The first twentieth-century archelogical dialectic I will look at is existentialism, associated with a loosely related set of philosophers from the late 1920s to the 1960s whose work was influenced by Søren Kierkegaard. Like Marx, Kierkegaard had a complex relationship with Hegel: whereas Marx didn't care for Hegel's idealism, Kierkegaard resisted the view that the individual was subsumed in the absolute Idea.[3] Also like Marx, Kierkegaard retained the powerful idea of dialectic, which existentialists moved toward the archelogical: "That fundamental contradictions remain 'unresolved,'" says Robert Denoon Cumming, "is a distinctive trait of existential method, as opposed to many other dialectical methods" (129).

As a way of understanding that archelogical method, I will use Cumming's *Starting Point: An Introduction to the Dialectic of Existence.*

Though he calls this book "an introduction," he certainly does not use that term in its typical sense, a simplified overview for novices. Rather *introduction* emphasizes the idea of existentialism as a philosophy of starting point. He says, "One reason why an introduction to existentialism has seemed warranted is that existentialists have been preoccupied with the problem of starting out" (399). In fact, one of Kierkegaard's chief objections to Hegel is that the latter promotes a philosophy of endings, of necessary conclusions. Kierkegaard counters with his own philosophy of beginnings, defined by the disturbance that marks the intersection of contradictory forces. This intersection is what Cumming means by "starting point" in the title. "Indeed," he points out, "the difficulty we face with existentialism is to reach a conclusion that would be as warranted as an introduction has been" (399).

One of the crucial issues in the study of existentialism is whether it is a philosophy at all or, as its Anglo-American detractors have claimed, merely the personal masking itself as philosophy. From its roots in Kierkegaard, existentialism has been characterized by this contradiction: a philosophy that has set itself *against* philosophy, locating itself in the gap between personal experience and technical philosophy (Cumming 65–67). In existentialism, that gap "becomes itself a philosophical experience—that is, an experience which is allowed to pose problems internal to philosophy" (67). Among the various contradictory forces that create existential gaps are, in addition to the subjective and philosophical, the particular and the general, the aesthetic and the philosophical, existence and essence, the personal and the sociohistorical, the physical and the psychological, and the contingent and the eternal (55–66). There is, then, an essential ambiguity in the very core of existential philosophy, an ambiguity dramatized by the "double character" of contradictory existence (66).

For existentialists, Cumming says, the subject matter of philosophical thinking is derived not in the categories of traditional philosophy but in contradiction itself, which explains why "a dislocated structure is generally characteristic of an existential experience" (143). To demonstrate the centrality of dislocation in existential thought, Cumming cites Heidegger's alternative etymology for the key word in existentialism—*existence*. Instead of the usual meaning of becoming actual or, literally, stepping forth into being, which implies a ground of being, Heidegger points to a different Greek root, *ekstasis*, which is derived from a verb whose passive form means "'dislocation,' 'displacement,' 'removed from its proper place.'" This is the meaning at work in *ecstasy*, "being moved outside oneself" (80). The existentialist moment, Cumming says, is defined by dislocation, a discontinuity, a subversive movement of disruption. It moves us outside meanings, relations, and explanations (82). With its roots in *ekstasis*, existentialism finds its beginnings in experience that is, as Cumming describes it, "dislocating and dislocated" (87).

This archelogical moment of dislocation is crucial to an existentialist philosophy of beginnings. "If the starting point for an existentialist is less a point than a movement, the movement is not simply a movement but a disruptive movement" (165). For Heidegger, this disruptive movement is represented as "discovery—a dislocated uncovering." The world is discovered through a break in the context in which we usually encounter the world. "In short," Cumming says, "the world has been there all along, but it is discovered as a 'context' only when a 'break' *(Bruck)* occurs, dislocating its structure" (98–99). For Kierkegaard, these existential movements are signified by the "passions" that "mark dislocating moments when some individual comes up against contradictions which disrupt the continuity of his life, leaving it fragmentary" (237). One source for this discontinuity is doubt: for Kierkegaard, the doubt that internal and external were the same, the doubt about Hegel's drive toward unity. Cumming points out that in Danish and German the word for doubt comes from *double,* which he calls in this case a "dialectical doubling." Kierkegaard's "doubt is an existential starting point both at the level of the philosophy it is fragmenting [i.e., Hegel's] and at the level where 'the life of an individual' is disintegrating" (240).

This archelogical movement of dislocation is at the core of existentialist thought: disruption, discontinuity, derangement, dialectical doubling, disintegration. Indeed, it is written into the dialectical experience itself. The very attempt to locate oneself "is dialectically implicit in the experience of dislocation—that is, implicit as the 'opposite,' the 'contradiction,' of the experience, in that we would not have this experience of dislocation if we were not making an attempt to locate" (143).

Such a dialectical experience is strikingly illustrated in what Cumming calls Sartre's "bifocal vision," the ability to hold contradictions in tension. In this double and doubling vision, the existential object becomes

> a *contradictory composite* which is characterizable more dynamically as the actualization of a structure which is *ambiguous, contradictory,* and *unstable.* . . . This process of actualization is itself a dialectical *development:* the structure first displays the *ambiguity,* which then sharpens into a *contradiction,* which eventually renders the structure *unstable,* until its "collapse" finally supervenes. (209)

This dialectical method exposes a world that is composed of contradictions and that is therefore indefinite, abstract, dynamic. Thus, the existentialist starting point offers a very uncomfortable place to begin a philosophy: "the starting point which would require a juxtaposition of opposites must itself be the opposite of the lucidity which is sought; it must be some confusion" (301). The act of defining undefines; the act of locating dislocates. The existential principle of beginnings, then, is not merely a problem to be solved; it is the state of being real, the confusion that derives from the recognition that reality is contradictory and thus can never yield to logical solutions.

The way Cumming presents it, existentialism finds its unifying theme in archelogical dialectic. It is an attempt to understand what it means to live in a reality in which contradictions remain unresolved in a dialectical tension. And located in the gap or break created by that tension is beginnings. This is one way of understanding the threshold event of beginnings, focusing on the anxiety created in that moment of finding oneself on the brink, an opening in the universe that demands a defining act.

An Archelogical Dialectic of Ideology

Existentialism represents one branch of the modern dialectical tradition, extending from Hegel and Kierkegaard to include Heidegger, Camus, and Sartre. Another branch stems from Marx. And just as existentialism is, as I see it, a recovery of the archelogical dialectic implicit in the early Hegel—Kierkegaard's rejection of the teleological Hegel but retention of the dialectical method—much of twentieth-century Marxian thought may be seen as a recovery of the archelogical potential in Marx. One of the clearest statements I know of this archelogical potential is post-Marxist Paul Smith's *Discerning the Subject*. Smith's understanding of agency defines an archelogical dialectic influenced by Marx.

The problem with the Marxist tradition, Smith says, is that it offers no theory of subjectivity and therefore no possibility for individual agency in the form of resistance to ideology. The main difficulty is Marx's conception of ideology as a monolithic, negative force, which does not allow for agency (5–13). Althusser's notion of subject positions was a major step away from the teleological Marx, but Smith points out that though Althusser's theory of subjectivity provided a basis for agency, he refrained from taking that step because he was still bound to a broader conception of ideology, that ideologies themselves reflect a dominant ideology. Again, such an ideological construction allows for no agency (15–21).

Smith uses the groundwork laid by Althusser to build what I see as an archelogical theory of the subject. Taking advantage of the ambiguity of *subject*, Smith points to two opposing concepts of the word. First is the traditional subject as a privileged entity, manipulator of objects and originator of all action and meaning. This is the form of the subject he represents graphically in quotation marks as "individual," the humanistic ideal of the whole, undifferentiated, and self-contained actor. Added to the long-lived Marxist suspicion of the "individual," this idea of subjectivity came under attack in the last several decades by poststructuralists, who portrayed the subject as interpellated in texts. The second understanding of subject is the more literal, that which is *subjected* to forces that dominate it, such as economic, political, social, and linguistic forces. Opposed to the "individual," this idea of subjectivity as "subject," is identified, Smith says, with Althusser, Lacan, Derrida, and the Frankfurt School, all of whom privilege the *subjected* state of the "subject" (xxviii–xxxi).

The trouble with this latter perspective, Smith contends, is that in their rush to unbind subjectivity from the "individual," many poststructuralists followed in Marx's original error and have rebound subjectivity to ideology, a monolithic and determining ideology. Subjected thus to ideology, the "subject" bears the same burden as the "individual," both projecting what Smith describes as a circumscribed, or "cerned," subjectivity, a false sense of completeness and stasis that denies any opportunity for resistance to ideology (xxxi–xxxiv). Hence the eponymous goal of the book: dis*cerning* the subject, coming to an understanding of subjectivity that breaks open the determinism that encircles the "subject."

It is this idea of resistance that brings Smith to the core of his work: "The human *agent*," he says, "will be seen here as the place from which resistance to the ideological is produced or played out, and thus as *not* equivalent to either the 'subject' or the 'individual'" (xxxv). The solution to the problem of agency, then, is not either-or but both-and, an archelogical relationship maintaining the dialectical tension between "individual" and "subject." By virtue of this dialectical tension, subjectivity is a contested site, never entirely subjected to social formations of ideology nor entirely free of them (xxxiv).

What we find in Smith is a powerful model of an archelogical dialectic. On one level there is the dialectical tension of "individual" and "subject." The "individual" is dialectically balanced against the "subject," which is composed of competing ideologies; the "subject" is dialectically balanced against the "individual," which momentarily and tentatively exists in the "choice" of one subject-position represented in the resistance to others. On another level, however, a dialectical tension exists among multiple and contradictory ideologies, whose gaps and fissures offer the potential for agency. Reality, as represented by ideology, is itself multiple and contradictory; subjectivity, then, is also inherently multiple and contradictory. Resistance, thus, is not *against* ideology, can never take place *outside* ideology; resistance, rather, is a function of the multiple and contradictory nature of ideology.

Smith finds the best possibility for a dialectical theory of subjectivity in contemporary feminism. He points to the major division in feminist theory between the Anglo-American movement, which is more practical and focuses on woman's experience and identity, and the French movement, which is more theoretical, drawing on psychoanalytical ideas of the woman (134–38). Instead of being a liability, however, Smith argues that the power of feminist thought lies in the tensions and contradictions generated by these two approaches. He emphasizes

> the possibly productive contradictions in this opposition out of which, it seems to me, there comes a kind of double feminist strategy capable of providing some important cues for the question of how an active political agent can be discerned from the sub-jected "subject." (135)

Such a "double strategy" is crucial to a theory and practice of resistance. The contradictions among diverse and competing subject positions render impossible any sense of the subjected "subject." But these contradictions also generate the negative movement that allows the subject to exploit those differences and thus encourages resistance.

> That is, the interpellation of the "subject" into oppressed positions is not complete and monolithic; rather, interpellation also produces contradiction and negativity. The necessary existence of various and different subject-positions in the interpellated "subject" produces resistance to the logic of domination while still being in a sense part of, or a by-product of, that logic. (152)

It is through this negative movement that Smith discerns the "subject" and thus creates the opportunity for agency. Agency depends on a theory of subjectivity that exploits the archelogical nature of ideology: the opposing forces of "individual" and "subject" existing in perpetual tension, each marked by its own internal contradictions. Agency is constructed in the seams and fractures inherent in the competing claims of opposing ideologies. It is in these seams and fractures, these moments of contradiction, that there is an opening and thus an opportunity for resistance.

An Archelogical Dialectic of the Middle

One of the defining issues in dialectical theory is the problem of identity and difference in the relationship between contradictory forces. *Archê*, as used by John, represented the balanced relationship between identity and difference: Jesus as God and human, both fully different from God and human beings as well as the same as God and human beings. The Kantian dialectic of doubt stresses the dialectic of difference in the antinomies of pure reason. The works of the teleological Hegel and Marx emphasize the dialectic of identity in the sublimation of difference. As I have argued, dialectical theory of the twentieth century tended to move toward a more archelogical understanding of dialectic. Perhaps the most purely archelogical statement in the modern dialectical tradition may be found in the systematic philosophy of William Desmond.[4]

For Desmond, the dialectical problem of difference and sameness is played out in the philosophical issue of otherness: that human beings find themselves different from the other, "estranged from being, different from things, alien to" themselves (*Desire* 5). The problem, as Desmond sees it, is how to avoid the two extremes either of projecting difference as so radical that any true mediation of difference becomes impossible or of raising identity to such a power that all difference is sublimated in the transcendental. Neither of these approaches offers a way to understand fully what Desmond calls our human "openness to otherness," the rich potential for openness that lies in the dialectic of sameness and difference, unity and diversity. To solve this problem, Desmond offers a philosophy that revolves around what he calls the *metaxological,* a philosophy of the middle (from the Greek *metaxu,* "in between" or "middle"). To understand the archelogical potential in this philosophy of the middle, it will be helpful to look at it in the context of forms of being other than the metaxological, that is, being as defined in various relationships between self and other.

The first is what Desmond describes as a univocal sense of being, which emphasizes a naive sameness at the cost of difference. There is, thus, no difference between self and other to be mediated. Desmond associates this radical oneness with reductive interpretations of Plato, Spinoza, and Hegel and with modern positivism. The problem with this approach is that it ignores the power located in differences. The second approach he calls the equivocal sense of being, which is the opposite of the first in that it stresses the radical difference between self and other and thus the impossibility of mediating them. The emphasis of this perspective is on the plurality of being and the suspicion of totalizing oneness associated with the centered self or the centered other. For Desmond, such fragmentation of being characterizes a philosophical line that includes Nietzsche, Heidegger, and post-Heideggerean deconstructionists, all engaged in the radical questioning of logocentrism. A third approach is the dialectical sense of being, a mediation of self and other that acknowledges the ambiguity of difference and at the same time resists the tendency toward dualistic opposition. The problem, Desmond says, is that dialectical thought has tended to vacillate between the negative and the positive, between the poles of univocity and equivocity. Hegel, for example, is dogged by his attraction to sameness, the mediation of self and other as *self*-mediated, resolving all difference in thinking itself, the Absolute Idea of philosophy (*Desire* 6–7; "Being Between" 317–19).

The fourth sense of being, the metaxological, is Desmond's attempt to create a truly archelogical dialectic, preserving the potential for productive difference he finds in dialectic while avoiding the tendencies to move toward naive sameness or radical difference. This middle way is characterized by a new relationship between the self and the other, what Desmond describes as "a double mediation," an alternative to dualistic oppositions and to the single-sided self-mediating tendencies of Hegel. The middle can be mediated from both the position of the dialectical self and the position of the dialectical other. Thus the middle is plural, communal, defined by the intermingling of contradictions. Indeed, self and other are themselves plural, marked by internal difference, which creates a middle space within each. The metaxological dialectic is a communal interplay of self and other, each fully, though differentially, one and in dialogue with its contrary, an intermediation of oneness and diversity, separateness and togetherness, identity and difference, univocity and equivocity (*Desire* 7–8; "Being Between" 319–21). The middle, then, is archelogical, marked by the dialogical difference of self and other which itself represents the differences *within* self and other. *Archê* is captured in the double mediation of self and other, each reaching toward its contrary to create a middle.

Desmond's fourfold unfolding of the layers of relations between self and other forms the framework for a rich and complex philosophy that I certainly cannot do justice to here beyond touching on a few points that provide some indication of the sense of the archelogical that pervades his work.[5] One is the crucial role of desire in his philosophy, which he describes as "a metaphysical openness to being, being in its otherness, as well as the self-development of the human being in its own ineluctable search for its own wholeness" ("Being Between" 314). Desire, however, should not be seen as merely a response to lack. Far more significant than that, desire represents the double movement of intermediation. It is both the drive toward completeness in the other and the drive toward a greater fullness of the self ("Being Between" 315).

Desmond points to another double movement in his philosophy of the middle. One he describes as the movement from the exterior to the interior: it is in the exterior middle, the space between self and other, that we find a potential openness into our own beings. The second movement is from inferior to superior: it is in the interior middle, composed of differences in the self, that we find a desire to transcend the self and seek after an other that is ultimate and cannot be reduced to ourselves. Even this movement is marked by its own double mediation, consisting of, in addition to "our own erotic quest of the ultimate," the drive toward the communal middle by the ultimate other "out of its own excessive transcendence" ("Being Between" 316). These various double movements are extrapolations of the double mediation of self and other, the interrelation of contradictory movements.

The last important point to make about Desmond's philosophy is that he doesn't shy away from the idea of a transcendent other, or what he labels "the absolute original." Though it is reminiscent of Hegel's Absolute Idea, which became the all-subsuming teleological force of identity in difference, the absolute original is more like Hegel's search for beginnings, the productive tension of identity and difference that generates opportunities for openness. Desmond describes the absolute original as a metaphor for the middle, the dynamic state of being both and between; as ultimate openness, the overflowing affirmation of being over nothing; as the "generous yes" of primordial and continuous creativity;

as both centripetal finitude and centrifugal infinitude (*Desire* 179–207). The absolute original takes on the characteristics of beginnings, neither the beginning nor the end but beginning *and* end. It cannot be limited to any one event, Desmond says, such as the beginning or end or any other one point or duration in time; instead, it is "a kind of perpetual beginning . . . an anarchic origin that gives time's beginnings, without itself being a first moment or a temporal product" (196). It is a beginning that is not *the* beginning, an end that is not *the* end, rather

> an indeterminate limit, at which the point is not to come to a dead halt but to begin to create. This end is no end, because it gives the open space that solicits new beginnings. This end cannot be a closure, since it is the opening up of originating being to what is ultimate. (197)

Certainly the language Desmond is working with seems to tie the absolute original to beginnings. Those ties to the archelogical are cinched for me, however, in the archelogical terms he uses to describe the absolute original, "a kind of inexhaustible wholeness of being, in which the eternal ruptures normal time and subverts its smooth flow with a dislocating, yet fulfilling, *perípeteia*" (198).

There is a powerful sense of an archelogical dialectic in Desmond, presented in the idea of the middle as a doubly mediated space created by contradictory worlds and the idea of the transcendent or the absolute original, which is also doubly mediated by the self. His work is important in my attempt to establish a theory of beginnings, but at this point all I can do is suggest the full archelogical potential in it. I will return to it in chapter 7 in an investigation of creativity and writing.

So far in this chapter I've explored three archelogical dialectics in my attempt to define more clearly the concept of beginnings. Two important features characterize this form of dialectic. One is the balance or tension of contraries, which is, as I have argued, what John is trying to get at in his gospel with the concept of *archê:* contrary forces held in productive tension, an interpenetration, neither resolving fully into the other. Among existentialists this tension of opposites is captured in the contradictory nature of experience created in the interplay of the personal and the philosophical, the internal and the external, existence and essence, et cetera. In Smith's post-Marxist theory of subjectivity, contradictions in experience are rendered both in the juxtaposition of "individual" and "subject"—always balanced against each other, no person ever fully individual or fully subject—and in the contradictory ideologies competing to define and undefine us. And in Desmond's philosophy, the middle itself is a function of the double mediation of self and other, each fully in dialogue with its opposite, both identical and different, one and diverse.

The other feature is the sense of openness—impending potential, possibility for newness—that is created in this intersection of contradictory forces. According to Cumming, existentialists portrayed this openness as a dislocation, a starting point conceived as a disjunctive movement in which the universe seems to open up, a disruption of the quotidian and commonsensical that demands an act of self-definition. For Smith, these moments of openness are opportunities for agency realized in the acts of resistance to subjugation by particular ideologies. Desmond's metaxological dialectic seeks to represent what he sees as a fundamental openness to being, an openness of self to other and other to self. This openness is emblematic of the openness *within* both self and other and the transcendent openness of self to the ultimate other and the openness of the ultimate other to the self. In all these cases, it is the tension of contradictory forces that creates the potential for openness.

What I am talking about here, of course, is beginnings. I have used Cumming, Smith, and Desmond to offer a way of understanding what it means to conceive of a universe marked by beginnings, the threshold experience of dislocation or agency or openness to being. This understanding of the universe is in direct contrast to a universe of *the* beginning, characterized by order, stability, and necessity, in which reality is not contradictory. Do we actually live in a universe marked by beginnings? Next I will look at a scientific description of an archelogical universe as set forth in chaos theory, also known as complexity theory—the science of beginnings.

An Archelogical Dialectic of Nature

It is a commonplace to begin talking about chaos theory by pointing out that the name is actually a misnomer: it is not really about chaos as we commonly think of it—an uncontrolled and senseless tumult—but rather about the surprising orderliness in apparent disorder.[6] The name is derived from mathematician James Yorke's search for an attention-getting title for his 1975 paper, "Period Three Implies Chaos," and was cemented in the public imagination by James Gleick's popular *Chaos: Making a New Science*. Thus chaos in its scientific usage carries a pleasingly ironic twist. Though it may bring to mind images of mad scientists working away in darkened laboratories investigating the forbidden, it is not that at all. This is hard science.

Understanding chaos theory depends on two key concepts. One is sensitive dependence on initial conditions. Traditional science has conceived of the world in terms of highly predictable linear systems, those in which small disruptions have proportionately small effects. You can imagine these linear systems as described by the simple curved line of a trajectory. At any point along the trajectory there is enough information to allow the observer to know the originary conditions of the system and to predict the state of the system at any point in its future. These are systems delineated by origins, the ideal of classical physics, a universe of stability and equilibrium.

Chaotic systems, however, are nonlinear and therefore are ultimately unpredictable; neither past nor future can be calculated with accuracy. The dominant characteristic of such systems, and the reason they are unpredictable, is what scientists call their sensitive dependence on initial conditions. This means that even the slightest disturbance in the system may have disproportionately large effects.

The weather is a classic example of such a chaotic system. Not too long ago, meteorologists believed that weather was ultimately predictable; all they needed was enough computing power. But Edward N. Lorenz, a meteorologist with a strong mathematical bent, stumbled on a finding that would dash all these hopes. Lorenz, using an early computer for modeling weather systems, was working on an experiment that required two identical models. For the first one, he entered the initial conditions for the system to six decimal places, but in the second he took what he believed to be the inconsequential shortcut of rounding off the initial conditions to three places. The results astonished him: two trajectories that began in similar patterns but over time deviated dramatically. Such a seemingly insignificant difference at the beginning of the two models led to a dramatic difference in the subsequent computer-modeled weather patterns. Weather, he realized, could never be precisely predicted because it is an inherently dynamic and unstable system. Even the slightest event can have considerable consequences, and there is no way to calculate every slight event in the world. In 1972 Lorenz presented a paper on his findings whose argument was not quite as hyperbolic as it sounded: "Does the Flap of a Butterfly's Wings in Brazil Set Off a Tornado in Texas?"[7]

For Lorenz and many other chaos theorists, sensitive dependence on initial conditions is a crucial defining feature of chaos. *Initial* conditions, however, are not to be confused with origins. Lorenz points out that in nonlinear systems *truly* initial conditions are possible only in the lab. In most complex systems, initial conditions "may also be the ones at the beginning of any stretch of time that interests an investigator, so that one person's initial conditions may be another's midstream or final conditions" (9). Indeed, one of the reasons chaotic systems are interesting to me in my study of beginnings is that these are systems whose origins cannot be told, whose origins have lost all deterministic influence. At any point in the life of the system there is the potential for beginnings, disturbances that have the power to initiate new conditions within the system.

The other key concept in chaos theory is bifurcation. The weather is a system that is in a constant state of instability and disequilibrium, but many other dynamic systems perpetually cycle from disequilibrium to equilibrium and back. It is in such systems that bifurcation theory is useful.

Literally a double forking, *bifurcation* is derived from a pattern that emerges in tracing the line of a system's trajectory, a pattern in which that line forks into two lines. Such a pattern was noticed by Robert May, a biologist using mathematical modeling to try and understand the boom and bust patterns of wildlife populations. As his modeling responded to higher degrees of fertility, it showed, after a period of stability, an apparently random series of boom and bust years. To May's surprise, however, he noticed within these data an unexpected regularity. As he carefully raised the fertility parameter—and thus the stress on the system—the line of the population trajectory split in two, oscillating between two different population numbers on alternating years. Then, as the parameter was raised even higher, both lines of the trajectory split in two, indicating a four-year cycle. At yet a higher level, these lines forked again, marking a periodic behavior of eight years. This "period-doubling" bifurcation revealed within what seemed to be an aleatory series of numbers a pattern characterized by bifurcating trajectories, one that defines many dynamic systems. At its most general, bifurcation refers to a broad scheme of change in a system; each individual bifurcation describes a point of unpredictable change from a relatively simple to a relatively complex order (Gleick 69–76).[8]

Sensitive dependence on initial conditions and bifurcation are two of the central attributes of chaos theory. Together they offer a powerful model for beginnings. For such a model, I turn to the Nobel prize–winning chemist Ilya Prigogine, whose *Order out of Chaos: Man's New Dialogue with Nature*—written with philosopher of science Isabelle Stengers—is both a metaphysics and a physics of chaos. Indeed, if Engels's dialectical materialism represents the modeling of a teleological dialectic in nature, Prigogine's science of chaos represents the same for an archelogical dialectic.

Prigogine opens his work with a paradox. He points to the second law of thermodynamics, which describes a world in which entropy is increasing, that is, the universe is becoming more and more disordered. This view seems to be contradicted, however, by the biological and social sciences, which describe a world that is becoming more and more complex, moving toward greater order. How, he asks, can increasing complexity arise from increasing disorder (xxix)?[9]

Thermodynamics, the science of fire, was the first important challenge to the static order of classical physics. The nineteenth-century fascination with the steam engine formed the basis for this scientific understanding of the conversion of heat into work, out of which came the second law of thermodynamics. It was an attempt to account for the inevitable loss of energy in an engine: entropy was a way of describing the dissipation of energy which, because of friction and other forces, was not converted into work and thus would eventually lead every system to cool to a final state of thermal equilibrium in which no energy could be expended and no work possible. This dissipation of energy came to be applied to all closed systems, and when applied to the closed system of the universe, it prompted the inescapable conclusion that it also was running down. Such a conclusion stood in direct contrast to Newton's idea of an unchanging, stable, linear universe ruled by gravitation (103–26).

Prigogine uses chaos theory to offer a third option, a view of systems that exist in the dialectical tension of both order and disorder, stability and instability, necessity and chance, the global and the local. He uses bifurcation theory to describe those critical points at which a new and more complex equilibrium emerges out of an older and more simple one. But it is the source of this complexity that is especially interesting. Written into all systems, according to the second law of thermodynamics, is entropy. Every equilibrium is thus defined by nonequilibrium. At the point at which a system has been pushed by entropic forces to the threshold of instability, what Prigogine calls "far from equilibrium," the system becomes chaotic, characterized by radical disequilibrium, completely unpredictable (165–75).

It is at this point that the exquisite sensitivity to initial conditions in chaotic systems comes into play. Unstable systems are ripe for change, says Prigogine, "because the amplification of a microscopic fluctuation occurring at the 'right moment' result[s] in favoring one reaction path over a number of other equally possible paths" (176). At the point of instability, a system is susceptible to the influence of even the smallest event, which could amplify throughout the system and thus determine which aspects of the system will dominate in the resulting bifurcation, a new order. Such fluctuations can come from within the system or from adjoining systems. It is because of the chaotic instability of the system that small fluctuations can have such a disproportionately large effect on the self-organization of a new and more complex stability. Hence what Prigogine calls "one of the main ideas of this book: Nonequilibrium as a source of order" (180). The universe as a whole is defined by increasing disorder, but it is the entropy itself that, on the local level of particular systems, creates the potential for greater order in those systems.

What we find in Prigogine's use of chaos theory, then, is a strong sense of archelogical beginnings: disturbances in an old order at the point at which opposing forces are juxtaposed, where stability and instability, order and disorder, being and becoming meet; disturbances that provide the potential for something new and unpredictable, a more complex order. Every dynamic, nonlinear system tends toward nonequilibrium, out of which new order is born or, rather, because of which a new order is possible (the dissipative forces perhaps spelling the end for unhealthy systems, those that lack resilience). The disturbance in the system can act as a source of order because it is in periods of instability that the butterfly effect becomes operational and a small force may have a large impact on the defining features of the emerging new order in the system. In the chaos that results from disruption in the old order lies the seed for a new and more complex order, part of a continuous pattern of beginnings.

Prigogine offers a number of examples of this generation of new structures on both the molecular and supramolecular levels (140–203), but what interests me most is his treatment of change on the human scale. From the perspective of classical physics, he says, the individual is destined to insignificance within the linear structures of larger systems. From the perspective of bifurcation theory, however, it can be seen how individuals or small groups can have a revolutionary effect on a system. He points out, though, that not just any fluctuation lends itself to amplification in regions of chaos.

> Even in those regions, amplification obviously does not occur with just any individual, idea, or behavior, but only with those that are "dangerous"—that is, those that can exploit to their advantage the nonlinear relations guaranteeing the stability of the preceding regime. Thus we are led to conclude that *the same* nonlinearities may produce an order out of the chaos of elementary processes and still, under different circumstances, be responsible for the destruction of the same order, eventually producing a new coherence beyond another bifurcation. (206)

This understanding of social and political realities is not only powerful and empowering but also, perhaps, frightening. There are no origins, no immutable givens, no ultimate foundations for any nonlinear system because every such system is formed by the same destabilizing forces that may eventually become the source of its own undoing, providing the opportunity for a new beginning.

This potential for beginnings in chaos theory has been picked up by others, such as Ervin Laszlo in *The Age of Bifurcation: Understanding the Changing World*. He defines bifurcation as "the transition of a system from the dynamic regime of one set of attractors, generally more stable and simple ones, to the dynamic regime of more complex and 'chaotic' attractors" (6). This concept, he says, is likely to become one of the most important ideas driving futures studies because it represents a powerful model for change. It is necessary to understand bifurcation because, he points out, we live in an unstable world susceptible to nonlinear change.

As a model for social change, Laszlo uses bifurcation theory to explain why it is that political and cultural transitions are so unpredictable, why it is that they so often surprise trained observers. Specific change may be ultimately unpredictable, he says, but that doesn't mean we cannot discern the broader characteristics a system will display over time. Those broader characteristics are provided by bifurcation theory.

> In a chaotic condition, society is sensitive to every small fluctuation, to every new idea, new movement, new way of

> thinking and acting. In the final analysis chaos in society spells human freedom—freedom to change the structures and institutions in which people live their lives. The heavy hand of the past is lifted, and individual creativity has room to unfold. Not dictators, armies and police forces, but the changing values and ideals of people are the butterflies that, flapping their wings, determine which way society will grow and develop. (53–54)

In *The Creation of Chaos: William James and the Stylistic Making of a Disorderly World,* Frederick Ruf shows the same pattern at work in individual consciousness. Ruf also conceives of chaos in terms of a dialectical tension, always existing relative to some order but also always challenging it (28). In his study of William James, Ruf seeks to understand the productive potential of chaotic disorientation on the individual.[10]

In James, Ruf says, "the chaotic . . . tends to undermine the certainty of any particular orientation by dissolving its demarcations of identities, roles, definitions, and directions" (131). He associates this disorientation with liminality, the threshold experience of old identities falling away and the opportunity for new identities presenting themselves (132–33). Disorientation, then, is woven into orientation, a dialectical relationship that possesses the possibility for creative chaos. "It seeks to counteract such notions as finality, ultimacy, determinacy, security, permanence, totality, mastery" (133). Chaos is the dislocation that may occur when experience becomes meaningless or oppressive. "It presents the possibility of dissolving structures, orders, and forms that have become inflexible, tired, or oppressive by countering them with fluidity, vagueness, indeterminacy, and fragility" (135). Just as in Prigogine's observations of nature, chaos for Ruf represents the potential for newness that comes of the tendency toward instability in an old order. It is this intersection of the old and the new that marks beginnings.

Beginnings, then, may be understood as integral to this pattern of disorder and order: disturbances at the point of juxtaposition of contradictory forces that hold within them the seed for something new, a creative potential. In this pattern of beginnings we discern the conceptual link between chaos theory and *archê*. It is certainly clear that contradictions play an important role in chaos theory.[11] Prigogine speaks of chaos as representing stability and instability, order and disorder, determinism and freedom, necessity and chance, being and becoming, among others. Chaos, then, occurs at the threshold, a point that is far from equilibrium where order and disorder meet and a new and surprisingly different order is possible. Chaos, because it is a region susceptible to the butterfly effect, is a source of the new. It is a newness that is ever renewable, however, because in nonlinear systems, every stability holds within itself the potential for an instability, every determinism the potential for freedom, and every beginning the potential for new beginnings.

This broad pattern of beginnings is by no means philosophically neutral. In it lies a powerful vision of a world and thus a way of knowing and being in the world. Chaos theory is attractive to me because it points to a pattern of beginnings *in the world*. It enables me to take a philosophy of beginnings derived from the ancient principle of *archê* and apply it widely to the world. It is a pattern that may be identified in the physical world (Prigogine), in the social world (P. Smith; Laszlo), and in the world of the individual consciousness (Cumming; Ruf). The principle of beginnings suggests a reality that is contradictory and therefore fluid and indeterminate; a reality that is unstable and therefore ripe with the possibility for newness; a reality that is multiple and refracted and therefore susceptible to new beginnings. It is a reality ruled by *archê*, not *telos*.

Conclusion

Part one of this book has focused on the concept of beginning. I started by viewing beginning through the lens of writing, attempting to establish where writing begins first as an initiating point in time and then as an origin or foundation. What I discovered is that writing deconstructs beginning as a temporal concept, which seemed to put this whole project in jeopardy: how could I ever determine where writing begins if the beginning is itself a meaningless term? This deconstruction of the beginning, however, created an opportunity for a reconstruction as suggested by John's use of *archê*, the interpenetration of contradictory worlds that holds the possibility for a new reality. In part one, beginning has gone through a conceptual shift from the beginning to beginnings, represented in this chapter by the archelogical dialectics described by Cumming, Smith, Desmond, Prigogine, and others. These archelogical dialectics help to establish the viability of *archê* as a principle of beginnings and to generate a model for beginnings to be used in the rest of this book.

It is fitting, then, to conclude part one with a brief description of the most radically archelogical vision of the universe I have found and one that will play an important role in parts two and three. During the 1927–1928 term at the University of Edinburgh, Alfred North Whitehead gave a series of lectures that were later collected and expanded in *Process and Reality: An Essay in Cosmology*. What I find especially intriguing about this work is the last chapter, "God and the World," which I see as a return to the ancient philosophical issues surrounding *archê*.

The question at hand is the relationship, if any, between the world of the divine—pure, static, ideal, infinite—and the world of the material—corrupt, mutable, real, finite. Whitehead represents this dichotomy as God and the World. He opens with a rejection of the idea of a transcendent Creator-God separated from the World in the very act of creation, "the fallacy which has infused tragedy into the histories of Christianity and Mahometanism" (519). Whitehead proposes a completely different understanding of the relationship between God and the World, one that he believes would eliminate the tragedy of creation. God, he says, cannot be conceived as the exception to all physical and metaphysical principles; Whitehead proposes instead a naturalistic God, one that is "not *before* all creation, but *with* all creation" (521). This does not mean that God is in essence the same as the World, not a form of animism. Rather, God is primordial creativity, meaning that God "is the unlimited conceptual realization of the absolute wealth of potentiality" (521). Whereas God is conceptual and potential, the World is physical and actual.

What is important for Whitehead is that the essential qualities of both God and the World are deficient in and of themselves: the conceptual and the physical, as well as the potential and the actual, are each incomplete without the other. God and the World may be essentially different, but each requires the other for its own completion. Whitehead describes this interrelationship in a way that hearkens back to *archê:*

> Conceptual experience can be infinite, but it belongs to the nature of the physical experience that it is finite. An actual entity in the temporal world is to be conceived as originated by physical experience with its process of completion motivated by consequent, conceptual experience initially derived from God. God is to be conceived as originated by conceptual experience with his process of completion motivated by consequent, physical experience, initially derived from the temporal world. (524)

This archelogical relationship is, as I see it, similar to Marx's dialectic of contradictory essences: God and the World, though contradictory in essence, exist in an intimate mutuality that goes far beyond the *archê* imagined by the ancients, and perhaps even by John.

In the ancient philosophical debate surrounding *archê,* the primary goal was to establish a route to Reality, usually located in the ideal world. For Whitehead, there is no such Reality in which one world is sublimated to the other. Reality is truly archelogical, God and the World existing only in and through the other. Indeed, as if in answer to Kant's dialectical antinomies of pure reason, Whitehead offers his own set of "antitheses, whose apparent self-contradiction depends on neglect of the diverse categories of existence":

> It is as true to say that God is permanent and the World fluent, as that the World is permanent and God is fluent.
>
> It is as true to say that God is one and the World many, as that the World is one and God many. . . .
>
> It is as true to say that the World is immanent in God, as that God is immanent in the World.
>
> It is as true to say that God transcends the World, as that the World transcends God.

> It is as true to say that God creates the World, as that the World creates God. (528)

Whitehead begins with the opposition of God and the World, but critical to his understanding of God are the oppositions in God itself. God is both primordial and consequent, the one and the many, the infinite and the finite, the conceptual and the physical. God is, like the World itself, composed of opposites. "All the 'opposites' are elements in the nature of things, and are incorrigibly there. The concept of 'God' is the way in which we understand this incredible fact—that what cannot be, yet is" (531). God, then, serves for Whitehead as emblem of both the reality of contradiction and the contradictions in reality.

Whitehead's treatment of the archelogical relationship between God and the World is beneficial to this study of beginnings because it provides a valuable link to ancient uses of *archê* in the philosophical-theological tradition. He also is trying to explain the connections between the divine and the material. Whitehead goes much further than the ancients, however, in offering a detailed account of the *process* by which that connection is constructed, the basis for his process philosophy. It is the process of beginnings.

For Whitehead, the universe exists not as a fluid stream of events in time but as an infinite series of discrete occasions or pulses or packets of time. Each of these occasions is a moment of actualization, a moment of creation or of becoming-concrete, which he describes as a four-phase process. The occasion is initiated in the conceptual potentiality of God. Next, the physical actuality of the finite world, consisting of all previous moments of actualization, is brought into the sphere of the conceptual, the opposing forces of material existence and divine potential held in tension. The third step is the completion of that potential, in which the many—that is, all the previous moments of actualization—become one in an act of unique creation. This is the primary creative event in the process, in which the conceptual influences a new actuality and the actual becomes the embodiment of the conceptual. In the fourth phase, the actualized event passes into the past, immortalized into objectivity to become one of the many which in the future will become part of another one (532).

I will elaborate on this process considerably in later chapters, but for now I will simply point out that what makes Whitehead's process philosophy so radical is that each moment of existence is archelogical. Each pulse of time is constructed in the interpenetration of God and the World: of the conceptual and the physical; of the potential and the actual. In that moment of the intersection of the finite and the infinite, the infinite is made finite and the finite made infinite. In that moment the universe is opened as the conceptual principle frees the occasion from the deterministic tendencies located in the physical, the accumulation of past occasions. Most dramatically, in that moment both God and the World may be made new. Each completes and thus creates the other. Thus, creation is a shared process, continuous, occurring moment by moment. Instead of Creator-God, God is both creator and created, as is the World: cocreators cocreating (522–30).

This cosmology certainly takes us a long way from the beginning as represented in the big bang and the majestic act of the God of Genesis 1. It projects a universe in which there is no ultimate beginning, only an infinity of beginnings.[12] It is a radically archelogical universe, one in which every moment offers the potential for existential dislocation and for ideological agency; every moment is a construction of the middle formed in the interrelation of self and other as well as self and ultimate other; every moment carries within itself the seed for greater complexity. This is a model of beginnings I will apply to writing.

The shift in beginning from the beginning to beginnings clearly has a significant effect on my guiding question, Where does writing begin? No longer a question about the temporal nature of writing, it is now a question about the relationship between writing and beginnings, how writing participates in beginnings. In what way is writing constructed in the interpenetration of contradictory forces? In what way does writing represent an opening in the universe, the potential for a new creation? These are the questions about beginning that will guide me as I explore what it means to write and teach writing and the value of writing and teaching writing.

Part Two
Writing

6 Defining Writing

> More and more I find myself reflecting on writing as languishing in language, a dance of oppositions, a labyrinthine journey, a game of *Scrabble,* a chorus of conflictual voices, an ontological enterprise, a (w)hole and seam(less) web of textuality, (con)fusion, dis-ease, textual intercourse, dispersing dissemination/not determinate destination, a germinating and gestating blank page, glossolalia, textual acrobatics, polyphony, ventriloquism, (a) play.
>
> —Carl Leggo, "Questions I Need to Ask Before I Advise My Students to Write in Their Own Voices"

A few years ago, I took my nieces and nephews on a quick tour of my campus, the high point of which was, for them, the snack bar. Along the way, we got to talking about the kinds of courses university students take, and they wanted to know what I taught. I told them that I teach writing. Cathleen, the first-grader, said with authority to four-year-old Claire, "That means he teaches his students how to make letters." "Not exactly," I said, "I teach what you might call advanced writing." Cathleen's eyes widened with newfound respect. "You mean you teach *cursive?*"

Some time ago, I served on a university committee charged with looking into the way writing is being incorporated into upper-division courses at our university, particularly in light of a proposal for writing-intensive courses in the junior and senior years. We interviewed representatives from every department and visited with every college-level curriculum committee and in the process endured hour after hour of the usual grousing about writing. Faculty in the disciplines certainly couldn't be expected to focus on writing because they didn't have the time and didn't feel comfortable correcting spelling, grammar, and sentence structure. Besides, their students wouldn't need more instruction in writing if the English department were doing its job in the first place. Why should they take class time away from the content of the course to make up for the failure of freshman composition to teach writing? And so on, and so on.

These two experiences have at their root a common conception of writing. As I sat in those meetings with faculty from other departments, I was struck once again by the conceptual gap—no, abyss—that exists between my understanding of what it means to write and teach writing and theirs. I realized that I had just about as much chance of explaining my vision of writing to the grousers as I did to Cathleen. The problem is that we, as a culture, think of writing in terms of the physical existence of marks on a page and the physical act of making those marks. Cathleen's concept of writing as lettering and the grouser's concept of writing as spelling, grammar, and syntax are both linked to the technology of text; it is language made visible and thus defines itself by what is seen on the page.

But I also know that this understanding of writing is perfectly natural. Indeed, it is written into the very word *to write,* which traces its long pedigree back to a Sanskrit word meaning to wound, tear, or cut, a sense developed from the earliest forms of writing in which sharp implements were used to cut marks into stone or bark (Onions). This "wounding" of stone or bark leaves traces of itself, the scars that remain after the act and continue to speak of the act. What makes writing writing is that it leaves these marks. Even with all the technological changes that have brought us from bark to computer screens, writing is still conceptually bound up in the scars left on the face of bark or stone. Writing is those marks and the act of marking.

As people who profess writing, this issue is important to us because who we are and what we do is determined by what it means to write. If writing is an act defined by the markings of text, then we are defined by those marks, accountable for what is most obvious about writing. But if writing is also something else that is beyond the technology text, then we are defined by that something as well. I think that one of the issues that has occupied us as a discipline for the last forty years or so is defining that something beyond the text. We challenged the hegemony of text by declaring writing a process; we have labeled it a cognitive act, a social act, an ideological act. It could be argued, in fact, that our field has been profoundly shaped by the firm belief that writing is much more than text.

Defining writing has been one of the recurring themes of this study, a function of Dobrin's question at the opening of the preface: What is writing? In chapter 1, I investigated the starting point of writing as literally the defining moment of writing. Then in chapter 2, I looked at the way we as a profession have used various interpretations of origin to define writing, centered particularly on the foundational belief underlying the discipline that writing *can* be defined. In this chapter, I return to that theme but this time with a completely different set of preconceptions about definition. The shift in beginning from the temporal to the ontological recasts the question of where writing begins, now a question of the ontology of writing, what writing *is.*

When I began this investigation of where writing begins, I simply assumed the *writing* part of the question. The problem lay in the predicate: Where does writing *begin?* Asking this question about beginning did not pose deep ontological issues about writing because I saw *beginning* as an ontologically neutral term, a temporal boundary or foundation. A starting point or an origin may have some influence on how we perceive writing, but neither one ought to define what writing is. However, the deconstruction and reconstruction of beginning changes the emphasis of the question: Where does *writing* begin? Beginnings itself has the power to deconstruct writing, to defamiliarize it and thus to place it in ontological doubt. Beginnings is a state of being; so to ask where writing begins is to ask what writing itself is, that is, in what way writing participates in and is thus defined by that state of being.

My response is that writing *is* beginnings. Beginnings deconstructs writing but is also the conceptual source for a reconstruction of writing. So the ontological question I will pursue in this chapter may be put this way: What is writing that it is beginnings? To answer that question I will present two definitions of writing, two ways of understanding writing as beginnings, the second a more radical reconstruction of writing than the first. By exploring the ways in which writing is defined by beginnings, I am also trying to define that "something else" that is writing and which defines us as people who profess writing.

Writing Is Beginnings

I admit that the claim that writing is beginnings seems suspiciously tautological. After all, how can I make an argument about where writing begins if writing is itself beginnings? But that, of course, is the point. Beginnings both undefines and defines writing. Perhaps it would be helpful to put my initial argument for the claim in the form of an enthymeme:

> archê *is beginnings;*
> writing is archelogical;
> therefore, writing is beginnings.

Since I've already established (persuasively, I hope) the major premise, the burden of proof rests on that minor premise. What possible evidence could I find to support it?

Actually, this is a surprisingly easy task because scholars in composition have for a long time been using the concept of *archê,* if not the term itself, to talk about writing. It has played a key role in our attempts to understand what it means to write ever since we started to take writing seriously enough to define it apart from the textual obsessions of current-traditional rhetoric. During this time, many composition teachers and theorists have demonstrated a strong sense that writing, or at least "good" writing, is somehow associated with the productive juxtaposition of opposing forces, that writing is defined by discontinuity or disjunction, the threshold experience of doubleness and betweenness that I am calling archelogical.

To back up that statement, I will look at some of the literature in our field that has defined writing or "good" writing as archelogical. It's not hard to find because there is so much of it. I have chosen pieces that represent a wide range of both our history and our theoretical assumptions.

Because my argument depends so much on the particular words used to describe writing, I will rely to a large extent on quotations to show how the language, as well as the concepts of these composition scholars, echoes the archelogical dialectic described in the previous chapter.

The sense of writing as archelogical may be found in the work of some of the earliest contributors to contemporary composition theory. D. Gordon Rohman, for example, defines good writing as self-actualization, which he opposes to the bad writing associated with textbooks promoting "Letters for All Occasions" (107). To encourage good writing, he uses two strategies to stimulate discontinuous thinking: meditation techniques that offer a "'puzzle form'" for discovery and analogical thinking, which encourages "the *'bisociation'* of all experience" (109–12; emphasis mine). Ken Macrorie says that one of the characteristics of good writing, in contrast to "Engfish," is that it incorporates *"[o]pposition between facts that create tension."* To help students write well, he asks them to observe "fabulous realities," disjunctions that generate tension. "Two things that do not belong together touch in some way. And their touching creates waves of further suggestion that are not stated" (48). He recommends a number of strategies to help students find oppositions and bring those oppositions into their writing (89–97).

Perhaps the most consistent theme in Peter Elbow's career is the productive use of contraries. In *Writing Without Teachers,* for instance, he portrays freewriting as a method that encourages "chaos and disorientation," which lead to growth and change (30–35). To explain how this occurs on the microcosmic level of writing, Elbow uses the metaphor of cooking, the "anti-entropy" that is produced in "the interaction of contrasting or conflicting material" (48–49). To get students' writing to the point of cooking, he advises them to "encourage conflicts or contradictions in your thinking" (50) and offers extensive advice to aid them in discovering these conflicts and contradictions (49–70). The archelogical nature of writing is most clearly revealed in Elbow's *Embracing Contraries,* in which he explores a myriad of oppositions that define writing.[1]

I have already mentioned in chapter 1 the role of dissonance in Young, Becker, and Pike, the most archelogical of the starting points I discussed there. They describe writing as an art of inquiry that arises out of an incongruity or tension:

> a paradoxical "fact" that doesn't make sense, a situation that is incompatible with a person's values, an apparent opposition of two respected authorities on an important issue, the seeming inadequacy of a strongly held theory, a clash of two sets of values to which a person is deeply committed. (72)

In association with this perspective, Janice M. Lauer provides a theoretical foundation for writing as inquiry, which she describes as occurring "when students raise meaningful questions about incongruities in their own worlds" ("Writing" 89). Such incongruities have been described by theorists using different archelogical terms: "tension" for Lonergan, "disequilibrium" for Piaget, "cognitive dissonance" for Festinger, "janusian thinking" for Rothenburg (90).

We can also see the concept of *archê* in the early work of Sondra Perl and Nancy Sommers as they each tried to understand the generative potential of revision. Perl uses "felt sense" to describe what it is, in the recursive nature of writing, that writers "go back to." This is a key to the creative nature of writing, a process, she says, in which "we begin with what is inchoate and end up with something that is tangible" ("Understanding Composing" 366–67). In a later piece, Perl continues to explore felt sense, this time with psychotherapist Arthur Egendorf, by focusing on the question, "What happens when writers sit down and begin to write?" (257). Perl and Egendorf suggest that creativity has its beginnings in the paradoxical state of "knowing but not knowing" (251), the contradictory quality of "turning toward and engaging the sense of what lies beyond one's current capacity to express" (254). "Thus *writing*," they say, "is what makes discovery possible by creating the possibilities for discovery" (258–59).

Sommers expresses this threshold experience of knowing but not knowing as dissonance, "the incongruities between intention and execution" that spark revision ("Revision Strategies" 387). In experienced writers, the productive potential of dissonance makes writing "a repeated process of beginning over again, starting out new" (387). The ability to recognize dissonances makes writing a series of beginnings; dissonance "confuses the beginning and end, the agent and vehicle; it confuses, *in order to find,* the line of argument" (384). In an essay published more recently, Sommers amplifies this archelogical view of revision by applying it to life and love as well as to writing. She uses the image in her title, "Between the Drafts," to question the either-or mentality that separates the academic from the personal, fact from feeling, work from home. Our authority as writers and human beings comes, she says, when we avoid either-or thinking with its apparent immunity from ambiguity and uncertainty. "Only when I suspend myself between either *and* or can I move away from conventional boundaries and begin to see shapes and shadows and contours—ambiguity, uncertainty, and discontinuity, moments when the seams of life just don't hold." It is in negotiating these uncertainties at the threshold marked by opposing forces that one finds authority. Her life and writing may be marked by discontinuity, but she observes that she has come "to see discontinuous moments as sources of strength and knowledge" (29). The space between the drafts becomes a symbol for the place where we live and write, the ambiguous territory of *archê.*

Writing as a threshold experience is also captured by Kurt Spellmeyer, who uses Foucault to express the nature of writing as beginnings. For Foucault, he says, knowledge structures are not unified and unchanging but are composed of discontinuities, which tends to problematize those knowledge structures. According to Spellmeyer, Foucault's "Discourse on Language" portrays "writing as an 'event' through which the familiar becomes problematic—a 'crack,' an 'irruption,' an 'incision' in the structure of knowledge" (716). Neither completely open nor completely closed, "discourse emerges instead from the eventful conflict between openness and closure, between what Foucault terms 'desire' and 'constraint'" (716–17). Spellmeyer points out that some people have used Foucault to overstate the role of the discourse community in writing. He contends, however, that Foucault is making a far different claim: "The subject always speaks from a 'discontinuity,' from a point of intersection between divergent interests, channels, and communities" (720).[2]

Another way our discipline has tried to understand writing as archelogical is by using Bakhtin. Joy Ritchie, for instance, takes Bakhtin's concept of heteroglossia as a way of understanding the productive conflict of the writing workshop, in which student writers are caught between the self and the other, "trying to resolve the dissonance among the voices they hear in the social network, and attempting to construct their own evolving voice" (154). As opposed to what Bakhtin calls "authoritative" or monologic discourse, the workshop encourages students to negotiate the cacophony of discourses that is heteroglossia, the conflicting, contending, dissonant values and purposes that they find in the social relations of writing. Geoffrey A. Cross uses another Bakhtinian concept to highlight the productive conflict in discourse: the centripetal and centrifugal forces in language. These forces of acquiescence and unity on the one hand and disagreement and disunity on the other create a conflict in discourse itself that, Cross says, citing Bakhtin, "'expose[s] it as a contradiction-ridden, tension-filled unity of two embattled tendencies in the life of a language'" (175). It is at the intersection of these forces, Cross argues, that writing takes place.

The archelogical dialectic at the site of writing has also been addressed by neo-Marxist composition theorists. In "From Silence to Words: Writing as Struggle," Min-zhan Lu contends that problems arise when we try to make the scene of writing pure and unconflicted; silencing the conflicts may have the effect of silencing the writer. And in "Conflict and Struggle: The Enemies or Preconditions of Basic Writing?" Lu argues that the founding tenets of basic writing have established the teacher's job as acculturation and accommodation, avoiding conflict and struggle at all costs. She offers instead the image of basic writing students as residents of a borderland, those who possess "a tolerance for contradiction and ambivalence, learning to sustain contradiction and turn ambivalence into a new consciousness." We must recognize, she says, "that reading and writing take place at sites of political as well as linguistic conflict" (888).

James Berlin uses a cultural studies approach to teach writing in what I think could be called an archelogical pedagogy. The purpose of a writing course, he says, is to make students aware of the conflicting cultural codes or discourses that compete to define their consciousnesses and then to provide the opportunity for students to negotiate among those conflicting ideological formations. Conflict, then, should be at the center of teaching writing. In order "to prepare students for critical citizenship in a democracy," writing teachers must "problematize students' experiences, requiring them to challenge the ideological codes they bring to college by placing their signifying practices against alternatives" ("Poststructuralism" 31).

Continuing the theme of archelogical conflict, Kathleen E. Welch describes a writing course based on the "productive clash" of dialectic. She sees dialectic as useful in helping students internalize the conflicts of writing and transform writing problems "into productive contraries that are embraced" (133), which she describes as "the movement forward to new insight from the pairing of oppositional forces" (134). Matthew Wilson also recommends "a productive disorientation; it is a move that alerts students to the fact that dis-sensus is not only possible but necessary" (673). The teacher creates that "dis-sensus" in part through the act of rewriting, which "becomes, then, a site of local struggle where the teacher tries to disrupt the safety of narrative by pointing to sites of contestation and where the student's effort is to preserve narration while trying to account for the dissonance created by the instructor" (677).

James Seitz explores the archelogical aspects of writing from a different angle, the role of metaphor and fragments. He chides composition teachers for treating metaphor as merely a figure of speech, something added to language or something to be avoided in favor of the literal. Metaphor is, rather, "a semantic tension which sustains both unity and disruption of meaning" ("Composition's Misunderstanding" 297). Writing teachers, he says, "should not ignore the potential value of disturbance, of tension in writing and reading" (293). Our obsession with clarity and accessibility of writing ignores "the power of *de*familiarization found in metaphor . . . its violation of our established order" (296). In another article, Seitz decries what he sees as the composition teacher's peculiar distrust of the fragment, our tendency "to disregard or even actively discourage the rupture and dislocation created by fragmentary texts" in favor of coherence and completeness that normalize discourse ("Roland Barthes" 816). He suggests that we encourage students to engage in the reading and writing of fragmentary and ambiguous texts, texts that "reveal the rhetorical and aesthetic power generated by disruption, discontinuity, and disorder" (823).

I suspect that by now my point is abundantly clear: we have, as a profession, expressed a long-lived and continuously iterated understanding of writing as archelogical, writing as participating in beginnings. Of course, we haven't used that terminology, but we have, I contend, made extensive use of the concept. I hope it is also clear that when we have talked about writing as archelogical we have usually done so not always in abstract and philosophically vague terms but also in terms of particular teaching strategies for encouraging productive contradictions in student writing.

Let me return now to the claim that writing is beginnings. I have argued that claim by presenting evidence, in the form of a review of some of the pertinent literature in composition, that writing is archelogical, the minor premise in my syllogism. But I would also like to make this argument more recognizably definitional by following the classic *topos* of definition, which starts by placing the definiendum (writing) into the larger class of the definiens (beginnings).[3] When I say that writing is beginnings I mean that writing is part of a larger set of phenomena that adhere to the pattern of beginnings as modeled by the archelogical dialectics in the previous chapter. Writing, then, is defined as a member of the broader category of beginnings.

The second step in the definitional *topos* is to distinguish the definiendum from other members of the definiens. The primary characteristic that distinguishes writing from other instances of beginnings is that writing involves literate composition (as opposed, say, to those forms of beginnings that occur on the submolecular and molecular levels as described by Prigogine or acts of agency described by Paul Smith in which literate discourse plays no direct role). Thus the definition: *writing is a form of beginnings that involves literate composition.* The pieces I have reviewed here offer multiple examples of the way the principle of beginnings is manifested in literate composition.

This definition has the advantage of helping us to see writing in a new light, or rather to recognize the broader implications of what we have been saying about writing all along. Writing is a powerful act that brings to us as writers and teachers of writing the opportunity for participating in beginnings, the threshold experience of archelogical dialectic. Seeing writing as beginnings also enables us to discern a common thread that runs through our discussions about writing, a thread that is otherwise obscured by our many disagreements. I think that all of the teachers and scholars in the preceding review are saying basically the same thing about writing; they recognize a similar source for the power of writing. Our disagreements arise from the different *perspectives* on that source of power. Yes, self-actualization and neo-Marxist cultural studies come out of radically different schools of thought, but within the broader context defined by *archê,* the differences seem relatively superficial—or at least not quite so divisive. Labeling both as acts of beginnings reveals a surprising commonality underlying them, which helps us to see what is important in our understanding of writing, what it means to write.

The definition I offer here brings with it some important benefits, I think, but there are two key problems with it. The first is the problem of overinclusiveness, a natural problem with definition. By saying that writing is a part of the class of beginnings that involves literate composition I am saying that all literate composition participates in beginnings. As writing teachers, however, we are acutely aware that much (if not most) of the writing our students do comes nowhere near the lofty ideals described in the review. Indeed, most of the authors of those pieces describe writing as archelogical in opposition to writing that is not. The implications of defining writing the way I have is that it includes all literate composition. So if the case can be made that most literate composition is *not* beginnings, that it does not place the writer on the threshold between knowing and not knowing, an act of disruption and alienation, then my definition is not very definitive. I can't define writing as beginnings when so much of what passes for writing is clearly not.

The second problem is even more troublesome: What do I do with the ludic postmodern critique of writing, particularly its challenge to the very idea of defining writing? You may recall from chapter 2 that the difficulty was the way definition makes writing finite, portraying the order that is writing in terms of something that lies outside writing. The ludic critique rejected the possibility of defining writing altogether, not only because the order in writing cannot be defined by something outside of it but also because there *is* no order in writing. Perhaps my definition of writing as beginnings falls into the same trap as other attempts to define writing.

These problems represent a challenge to my initial definition of writing as beginnings, but they also provide an opportunity to explore further the ideas of definition and writing and, thus, the opportunity for a more radically reconstructed understanding of what it means to write. I will address the ludic challenge first and then the problem of overinclusiveness.

The Ludic Critique of Definition: (Un)defining Writing

In chapter 2 my review of the ludic critique of composition focused on its suspicion of the beginning as origin in writing theory, particularly the way we have defined writing by establishing foundations for it outside writing itself. Worsham, Vitanza, and Davis challenged not only our definitions of writing but also the very idea of defining writing, an unwarranted act of setting limits around it, of making writing definite. To a large extent, the problem with writing is in writing itself, that is, the written text. The definiteness of marks on the page engenders the illusion that writing is itself definite, defined by that materiality. This quality of text leads to an understanding of writing as founded in substantial premises that lie outside writing.

But there is another aspect of this argument that I did not get into in chapter 2. My sense of the ludic critique is that it's not just that text defines writing but that writing as text also defines a way of knowing and being in the world, an epistemology and ontology of definiteness, of foundations. The image of solidity and permanence created by the text has helped to generate and continues to prop up the cultural metanarratives of solidity and permanence that anchor modernity. The title of this chapter, "Defining Writing," is a way of rendering both the issue of how to define writing as well as the defining nature of writing. Writing is defined by text but also defines *as* text, that is, defines the ways of knowing and being in the world associated with the modern.

From this perspective, the ludic critique of defining writing takes on greater import. But this critique is much more than a simple dismissal of all attempts at defining writing. Rather, Worsham, Vitanza, and Davis seem to suggest that a different way of thinking about both definition and defining writing may be consonant with the ludic postmodern project. Theirs is an argument for a reconceptualization of writing that frees it from the tyranny of text.

In "The Question Concerning Invention," Worsham distinguishes writing as a question of Being from writing as a question of being. The former participates in Heideggerean Being; the latter is foundational, writing that is defined and is defining, writing that gives the false impression that the truth inhabits it. "But the truth that writing brings into being," says Worsham, "is not carried *in* any statement a text makes; indeed, the truth that happens in writing leaves no trace of itself in any explicit sense" (233). As a way of separating writing as a question of Being from the definiteness of text, she calls upon the model of oral discourse:

> What happens in writing, in other words, is not itself *written*. Writing is as ephemeral as the sounded word and . . . hides itself in what it brings to light. . . . In this moment, the distinction between "oral" and "written" dissolves and the interior structure of Being is registered as event. (233)

In "Writing Against Writing," Worsham creates a similar distinction, as the title suggests, but this time between *écriture féminine* and academic writing. The idea of two kinds of writing is established in her epigraph from Hélène Cixous: "to get to the point of writing a paper, I had to combat the writing in me." Like writing as a question of Being, *écriture féminine* is described in terms of its link to orality. "In particular, *écriture féminine* disturbs the logic of academic language, which depends on a scission between oral and written text, by working with the oral otherness of discourse, the nondiscursive possibilities of voice and rhythm" (90–91).

What Worsham does to resist the textual imperatives of defining writing is to project a form of writing—characterized as a question of Being and *écriture féminine*—in terms of orality, loosening this form of writing from the confining definitions of what we normally think of as writing. Vitanza and Davis make similar projections, though without moving writing explicitly toward orality. Vitanza does this by distinguishing between modern and postmodern views of writing. He uses a quotation from Deleuze and Guattari's *Anti-Oedipus* to describe the latter as

> writing inscribed on the very surface of the Real: a strangely polyvocal kind of writing, never a biunivocalized, linearalized one; a transcursive system of writing, never a discursive one; a writing that constitutes the entire domain of the "real inorganization" of the passive syntheses, where we would search in vain for something that might be labeled the Signifier—writing that ceaselessly composes and decomposes the chains into signs that have nothing that impels them to become signifying. (151)

Davis contrasts writing in the humanist tradition with a posthumanist "writing itself," or genuine writing.

> This writing refuses to weave another thread into the myths of community [common-being] upon which the ideal of "good writing" is usually built. This writing instead works at the weave, yanking, pulling, ripping . . . exposing the infinite finitude that rhetorics of "the social" and "the individual" attempt to cover over. (238)

It is writing that is not specifically addressed to anyone and has no message or driving purpose other than the play of language that undercuts the humanist urge for meaning making (236–40).

What we find in this ludic postmodern rethinking of writing is the possibility of a writing that is not trapped in the foundations of modernist metanarratives. These ludics express that possibility by proposing two conceptions of writing: on the one hand there is writing as a question of being, academic writing, modernist writing, and humanist writing; on the other hand there is writing as a question of Being, *écriture féminine,* postmodern writing, and writing itself. This differentiation between forms of writing allows for a writing that lies outside our usual conceptions of it as tied to text. So the ludic postmodern project in composition holds out the possibility for a definition of what it means to write that moves beyond defining writing.

Let me explore this issue more deeply. In chapter 2, I argued that Worsham, Vitanza, and Davis deconstructed not only all of our definitions of writing but also the very possibility of defining writing. However, it seems to me that their attempt to delineate a postmodern form of writing offers the opportunity for a reconstruction of both writing and defining writing. Because this reconstruction is only hinted at here, I must extrapolate on what is given. Obviously, a definition of what it means to write that moves beyond defining writing is not what we commonly mean by *to define,* to make finite, to set conceptual boundaries around a phenomenon. What these postmodern critics are doing is just the opposite: they are—by making writing indefinite, by unlinking it from the illusory definiteness of the text—defining writing as both undefinable and undefining. One way to capture this paradox is to say that their definitional method is to (un)define writing, a both-and solution to the problem of definition. A postmodern writing is (un)defined as an indefinite and undefining act. Thus the idea of defining writing shifts dramatically. A ludic writing, liberated from the illusory definiteness of the text, defines its own way of knowing and being in the world.

And this reconstruction of writing and defining writing helps us understand what it means to say that writing is beginnings. The principle of beginnings is itself (un)defined by contradiction. The threshold event both defines and undefines, as modeled by archelogical dialectics in the dislocating moment of an existential starting point or resistance or the intermediation of opposites that forms a middle. The order of a nonlinear system is (un)defined by the very principle that defines it. For Whitehead, each of the infinitely recurring interpenetrations of God and the World is an instant that has the potential to undefine previous definitions of the conceptual and the actual and thus allows for new definitions of each. In beginnings is the archelogical dialectic of disorder and order, discontinuity and continuity, disjunction and junction. So when I say that writing is beginnings, the *is* is not a simple equal sign at all. What I really mean is that writing is (un)defined by beginnings—which is the very nature of beginnings. In this way, the (un)defining characteristic of writing is located in beginnings.

The Problem of Overinclusiveness: Writing and Scribing

The other issue associated with my definition of writing as a form of beginnings that involves literate composition is that it includes too much to be effectively definitive. The problem lies in the second part of the definition, in which I distinguish writing as beginnings from other forms of beginnings. This move raises the question, how can I define writing as beginnings when it is clear that so much literate composition is not marked by beginnings? The solution to this problem, however, has already been suggested by the ludic critique and its recognition of the possibility of a writing that may be set apart from another kind of writing, what I have for the time being labeled text-based writing. But this recognition of the polar nature of writing is by no means limited to the radical project of ludic postmoderns. Indeed, the composition scholarship that I reviewed earlier in this chapter also reveals a strong sense of this duality in writing.

Rohman, for instance, distinguishes writing as self-actualization from writing as "Letters for All Occasions." In Macrorie it is real writing versus "Engfish," and in Elbow writing without teachers versus an implied writing with teachers. This pattern is also apparent in most of the other articles in the review, as a few other examples will illustrate: for Perl, it is writing that is marked by the paradox of knowing but not knowing as opposed to the orthodoxy of knowing; for those using Bakhtin it is dialogic as opposed to monologic or authoritative; for Lu it is conflict and struggle as opposed to acculturation and accommodation; for Seitz it is the metaphorical and the fragmentary as opposed to the literal and the unified.

This duality certainly disturbs my definition of writing. Now admittedly, the duality represented in these articles sometimes masks itself as evaluative—"good" writing versus "bad" writing—but I think the division that is being described goes much deeper than that; it is epistemological and ontological, two wholly different conceptions of what it means to write.

Let me step back for a moment and look at the implications of what I've just said. The way I'm defining writing has made an unexpected twist. I had originally said that writing is a kind of beginnings that involves literate composition, placing writing under the larger category of beginnings and distinguishing it from other kinds of beginnings. Now, however, that definition has been reversed: *writing is a kind of literate composition that is marked by beginnings.* This reversal suggests a substantial change in the way we understand what it means to write because it points to a distinction between writing as beginnings—which I will claim as just plain *writing*—and a form of literate composition that is not (un)defined by beginnings. As we will see, this way of understanding writing and its other deconstructs the generally accepted idea of writing as defined by marks and the act of marking.

Claiming that writing is beginnings invites a whole new way of understanding what it means to write. What I propose here is a reconstruction of writing that extends the one I started in the previous section. To do that, though, I need to be able to make a clearer distinction between literate composition that is writing, (un)defined by beginnings, and literate composition that is not writing.

One useful model for making that distinction may be found in the linguistic differentiation between *utterance* and *text*. These terms are used by David R. Olson as a way of describing the different conventions of speech and writing. Olson mounts a kind of ontogeny-recapitulates-phylogeny argument by positing both the development of civilization and the education of children as the movement from the culture of utterance to the culture of text. George L. Dillon takes up Olson's terms and uses them to explain the difficulty many students have in writing classes, which he sees as the apotheosis of the culture of text. Dillon points to seven sets of opposing conventions that describe the poles of utterance and text: for example, whereas utterance has an immediate audience, is spontaneous, depends on implicit logical connectors, uses words without defining them, and values understanding, text has a distant and multiple audience, is planned, depends on explicit logical connectors, uses words as objects of scrutiny, and values correctness (22). Dillon is not, strictly speaking, referring to a division between speech and writing. Rather he is looking at how and why the conventions associated with utterance tend to populate student texts (24–49).

Edward Lotto observes, however, that underlying Dillon's distinctions between utterance and text are two different relationships to the language and thinking of a user's community. As Dillon describes it, in utterance, language users are expected "to reproduce accepted wisdom, attitudes, and values," to conform to received opinion, to "enact solidarity with their social group"; to use words in such a way that their meanings rely on "shared experience" and therefore need not be examined; to use premises "based on common assumptions and stereotypes"; to achieve "the sharing of experience." In text, however, language users are expected "to produce novel, even counterintuitive, facts and viewpoints" and to "enact membership in an *imagined* community of inquiring minds"; to use words in such a way that they challenge shared experience as they "are subjected to scrutiny and stipulative clarification"; to use premises that question common assumptions and thus must be made logical and explicit; to resist shared experience that demands "proving the correctness of its models of the world" (Dillon 22; emphasis added).

Text, then, represents a disruption of the conventions of utterance. Lotto makes the case that these conventional differences should become the focus of our composition teaching. The student writer who is caught up in the conventions of utterance has no way to see beyond cliché and generalization of his or her own sense of the way things are and thus no way to understand why their teachers resist that. "For that writer to analyze the cliché or examine the details that are part of the generalization is, in some way, to destroy reality" (679).[4]

Thus the difference between text and utterance lies much deeper than surface-level conventions, and this, I think, is what Lotto is getting at. The difference is epistemological and ontological; it is about different ways of knowing and being in the world. Utterance, Lotto says,

> functions to encourage assent among the listeners, thus affirming the speaker's place in the group as a person who partakes of the common set of beliefs. It will not do, however, to look at these beliefs too carefully, especially not in the light of the experience of the writer, since to do so could well mean bringing up counter examples to the commonly accepted beliefs. (679)

The issue, then, is not really writing versus speech. Utterance tends to be comfortable in that it reproduces what one knows, believes—in speech *or* in writing. Lotto points out that best-sellers are best-sellers often because they construct a comfortable vision that corresponds to the way most readers perceive the world (684). They are written-down utterance. Thus the distinction I am getting at may be rendered more accurately as "text" versus "utterance."[5]

This understanding of "text" and "utterance" is helpful because it models a way to distinguish writing that is beginnings from writing that is not. Particularly in Lotto's interpretation of the terms, the principle of beginnings is associated with "text," the act of dissent, of questioning, of challenging commonly held values and beliefs. "Text," then, describes a form of literate discourse that is marked by the threshold event of contradictory experience; "utterance" is a form of literate discourse that isn't. The problem, though, is that these terms, despite protests to the contrary and my use of quotation marks, still carry with them a speech-writing dichotomy and thus the tendency to essentialize that dichotomy. I want to avoid the difficulties surrounding the speech-writing issue; I want to be able to make an argument about the polar identities within literate composition itself, separate from the idea that "text" and "utterance" each may be used to designate both literate and spoken discourse as well as combinations of both.

As a way of making this distinction, I offer the terms *writing* and *scribing*, terms that are more indicative of the distinction I am drawing here because they are both associated with literate discourse.[6] The critical difference between them may be seen in their derivations. *To scribe* comes from the noun *scriba,* which is Latin for official writer, from *scribere,* "to trace characters." Its Greek precedents are various words that mean "to scratch an outline, sketch," coming from an older Greek word meaning "to cut, as in to shear."[7] My dictionary elaborates on this idea of official writer as referring more recently to clerks or those who keep accounts, secretaries, and people who take dictation. For most of us, though, the idea of the scribe is most closely associated with ancient copyists who laboriously transcribed holy scriptures.

The scribes of the ancient scriptoria were not writers in the sense that we would use the term now. Their job was to copy the sacred texts of their communities, sometimes illuminating them with exquisite designs, but still copying, tracing characters that already exist. Even *scripture* itself gives the sense of something copied, "dictated" by God, something sacred, beyond human production, to be maintained as closely as possible to the original and accepted form.

Scribing is the word I will use to signify the kind of literate composition that is characterized not by beginnings but by *the* beginning, a way of knowing and being in the world marked by continuity, equilibrium, orientation to that which comes before. Scribing takes place in a world that is ruled by linear systems and strict adherence to the laws of noncontradiction. It is writing as a question of being, as modernist, as humanistic. It is a sort of copying because, like "utterance," it is the generation of text without questioning, challenging, without upsetting, without interpretation, at best only ornamenting what is already there. Most of us would have to admit that in our experience as composition teachers, the literate composing done by our students tends to fall into the realm of scribing. This is what Lotto is talking about when he characterizes such student compositions as "utterance," the undisturbed reflection of the thoughts and beliefs of the community.

Writing is different in significant ways from scribing. Writing, as I noted earlier, has its roots in words that mean to tear, to wound, to cut. I used this derivation earlier to talk about writing as marks left on bark, stone, or paper, marks that in our culture define all literate discourse. But I want to shift the emphasis here. As opposed to scribing, making a sketch or an outline of something familiar, writing is tearing or wounding, making an incision, resulting in a cleft or gap. As Spellmeyer puts it, citing Foucault, writing is "a 'crack,' an 'irruption,' an 'incision' in the structure of knowledge" (716). Writing is defined by a rending or cutting—and thus by disjunction, discontinuity, disorientation. Again, in contrast to scribing with its implications of copying, writing is an act of interpretation that wonders about, questions, challenges that which is given—scripture. It is a question of Being, *écriture féminine,* postmodern, and posthumanistic writing itself. Writing is beginnings: an event that takes place on the threshold between order and disorder, the known and the unknown, being and becoming, location and dislocation.

Writing, then, is a word I am removing from its common to a special use. In this usage, writing is not synonymous with all literate composition. Rather, it is a form of literate composition that, in contradistinction to scribing, is characterized by beginnings. Let me hasten to say, however, lest I be misunderstood, that I am not making this distinction for evaluative purposes. Though some of the teachers and scholars in the review of literature couched their descriptions in terms of "good writing" as opposed to "bad writing," it is not, I believe, an issue of determining quality in the sense that we usually use the term, that is, of ranking within orders of the same kind. It runs much deeper than that, not qualitative but epistemological and ontological. Differentiating writing from scribing is not a representation of levels within the same kind; rather, they are wholly different ways of knowing and being in the world. Indeed, I strongly suspect that scribing is, generally speaking, more likely than writing to be labeled "good writing."

Writing is the ideal expressed by the teachers and theorists whose work I have reviewed in this chapter. For them and for many others, it is what we profess when we profess writing. I would guess that this is what has brought a lot of us to this profession in the first place: that ideal vision of what it means to write. We are at our best when we are driven by that vision, in both our teaching and our scholarship. So let's claim that ideal by calling *it* writing.

The problem of overinclusiveness may be solved, then, by recasting the definition of writing so as to focus on the way the principle of beginnings sets writing apart from the form of literate composition I am calling scribing. As I have shown, however, this sense of the polar nature of writing is certainly nothing new to the way we have conceived of literate composition. What I have done is to follow the lead of the ludic postmodernists, who deconstructed the very idea of defining writing but then left open the possibility of a reconstructed definition of writing that is not tied to the illusion of definiteness attached to marks on a page. (Un)defining writing as beginnings allows me to reconstruct it in a way that captures the threshold event of writing.

What It Means to Write

The deconstruction and reconstruction of what it means to begin points to the possibility of a similar deconstruction and reconstruction of what it means to write. Reconceived as beginnings, the question of where writing begins deconstructs writing by placing it in ontological doubt. The question, then, becomes, What is writing that it is beginnings? The two definitions I have presented to answer that question offer two ways in which we can reconstruct writing as beginnings. The first definition, writing as a form of beginnings that involves literate composition, finds its grounding in my review of literature, which shows that many teachers and scholars of writing have for a long time been describing writing as archelogical. There is, then, a lot of support in our professional literature for the concept of writing as a form of beginnings. There are also advantages to the field, I have argued, in conceiving of writing this way. It provides a powerful understanding of writing that cuts across many different theoretical perspectives, and it helps us to see how writing is related to other forms of beginnings.

This is, I suspect, the less problematic of the two definitions. The second, a radical extension of the first, is my contention that writing should be redefined as a special term: writing is a form of literate composition that is marked by beginnings—a definition that had necessitated my distinction between writing and scribing. This second definitional claim is a response to the deconstructive critique of defining writing by Worsham, Vitanza, and Davis, a critique that stood alongside hints that it may be possible to (un)define a reconstructed postmodern writing. I have acted on that hint by applying the conceptual shift from the beginning to beginnings, scribing defined by the former and writing by the latter. Beginnings, then, undermines our usual notions of writing and thus invites a radical reconsideration of it.

I readily admit that taking it upon myself to redefine writing is likely to be seen as a foolish enterprise; after all, as the Sanscrit roots of *to write* reveal, we have for many thousands of years conceived of literate discourse as a function of the definiteness associated with marks on a markable surface. How can I possibly expect to counter an understanding of writing that is so firmly established in our cultural consciousness?

I can't. To believe that I could really would be foolish. My ambitions, though, are limited to those of us who profess writing, not to the culture at large. In terms of that much smaller group, redefining writing is not audacious because the definitional crisis in the concept of writing is already very much a part of our consciousness. My argument is that we have for a long time conceived of writing as a special concept, somehow removed from what often passes for writing but isn't. The review in this chapter illustrates that; the ludic postmodernists provide the opportunity to crystallize it. All I am doing by claiming writing as a special term is giving linguistic validation to a concept that already exists in our conversations about writing.

This validation is important because, as I have pointed out before, we are people who profess writing. The usual definition of writing as any literate composition works against us in ways that most of us can readily see. We are defined by what is most obvious about writing, the technology of text—handwriting, spelling, grammar, syntax. As such, we are perceived as keepers of forms, upholders of "standards." It's little wonder that so many of our colleagues outside composition understand teaching writing solely as the diagnosis and treatment of error and syntactic infelicity. It's little wonder that our students understand writing simply as a test of how well they can conform to the confusing welter of textual niceties handed down to them over the years by English teachers. And it's little wonder that so many composition teachers are still consumed by the task of trying to extract from their students isolated performances of "good writing," inscriptions that adhere to some Platonic Ideal of textual conventions.

What we need is a stronger conception of what it is that we profess as professors of writing, a way to capture the sense of writing that already drives much of our teaching and scholarship. Defining writing as beginnings is my way of doing that. It gives me a way of conceptualizing the "something else" that is writing.

But it also does more than that: it provides a way to comprehend and express the source of the power that is writing itself. My argument for distinguishing writing from scribing is directed toward helping us understand and identify that source. This is, I think, the most important benefit in this reconstructed definition of writing. We are drawn to writing, most of us, because we recognize the power of writing, a power that vanishes when we think of writing merely as marks on a page. Understanding writing as beginnings associates writing with the power of *archê,* a power that is modeled in the archelogical dialectics of the previous chapter, one of the most accessible ways for people to participate in the dialectical experience of beginnings.

What are we to do about my niece, Cathleen, and the grousers from other departments and the age-old cultural understanding of writing that is so firmly set in the epistemological and ontological definiteness located in the marks on a working surface? I don't know. My chief interest here is in how *we* conceive of what it means to write, and I realize that the definitions of writing I have offered here would have little persuasive appeal to those others. But who knows, perhaps it may be possible to create a change in the broader concept of writing by understanding more clearly ourselves what it is we do—and by doing it well. Perhaps we could convince others that what it means to write lies not just in the marks but also in the "something else" that is writing, something that is beyond the technology of text. As Worsham puts it so well, "What happens in writing . . . is not itself *written*" ("Question" 233).

7 Valuing Writing

> Time is the continuous renewal of being in the discontinuous. . . . Creatures *within* creation age. They are given to themselves to refresh creation. Age is the dying of *this* creature, death the time when the renewed beginning passes beyond *this* creature. But the universal impermanence is still the time of beginnings.
>
> —William Desmond, *Being and the Between*

Surely I'm not the only composition teacher to find myself more than a little troubled by the common term for teaching students to write fiction and poetry—creative writing. It certainly *seems* innocent enough; we need some way of distinguishing fiction and poetry classes from other writing classes. But I don't see it as innocent at all. The implication is that what we teach in composition classes is *not*-creative writing.

The problem is that *creative* is itself a highly value-laden term in our culture. Margaret A. Boden, for example, describes creativity as "a socially sanctioned honorific" (Introd. 2). C. A. Bowers points out that within educational circles creativity has become a "godword," used and accepted unreflectively by people of quite different agendas and political stripes (159). Practically everyone would be flattered to be called creative—original, inventive, ingenious, imaginative. It's one of the highest attributions of value we can make about someone or something.

For me, then, nothing highlights the issue of value in writing more than the distinction between creative writing and, by implication, not-creative writing. This is clearly a value dichotomy, and as composition teachers, we know very well which side of that dichotomy we fall on. In this chapter, I turn again to value, the other theme, in addition to definition, that has driven this study. Definition is the answer to the *what* question: What is writing? Value, as I understand it, is the answer to the *why* question: Why write? or to put it a little more precisely, What is the source of the good in writing?

Of course, the issue of value has been extremely important in composition theory. In chapter 2 I pointed out that one of the most significant steps in the formation of our discipline was the shift in focus from extrinsic to intrinsic value, from value located in what makes writing good to value located in the good of writing. Though we have actively disagreed about what that good is—self-actualization, discovery, meaning-making, learning, knowing, participating in discourse communities, encouraging agency in the resistance of dominant ideologies—we have tended to agree that there is value inherent in writing.

As I also showed in chapter 2, however, the ludic postmodern critique of composition represents a radical challenge to our assumptions regarding value in composition and, by extension, to the value of the field. The charge is that we have fallen into the teleological fallacy of confusing the value of the thing itself, literate composition, with its goal or object: all those values listed above are not actually values of writing itself but values that are still extrinsic to it, located outside writing in what it can do or accomplish. We have, these critics claim, maintained writing as an instrument, merely a tool for achieving something else: self-actualization, discovery, meaning making, and so forth.

The ludic deconstruction of the ways we have valued writing is a deconstruction also of value itself. As with definition, however, there is in this deconstruction an opportunity for a reconstruction of value and of valuing writing. This opportunity is suggested by the ludic critics in their attempt to express a noninstrumental source of good in writing. Worsham is particularly eloquent in her description of that value. In an implicit response to the issue of the good of writing, she says that all language acts are poetical insofar as "they realize their essential function in bringing beings into unconcealment and in making truth (as a process of concealing and revealing) into a concrete historical happening" ("Question" 229). The value of writing, she suggests, lies not in its ability to generate knowledge but rather in its ability "to subtract the familiarity and alreadiness of what has been said, . . . to defamiliarize and denaturalize. Its task is to make strange and uncanny what is familiar and comfortable" (233). "Our emphasis," she adds,

> should shift from the notion of writing as a mode of learning to that of writing as a strategy, without tactics or techniques, whose progress yields "unlearning." . . . Writing would no longer function primarily as an agency in the articulation of knowledge and redistribution of power; instead, it would become an indispensable agency for making the world strange and infinitely various. ("Writing" 101–2)

We find a similar sense of value in Vitanza. As paralogical, writing "is not a means of achieving or accounting for consensus. It is, instead, a means of continuous 'dissensus'; it 'counterhopes' to achieve an occasional, if not permanent, place of misology (i.e., a distrust of *logos*)." The object of postmodern writing is "just drifting/gaming" (165). "For paralogy, the goal is not renovation but innovation. . . . Thinking paralogically, Lyotard says, means 'searching for the unintelligible'" (166).

Davis condemns the values of liberal education that most writing courses serve, what she refers to as E^3, "Enlightenment, Empowerment, and Emancipation" (211). Instead, she holds up the good of a writing course that has no other purpose beyond writing itself: "it would devote itself to a critical unworking of reactionism, an affirmative unraveling of pre-established truth/knowledge in a radical resistance to closure/totality" (235). The good of such writing would be in that it "costs us a myth . . . but then grants us [a] life" (235).

I am sympathetic to the ludic critique of valuing writing. There is something deeply wrong in the way we have consistently located the value of writing outside writing itself, which has the unintended effect of contributing to the devaluation of writing. I appreciate also the fact that despite their radical deconstruction of value in writing and despite the fact that their own language remains superficially instrumental ("function," "task," "means," "goal"), Worsham, Vitanza, and Davis do point toward a way of valuing writing that is somehow intrinsic to writing itself: located not in the *telos* but in the event of writing. But what does it mean to conceive of value in terms of a "process of concealing and revealing" or "'unlearning'" or "misology" or "'searching for the unintelligible'" or a "radical resistance to closure/totality"? I realize that these terms represent the struggle to put into words an understanding of value that counters the instrumental and thus counters the sense of value that dominates our culture. Unfortunately, such terms can do little more than invoke the possibility for a reconstruction of valuing writing. It is that invocation, though, that provides me the space for such a reconstruction.

There are, of course, many ways of thinking about value. I am going to focus my reconstruction on the value associated with creativity: it is a widely accepted term of value, it marks the devaluation of composition as not-creative writing, and it is conceptually linked to creation, which allows me direct access to beginnings. I will start by investigating two opposing conceptions of creativity. The first is the Creator tradition. Tied to *the* beginning, this tradition is the one that dominates our culture, promoting a perception of creativity that locates value outside the event of creation. The other I call the archelogical tradition. Linked to beginnings, this tradition provides a basis for conceiving of value as intrinsic to the creative event. I will use this latter understanding of creativity to argue that the writing our students do in composition courses may be valued as creative writing.

Ultimately, this is my answer to the value question: the primary value of writing is located in beginnings. Why write? Because writing is beginnings; it engages the writer in the threshold experience of beginnings. Let me take this a step further: writing therefore is, by its very nature (and in opposition to scribing), creative. This argument is, however, much more difficult to make than the definitional one in the previous chapter. There, I was able to call upon what we have been saying all along about writing and use that for support. In this chapter, however, I challenge our most dearly held cultural and disciplinary assumptions about value, shifting from the instrumental to the intrinsic, from the teleological to the archelogical, from the beginning to beginnings.

Creativity: The Creator Tradition

In *The Creators,* Daniel J. Boorstin makes a case for a definite link between the way we in the West think about creativity and our understanding of the act of creation, particularly as it is presented in Genesis 1. Boorstin says that Western culture, with its profound historical sense of a Creator-God, has developed an understanding of the possibility of the new that is fundamentally different from other cultures. This doesn't mean that other peoples have not also created works of art and engineering. Rather, the West has developed an "unusual hospitality to the new," a special understanding of what it means to create that is strongly influenced by the image of the Creator-God (71). My objective in this section is to explore the key characteristics of that understanding of creativity so as to establish more clearly its alternative.

As I suggested earlier, the first chapter of Genesis portrays the most radical form of creation imaginable—creation out of nothing by fiat. Though this understanding of creation is a complex and contested notion, it is still the idea of creation that has dominated Western conceptions of how the universe came into being. The Creator-God creating all there is out of nothing represents a daunting paradigm for creativity. "Ultimately," says Charles H. Long, "the creation from nothing emphasizes that the creation is not a mere ordering or even founding but has come forth as a powerful religio-magical evocation from a powerful supreme being" (95). According to Robert C. Neville, the generation of "absolute novelty" implied in the *ex nihilo* doctrine is an act of creativity that is utterly unique to God (*God* 109). Viewed from this perspective, creation is the ultimate mystery. It is a divine act of consummate power removed from human understanding.

Another indication of the absoluteness of God's creativity is that it has no parallel to human acts of creation. Unlike creation stories in other cultures and even elsewhere in the Bible—stories that may portray creation as a birth from primordial parents, a construction out of familiar materials, or a battle between cosmic forces—this creation seems to be totally removed from all human analogy (Westermann 39–40). It is the serenely majestic act of calling forth: God says let there *be* and there *is*. As I have pointed out, this act is significantly different from its Babylonian predecessor, the *Enuma Elish,* in which creation is painted in very human terms. Genesis 1 is a manifesto of the ultimate power of the Hebrew Creator-God. This special power of divine creativity is even reflected in the Hebrew word *bara* in Genesis 1 and elsewhere ("In the beginning God *created*") a verb exclusively used with the subject God (Drees 256; Towner 16).

These two conceptions of the act of creation—that it is unique to God and removed from human analogy—may be understood with more precision by describing them as monolithic and unilateral, representing the dramatic oneness of God. The monolithic nature of creation is expressed first in the fact that all that is was fixed by God at the point of creation. Creation was a momentous act, a once-and-for-all event; thus, God is the only Creator. It is also expressed in the interpretation of creation as out of nothing: the universe was not formed of preexisting material but spoken forth out of absolute emptiness. Thus, all that is is of God. Indeed, Boorstin points out the likelihood that the Hebrews' belief in one God made it easier to envision a Creator-God and thus a monolithic act of creation (44). The fundamental novelty of this creative event means that all there is and can ever be is already created by a God that existed prior to Creation.

In addition to being monolithic, the biblical act of creation is unilateral, that is to say, it occurred as a one-way event. The Creator-God is the only actor in creation, a concept that stands in stark contrast to other creation stories, which tend to be bilateral or multilateral, representing creation as a shared event in which two or more divine beings or even human beings participate in a creative act that is analogous to human acts of creativity. "According to this view," says theologian David Ray Griffin, "God has all the creativity, the world has none. The creative God is not present in the creatures, but is their external creator and controller" ("Creativity" 65).

This radical conception of creation and creativity came to dominate Western culture as what John Hope Mason terms the Creator tradition, a wedding of Judaism and the classical philosophical systems of Stoicism and neo-Platonism. The cosmology of the Stoics and neo-Platonists was formed on the belief that all the world was the emanation of the transcendent and perfect One. By portraying the vast multiplicity of all Creation in terms of the eternal One, these Hellenistic and Roman philosophers projected a universe that was totally identified with *logos,* the rational order that marked all goodness and morality. Similar to Judaism, creation as envisioned by the Stoics and neo-Platonists was the result of a founding order and unity: the universe was conceived as One (706–7). These two powerful sources of the Creator tradition, the Hebrew and the classical, came together in the first century CE. "The result of this process," says Mason, "was a view of the Creator which combined the poetic power of the Book of Genesis with the philosophical attractions of Platonism after Plato" (707).

The Creator tradition is associated with what I am calling the beginning, a single, one-way event of creation. For Mason, the Creator tradition has defined the way we in our culture have understood creativity, identifying it with morality and order (707–10). I think, however, that the relationship between the beginning and creativity is more complicated than that; indeed, the whole idea of human creativity, that special quality of being able to create, is, as Reto Luzius Fetz shows, a concept that is only as old as modernity (190). Before that, creativity was conceived of as a power possessed by God alone. For the Hebrews, the Creator tradition was reflected chiefly in the special relationship between a chosen people and their all-powerful Creator-God. This relationship was expressed most clearly in the demand for obedience symbolized in the law and covenant.[1] In the Christian West of the late classical and medieval periods, creation as the beginning defined a worldview Fetz describes as creatureliness, the dominance of the Creator in the Creator's relationship to the creatures, the objects of creation (191–93). It is a relationship of absolute dependence on God alone. Law and covenant and creatureliness descend from an understanding of the radical oneness and subjectivity represented in the Creator-God. Creativity as a quality was vested only in the divine One—monolithic and unilateral.

The modern era, however, represents a crucial shift in the way the Creator tradition has defined our worldview, a shift from theological creativity to what Fetz calls anthropological creativity (190). In other words, creativity is no longer thought of as the exclusive province of the Creator-God; in the modern era, we conceive of human beings as also possessing creativity. However, this modern conception of human creativity is heavily influenced by the continuing dominance of the monolithic and unilateral nature of the beginning. Creativity may have shifted from the theological to the anthropological, but it is a conception that still takes as its paradigm the divine act of the Creator-God in the beginning.

One of the principles that defines the Creator tradition is that the source of creation is outside Creation itself; that is, the Creator-God preexisted the created universe and thus creativity is originated from without, extrinsic to the event. This principle is associated with the monolithic nature of creation. The absolute power represented in this view of creation was reflected before the modern era in our relationship with the Creator-God—law and covenant and then creatureliness: all creativity is vested in God. But even in the modern shift to human creativity, the idea of a special connection with an external power has continued to characterize creativity. Of course, the idea of divinely inspired works of art has long been a part of Western civilization,[2] but under the influence of Renaissance humanism, that idea underwent a significant transformation. The possibility of *human* creativity led to the perception of human beings as more than just passive receptors of God's creativity, as is symbolized in the concept of the muse, but as creators in their own right. For example, the poet was described by Marcilio Ficino in 1482 as "god upon earth," by Julius Caesar Scaliger in 1561 as "another god," and later by Shaftesbury in 1711 as a "second maker, a just Prometheus under Jove" (qtd. in Burwick 22). Mason points out that this link between human creativity and Christian–neo-Platonic ideas "provided the materials from which the modern notion of the artist as a uniquely valuable creator was constructed" (710).

This link to an outside creative force is one of the principal reasons that creativity inspires such a reverence in our culture: genius, the quality of the few people who are set apart from the rest of us, specially blessed. *Genius* is a cognate of a large group of words having to do with birth, from the Indo-European *to beget*. Genius indicates special powers that come from outside a person. Indeed, it originally referred not to the gifted person at all but to the divine being who was said to have presided over the birth of that person. Genius literally names the divinity itself and only by association the person who is gifted. Later the word came to be associated with the person who was thus blessed at birth by the genius (Partridge 250; Weekley 632). Our present understanding of genius as an exceptional person of uncommon creative powers bears the connotations of the source of those powers as in some way external to the person.

In much the same way that the Creator-God was considered set apart and worshipful in previous traditions, the creative person is the object of special reverence in the modern era, somehow removed from the rest of us by an association with the divine or other extraordinary source of power. In the latter half of the eighteenth century in England, explanations for genius typically followed faculty psychology. William Duff, for example, identified the imagination as the faculty that most distinguished the person of genius. The imagination, he says, is that "which, by its plastic power of inventing new associations of ideas, and of combining them with infinite variety, is enabled to present a creation of its own, and to exhibit senses and objects which never existed in nature" (qtd. in Puccio 4). In the romantic era, the mysteries of creativity were represented in even more powerful terms, as a kind of possession or madness. In *Poetic Madness and the Romantic Imagination,* Frederick Burwick examines the idea of creative madness and the cult of genius that characterized the aesthetic thought of Germany and England during that period. Perhaps the best expression of that understanding of genius is Coleridge's description of the primary imagination in the *Biographia Literaria:* "The primary IMAGINATION I hold to be the living power and prime agent of all human perception, and as a repetition in the finite mind of the eternal act of creation in the infinite I AM" (395–96). Burwick argues that Coleridge was thus able to have it both ways: "He wanted to affirm the creative capacities of intuition and imagination without denying divine agency" (38).

Later, the poetic madness of the romantics came to be understood as madness indeed, as faculty psychology gave way to psychiatry, imagination to psychosis. By the end of the nineteenth century, Cesare Lombroso had compiled an encyclopedic analysis of genius, linking it to a wide array of mental illnesses. Emil Kraepelin, a professor of psychiatry in Germany, described a manic syndrome that freed artists from mental constraints and allowed them to produce art (Burwick 2–3). This link between creativity and madness has continued to have a powerful hold over our conception of genius, both in the popular imagination and in much of the recent research in creativity studies.[3]

The point is that modern notions of human creativity are still heavily influenced by the monolithism of the Creator tradition. In that tradition, the source of creativity is outside Creation; creativity is portrayed as unique to God and therefore special and mysterious, beyond our understanding. In the modern rereading of that tradition, people regarded as creative are thought of as special, set apart from the rest of us; creativity is a form of possession, something that can be explained only in terms of the divine or what passes for the divine, whether it is located in the realm of Christian neo-Platonism, faculty psychology, German Idealism, or psychiatry. The source of creative powers is in a creative force that exists outside the human creator.

Modern creativity, in addition to its monolithism, also reflects the unilateral nature of creativity in the Creator tradition. In the worldview of the beginning, the Creator-God possesses all the powers of creativity, which are expressed most palpably in the materiality of Creation itself. Creation, thus, is the object of God's radically creative Subjectivity. As Creator, God is the Subject and all else is the object, absolutely dependent on the Subject, a dependence that before modernity was represented in law and covenant and creatureliness. In the era of human creativity, however, the relationship between creator-subject and created object has maintained its unilateral nature, heavily influencing our concept of creativity. In the same way that the Creator-God's creativity is recognized primarily in the material object of Creation, the creativity of human beings is recognized primarily in creative objects—poems, plays, paintings, performance art, et cetera.

For most of us, this appears to be such an obvious relationship that it may seem ridiculous to point it out. The commodification of creativity has become an accepted part of our cultural understanding of what it means to be creative: to produce material objects that are deemed by the culture as creative. Notice, however, that what we label as creative is determined not by the act itself but by the product of the act. Creativity is defined by the estimation of novelty or beauty or other notion of the good we apply to the created object. We identify creativity by the object we call creative.[4]

Thus, the locus of value in modern creativity is extrinsic to the creative event itself, located in the creative force outside the creator represented by the idea of genius and in the creative commodity that marks creativity. This concept is highly limited in that it denotes the few set apart as geniuses and the rare works that achieve high cultural value. In this way, our modern idea of creativity continues in the Creator tradition that has long dominated Western culture. It is to a large extent because creativity persists in the paradigm of the Creator-God that it has achieved what amounts to worshipful status for us. Creativity is quite literally, as Bowers describes it, a "godword."

Little wonder, then, that creative writing is so narrowly defined and that what our students do in composition classes is, within this paradigm, emphatically *not*-creative writing. It is not-creative because it is not valued as influenced by a special source of inspiration outside the writer nor as producing a commodity that is culturally esteemed. But the case I am making here is that this not-creative label is attributable not to the act of writing itself but to a culturally specific understanding of creativity that happens to locate value outside the creative event.[5] If I am to argue that the writing students do in composition classes may be valued as creative, then I need to offer an entirely different paradigm of creativity, an alternative to the monolithism and unilateralism of the Creator tradition.

Creativity: The Archelogical Tradition

In "The Character of Creativity: Two Traditions," Mason provides the historical and philosophical background for a conception of creativity that opposes the Creator tradition. Mason points out that in contrast to the creation story in Genesis 1, most other creation myths involve one of two activities: either the sexual union of two divine beings or a series of cosmic conflicts or struggles—both of which he describes, quoting Mircea Eliade, as "'a disjunction which breaks the primordial conjunction'" (697). This disjunctive myth provides the basis for what I call the archelogical tradition of creativity, founded not on oneness but on the productive relationship of opposing forces.[6] It is an alternative understanding of creation, and thus of creativity, as beginnings.

The creative elements of sexuality and conflict are captured in two figures of inventive cunning and daring that recur in many mythologies, the trickster and the smith. "Both," Mason observes, "are regarded as essentially disruptive. The making of new life or entities or artifacts only happens through the disturbance of the status quo" (698). Mason traces this alternative notion of creativity through ancient Greek mythology and philosophy, showing how the ideas of productive opposition came to be supplanted by the ordering ideas of oneness, for example, the myth of Prometheus, in which that cosmic disrupter was overcome by Zeus, the cosmic orderer (698–703).

One of the strongest voices in this tradition was Lucretius, the first-century CE Roman philosopher-poet whose long poem *De Rerum Natura* Mason describes as "the clearest exposition of the view that conflict and disorder are productive" (704). In that poem, Lucretius elaborates on the atomic theory of Epicurus, a materialistic theory that was propounded in opposition to Stoicism by portraying the universe as an infinite space in which atoms fall in straight lines, except for a few instances in which a slight angle or declination of the trajectory of one atom, a deviation he calls the *clinamen*, sets up a turbulence in the atoms that leads to other turbulences and eventually accounts for the infinite variety of the universe. This theory is an argument for the creative power of disorder, a mode of creativity founded not in order and oneness but in chaos and the potential for novelty that lies in multiplicity.[7]

But Lucretius's vision of creativity was overwhelmed in our culture by the Judeo-Platonic-Christian creativity of the Creator tradition.[8] This latter tradition has dominated Western thought virtually unchallenged in any formal way until the publication of Whitehead's *Process and Reality*. As I see it, process philosophy—which I introduced briefly in chapter 5—represents a return to the archelogical tradition of creativity, the first fully formed philosophy of that tradition in the West since Lucretius's *De Rerum Natura*. The influence of process philosophy was significantly extended in the 1960s and 1970s by a group of theologians who seized on the theological implications in Whitehead as a source for what has become known as process theology.[9] For Whitehead and these process theologians, creativity is one of the central principles in process thought, an understanding of creativity that calls into question the entire Creator tradition.

As I mentioned earlier, process philosophy envisions time not as a smooth and seamless flow but as a succession of distinct actual occasions, each of which is an act of creation, a coming-to-be in the present. Whitehead describes the event of coming-to-be as a concrescence, a coming into concreteness or definiteness. A key to understanding the process model of creation lies in the "dipolar" nature of concrescence. One pole is what Whitehead refers to as the "physical pole." Each actual event is said to "prehend" or grasp the vectors of past occasions. That is, each event is influenced by previous events. The past is still very much a participant in the present because though every moment is perpetually perishing, it is also objectively immortal, able to influence a new present in the future. The past, then, is real, definite, always with us (Cobb and Griffin 14–24; Suchocki 12–19). The other pole is the "conceptual pole," which for Whitehead acts as the creative principle associated with God. Not only is each actual occasion oriented to the past, but each one is, in a way, also oriented to the future. In the future is openness, possibility. The future, then, is to be understood not as a distant prospect, perpetually removed from the present, but as an immediate presence in each moment, offering the possibility for newness (Cobb and Griffin 26–28; Suchocki 20–21). Thus each actual occasion may be understood as archelogical, existing at the threshold of these opposing forces and possessing the potential for a newness that is beyond the influence of the past alone.

The four-part process of each creative occasion has its beginnings, its "initial aim," in the conceptual pole, the prospect of what is possible for that occasion. This prospect is not, as William A. Beardslee points out, a part of some grand plan or determining metanarrative. Rather, it is "decentralized and localized in the actual occasions themselves. There is no one fixed aim in detail for the whole of things, but there are specific aims of specific occasions" (33). The second step is defined by the physical pole, the "objective aim," in which past events are brought to bear on the formation of the present occasion. Third is the "subjective aim," the point of concrescence in which the many events of the past are reconfigured as one in the subjective present under the possible influence of the conceptual future. In the last part of the process, the subjective event becomes an element of the objective past, a potential influence in the formation of another actual occasion. According to Whitehead's vision of the moment-by-moment creation of the world, the past is definite and has an influence on the present; the present is an eternal now; and the future is radically open.[10]

What we find in process thought is an understanding of creation that is entirely different from that of the Creator tradition. Instead of one massive creative event, this creation literally occurs in the present, in each actual occasion, an infinitude of creative events. Creation is ongoing and (dis)continuous: because creation occurs continuously, each moment represents the opportunity for a newness that, like Lucretius's *clinamen,* disturbs continuity. This creation is formed not in the beginning but in beginnings, each pulse of the universe a creative event on the threshold of past and future, definiteness and indefiniteness, what is given and what is possible.

This archelogical model of creation is an explicit rejection of *creatio ex nihilo,* a doctrine that makes absolutely no sense in process thought. Because every actual event must arise out of previous events, there can be no such thing as a state of no-thingness. The universe, then, has always existed; out of disorder came the gradual generation of order in a creative chain of innumerable actual occasions (Cobb and Griffin 65–67; Griffin, "Creativity" 77). This challenge to the Creator tradition also means that God is not all-powerful and not the upholder of status quo. "Process theology," say Cobb and Griffin, "understands God precisely as the basic source of unrest in the universe," the potential for creativity that defines each actual occasion (59). Thus God is not a controlling power, a Being that determines all actuality at the expense of worldly freedom; rather, God's power is suggestive—directional or orientational—not deterministic. The process God is the ground of all possibility instead of the ground of all power (Cobb and Griffin 28–29, 41–61).

Archelogical creation subverts the two basic tenets of creativity under the Creator tradition—monolithism and unilateralism. As ongoing and (dis)continuous, there is no one event of creation and thus no one author of all there is. Every entity in the universe—human and nonhuman, biotic and abiotic—engages in the moment-by-moment process of creation; thus every entity is, on some level, creative (Beardslee 51–53; L. Ford, "Creativity" 179). Instead of monolithic, then, this paradigm of creation projects an understanding of creativity that is universal. According to the Creator tradition, what placed creativity apart from the norm was a special connection to the divine or other external creative force. In process thought, however, the creative force of the divine intersects every moment of existence for every entity. There is no special creativity, the possession of a few geniuses; rather, creativity is radically universal, an essential characteristic of all beings. As Fetz describes it, being itself is "creative being" (198; Griffin, "Creativity" 70–76).

The idea that creativity is unilateral is based on the model of the Creator-God as ultimate Subject and Creation as object of creativity. Creativity flows one way. But that idea is turned on its head in process thought: this is a model in which, as Whitehead says, God creates the World as the World also creates God (*Process* 528). Thus, there is no real distinction between subject and object. Subjectivity itself is considered "derivative," based on the illusion of continuity over time. Because experience comes in discrete chunks, the subject is a formation of each actual occasion and thus a succession of subjectivities. There is no subject to hang the old idea of creativity on (Beardslee 34). Neither is there a traditional object. The universe is created in each pulse of time, a process in which an objectified past contributes to the creation of a subjectified present. It is a conception of creation that is utterly collaborative, no unified subject and no derivative, commodified object (Beardslee 31–32; Griffin, "Creativity" 73–74). Instead of unilateral, then, creativity in this archelogical model may be thought of as multilateral. It flows in all directions, erasing the division between creator-subject and created object and challenging the notion of value as located in the external creative commodity. No longer defined by the hegemony of the active creator over the passive created object, creativity is, therefore, universally participatory: every entity in the universe is both creator and created, subject and object, even God.

Creativity is one of the most important principles in Whiteheadian metaphysics, his term for the moment of concrescence, the fundamental event of all existence. It is embodied both in coming-to-be in that moment and in the possibility for newness that marks each beat of existence. For Beardslee, Whiteheadian creativity is a way of indicating the radical openness of the future, which is the source of hope in the world. "Not *because* he hopes does man create," Beardslee observes, "but by creating he comes to be involved in the open future, which at a certain level of awareness can come to consciousness as hope" (39). Hope is the belief that the potential for creativity has not been spent in one dramatic moment of creation, that the future is open to novelty (44). Each occasion, then, is free to find its own balance between the definite past that is present in each moment and the openness of the future (54–55).

By giving contemporary philosophical voice to the long-mute tradition of archelogical creation, process thought provides the basis for a reconstruction of creativity and for writing as creative. It is a way of reconceptualizing a universe under the aegis of beginnings. Creation is ongoing and (dis)continuous, ruled not by oneness but by diversity. Thus creativity is universal and multilateral. Relocated within the paradigm of beginnings, creativity is neither rarefied nor commodified. It is simply the state of being in the world, the state of creative being.

Archelogical Creativity: Enjoyment, Firstness, and Metaphysical Mindfulness

Though process thought offers a way of applying the paradigm of beginnings to creativity, there still remains the question of value, how are we to understand the value of creativity as a threshold event? Within the Creator tradition, the sources of value in creativity are clear: value resides in the connection to the mysterious power that guides the creative event and in the culturally notable commodity that is the outcome of that event. Both of these sources of value, I have argued, are extrinsic to creativity itself. The paradigm shift in creativity from the beginning to beginnings suggests to me the possibility of a dramatically different way of conceiving of the source of value related to creativity, value that is intrinsic to the creative event. Intrinsic value, however, is much more difficult to describe than extrinsic value, partly because it runs against the prevailing notions of value in our culture and partly because we have so few conceptual models to work with. What I will do here is to look at various descriptions of this illusive intrinsic value of archelogical creativity, relying on a composite of these descriptions to provide a better—though I cannot promise absolutely clear—understanding of this concept. The purpose is to explore the value intrinsic to participating in beginnings.

The term Whitehead uses to describe the value inherent in coming-to-be is *enjoyment*. On its surface, this seems to be a rather odd term for him to use as a label for the ultimate value that lies at the root of existence. Our normal understanding of enjoyment is grounded in pleasure or ego-gratification, embracing everything from mild delight to hedonistic sensuality. Indeed there is a sense of delight at work in Whitehead's term, but not a hedonistic delight. Rather, it is the pleasure that comes from participating in the creative event of concrescence. In other words, enjoyment is intrinsic to that moment in each actual occasion when the indeterminate forces of the past are brought into conjunction with the conceptual force of the future to become, in an instant of creative freedom, a concrete existence in the presence. We can think of the value of such enjoyment in three ways. One is the "receptive" value that comes of simply being associated with conditions that stimulate creativity. The second is the "achievement" value that comes from taking an active role in the self-creation of each occasion. And the third is the "contributory" value that comes from the anticipation of the creative effect that occasion can have on future occasions, the further enjoyment that may be experienced later by self and others (Griffin, "Creativity" 81–82).

Enjoyment, then, is Whitehead's way of expressing the potential value for every entity in the universe inherent in the creative event of each moment of the infinite process of time. The potential for enjoyment, then, is universal. This base-level sense of enjoyment becomes more complex, however, when consciousness is added to the mix. I'll take as an example the work of environmental ethicist Frederick Ferré, who uses process thought as the basis for proposing a radically different vision of what it means to be and the value of being, a shift from a physics model—which values the greatest simplicity—to an ecological model—which values the greatest complexity. Ferré accepts the Whiteheadian idea that all the entities of the universe are linked by the common creative act of becoming:

> The regular, rapid achievement of definiteness by energies pulsing at the level of the ultra-small and the ultra-simple produces its tiny share of value for itself. Intrinsic value, of whatever degree of simplicity or complexity, *is* this enjoyed achievement of definiteness from a moment of indeterminate possibility. (*Being* 356)

For Ferré, such value is best understood as *kalogenesis,* the generation of beauty. Beauty is his way of describing the subjective satisfaction that binds all entities, the harmony that is created in becoming definite (357–61). "Every pulsing element of our kosmos," he says, "is beautiful to some degree in itself and for itself" (359).

There is, then, a crucial link between the natural and aesthetic in the enjoyment experienced by even the most simple particle of existence in the universe. Some forms of existence, however, are able to experience enjoyment with a greater awareness than others. This difference, Ferré says, depends on consciousness. The *conscious* experience of *kalogenesis* represents a level of intrinsic value that distinguishes it from the subjective experiences of entities that do not possess consciousness (363). Consciousness, then, adds a very important dimension to the understanding of enjoyment—and enriches the idea of intrinsic value in creativity. Human beings share with all other entities the enjoyment of coming-to-be, of being a part of the creative process that both defines and gives value to existence. But human beings—and any other beings that may be said to possess consciousness—have the added capacity of being aware of that enjoyment, aware of the intensity and harmony in the marked contrast between the actual and the possible. This is what it means to be a conscious participant in creation, to be fully creative.

It certainly cannot be said, however, that all conscious beings exist in a perpetual state of creative awareness. Even in human beings it is primarily a potential. As a way of getting at the variable nature of human participation in enjoyment, process theologian Marjorie Hewitt Suchocki distinguishes heightened consciousness from rote consciousness. The latter is habitual thinking, dominated by an orientation toward the physical pole, the human tendency to resist the possibilities represented in the future and thus to reproduce the past. Heightened consciousness, in contrast, is marked by an awareness of the contrast that is always potential in each creative moment, the contrast "between the data at hand and possible ways in which the data might be ordered . . . between what is and what might be, between the past and the future" (54). Heightened consciousness, then, considerably intensifies the enjoyment of concrescence; it is an awareness of the creative event *as* creative event, valuable in and for itself (60).[11]

Thus one key to understanding the intrinsic value associated with archelogical creativity is Whitehead's idea of enjoyment. There is, as Ferré points out, a strong sense of the aesthetic in this valuation, which effectively distinguishes it from value attached to usefulness or any other extrinsic standard. Creativity is innate to all existence. In conscious beings, though, the intrinsic value of enjoyment in creativity may be amplified by heightened consciousness.

Another term that I will add to my composite portrait of the intrinsic value of creativity is David Lee Miller's "the firstness of experience." In *Philosophy of Creativity,* Miller seeks a broad understanding of creativity among many different philosophies—including those of Neitzsche, Kierkegaard, Marx, and Heidegger, as well as phenomenology, existentialism, and process philosophy—all of which stand opposed to the "paradigm of abstract reason, determinate form, and completed actuality" that has dominated Western thought.

Critical to this metaparadigm of creativity is the sense of firstness, which Miller describes as "the experiential core for the development of a philosophy of creativity" (97); that is, firstness is a way of articulating the *experience* of creativity, a powerful sense of immediacy, a keen awareness of the reality of each passing moment. Creativity is valuable in and for itself because it engages us in an encounter with firstness. Unfortunately, Miller says, human beings typically react to the firstness of experience in one of two negative ways. One is fear, the tendency to reject the powerful and unfamiliar. The other is to turn it into a product, to commodify it. Commodification is not bad in itself; it's just that conceptualizing creativity in the logical and material tends to distract us from firstness, limiting the value of the experience itself. Miller offers his philosophy of creativity as a way of helping us participate in the firstness of experience without fearing it and trying to limit it (99–101).

To express this firstness of experience more philosophically, Miller calls upon the work of Charles Sanders Peirce and Heidegger. For Peirce, firstness is a sense of the fullness in creativity characterized by those aspects of experience that exist prior to the application of categories; in

Peirce's words, it is a "quality of feeling [that] can be imagined to be without any occurrence. . . . Its mere may-being gets along without any realization at all" (qtd. in Miller 104). There is no greater reality behind this fullness of creativity (104). For Heidegger, firstness is an originary awareness that is best understood by the metaphor of the opening, particularly as in abruptly coming upon a clearing in the midst of a dark forest. As Heidegger puts it,

> the opening grants first of all the possibility of the path to presence, and grants the possible presencing of that presence itself. We must think *aletheia,* unconcealment, as the opening which first grants Being and thinking and their presencing for each other. (qtd. in Miller 107)

These images of firstness—opening, fullness, and presencing of presence—are ways of describing the intrinsic value of participating in creativity.

Miller also looks at the implications of Heidegger's treatment of the relationship between language and creativity, which is useful for the larger purposes of this study. Miller admits that in many cases language has the effect of deadening the experience of firstness, a threat to creativity because it is typically tied to what is known and settled, the alreadiness of living. Heidegger suggests, however, that it is possible for us to use language in such a way that it returns us to creativity, "learning to live in the speaking of language" (qtd. in Miller 114). What Miller sees in Heidegger is the possibility for language acts that engage human beings in the presencing of Being, in which language and Being are present in each other, each illuminating and transforming the other (109–14). "The freshness and firstness of language, then, is the opening, the presencing, the emerging and transforming of mere language, unheard language, jaded language, utilitarian language into the language of essential thinking" (114). Language, though it has the capacity for deadening the firstness of creativity, also possesses the potential for bringing us into the presence of that firstness.[12]

The ideas of consciousness of enjoyment and firstness of experience are offered in an attempt to capture both the event of creativity and the value intrinsic to that event. In addition to these terms, I will look at one more that characterizes the intrinsic value of creativity, William Desmond's idea of the metaphysical mindfulness of universal impermanence, which provides a direct link to beginnings. In chapter 5 I used Desmond's philosophy of the metaxological, or middle, as a prime example of an archelogical dialectic, a dialectic of the between. In *Being and the Between,* Desmond focuses his attention on the metaphysical implications of the between. Metaphysical mindfulness is for Desmond the perennial wonderment at what it means to be. Though the focus of his discussion is on philosophical metaphysics, it is clear that he is talking about a mindfulness that goes far beyond the confines of philosophers to project a way of being that is potentially available to all of us.

As you may recall, Desmond uses the concept of the metaxological to represent a relationship between self and other that is characterized by a double mediation, the self reaching toward the other and the other reaching toward the self, together constituting a pluralistic ground of being. Metaphysical mindfulness is similarly constituted at the threshold of two opposing modes of apprehension. One mode Desmond refers to as agapeic astonishment, a response to an awareness both of the sheer excess of being that surrounds us and of the excess of mind in us. This is an "overdetermined beginning" that comes of the sense of being double and in-between, of being in the middle of being and mind (4–13). The other mode he labels erotic perplexity, which instead of being defined by excess is defined by lack. The indeterminate astonishment of mind and being is opposed by the perplexity generated in the perceived gap between self and other and thus the desire to complete the self in the other, the drive to colonize the other (14–15).[13] Mindfulness is itself the broader metaphysical perplexity at finding oneself in the middle, between excess and lack. "This double mediation of our perplexity makes it *metaxological*," says Desmond.

> By this I mean that perplexity is itself a condition of mindfulness that is between: between nonknowing and knowing, between ignorance so complete it knows not its own ignorance, and a knowing so complete that is it not human at all but that of a god. Metaphysical perplexity is a *tense togetherness* of being at a loss *and* finding oneself at home with being. (6)

Metaphysical mindfulness is an intense awareness of being, which for Desmond means an awareness being in the middle, between excess and lack, knowing and nonknowing. What makes all this beneficial to my purpose, though, is Desmond's link between metaphysical mindfulness and archelogical creativity. For him, agapeic astonishment may be understood as origin and erotic perplexity as creation. By "origin," however, Desmond certainly does not mean the preexistent foundation that I discussed and dismissed in chapter 2. The question of origin in this case has nothing to do with a beginning in time or any other idea tied to a *definite* beginning. Rather, it is a question of why there is anything at all and not just nothingness (227). Origin corresponds to the indeterminate opening of mind, an indeterminate mindfulness of being. It expresses the ongoing creative capacity of the agapeic as beginnings: "a creative principle that does not just create at a momentous once and then deserts creation. The momentous once is now always. The act of creation is an always continuing origination and sustaining of finite being in being" (255). In other words, it is the indeterminacy of origin that allows for its own power of creativity, the endless regeneration of the finite in the creative power of being for itself (255–63).

Whereas origin is characterized by indeterminacy, creation is the actualization of being in the finite. For Desmond,

> [c]reation comes out of an origin, but that coming out suggests a doubleness; at once a giving of the plenitude of being, for creation is there; and yet a coming out shadowed by nothingness. For creation would be nothing, were it not for the giving of the origin. (269)

The doubleness of origin and creation is intensified by the doubleness of being and nothing, which means that their relationship is complicated by being both discontinuous and continuous with each other. "That is, the discontinuity and possible nothingness of the creation, as outcome, suggests the continuing of creation, as activity of agapeic origination" (270).

Like the consciousness of enjoyment and the firstness of experience, Desmond offers the metaphysical mindfulness of participating in creation as a way of describing the intrinsic value associated with creativity. It is an awareness of being, extended to an awareness of being creative: between the indefiniteness of origin and the definiteness of creation, the fullness of being and the emptiness of nothing, the continuity of ongoing creation and the discontinuity of each succeeding momentous once. Desmond also emphasizes the radical openness that comes of this awareness. The chief value associated with the mindfulness of being creative is what he describes as "the glorious gift of universal impermanence" (270). It is a gift of the creative moment, which locates one in "a middle world that is something given, but given full of a promise of its own openness beyond every closed totality, the promise of its own infinitude" (293). This is the promise of the possible Whitehead attributed to the divine, the concept of unconcealment Miller takes from Heidegger. An awareness of universal impermanence is the gift of archelogical creativity, the value intrinsic to it. As Desmond describes it, the value of that gift lies in its "continuing . . . *discontinuity*"; in its role as "the *disturber* of all finitude"; in its being "the slash between being/void" (294–96). Universal impermanence is the gift of beginnings:

> For we find in becoming an ever-renewed beginning: becoming reveals the power of being to begin, again and again. Every "once" is poised over its "never," but behold, it comes to be once again, renewed again. . . . There is disjunction [in] this continuity of again and again, the disjunction of the "never" that stands between the "once" and its renewal. (296)

The goal of this section has been to extend the reconstruction of an archelogical creativity to an understanding of value that is intrinsic to archelogical creativity. The challenge in this task is to find a way of articulating such an intrinsic value, a form that does not give itself over easily to words. To do that I have relied on a composite portrait: enjoyment from process thought, firstness of experience from Miller, and metaphysical mindfulness of universal impermanence from Desmond.

Some themes have emerged from this composite that help us better understand the value intrinsic to archelogical creativity. One is that creativity is not a special activity, removed from the everyday, a quality reserved for the few. Rather, creativity describes a state of being in the world, the potential value that exists for all beings in every moment of existence. Another is the role of awareness. In process thought, enjoyment is considerably intensified by heightened consciousness of it. For Miller, the firstness of experience is necessarily the "experiential core" of creativity. And Desmond's use of mindfulness follows a similar line of thought. Creativity, then, is a state of being creative, and the value intrinsic to that state is enhanced by an awareness of it.

An awareness of what, however? An awareness of the radical openness of the universe, the gift of freedom, the sense of possibility that exists in each creative moment. An awareness of the fullness of being, the plenum of existence underscored by the rich excess of creativity. An awareness of the presentness of the present moment of being. An awareness of the potentially disruptive nature of the creative event, a disruption of the given, the past, the known, the settled. And an awareness of the againness of existence, of the perpetual renewal of being. These attributes delineate the value intrinsic to creativity located in beginnings, the value of full participation in the ongoing and (dis)continuous creation of the universe.

Value: Creativity and Writing

This discussion of valuing writing may seem to have drifted rather far afield, deep into the more remote and obscure territories of philosophy and theology. But I've been led into those territories by the need to understand how it is possible for us to conceive of what we teach in composition as creative writing. To be able to make that claim, I have had to reconstruct creativity within the paradigm of beginnings.

Here's the path I've been following: If the universe does indeed exist in beginnings as opposed to the beginning, it projects an entirely different model of creativity; instead of monolithic and unilateral, creativity in the archelogical tradition is universal and multilateral. Because creation is ongoing and (dis)continuous, creativity itself is the chief source of the good, intrinsic to the ever renewable creative moment, in and for itself, and available to all entities in the universe. What sets human beings and other beings that may possess consciousness apart from entities that don't is not, therefore, our ability to participate in creativity but rather our potential for awareness of that participation and thus the sharpened sense of intrinsic value that comes of the apprehension of a full partnership in creation. In an effort to understand this value intrinsic to creativity I have called upon Whitehead's enjoyment, Miller's firstness of experience, and Desmond's metaphysical mindfulness of universal impermanence. Each of these terms represents an attempt to describe the dim outlines of archelogical creativity, an awareness of participating in beginnings, a value in and for itself.

All this is aimed toward understanding writing as creative. Right now, though, I must admit that I'm having a hard time associating the lofty ideals of archelogical creativity with the students in my eight A.M. MWF composition class. Is this writing class really enabling them to be full participants in the ongoing creation of the universe? Is their writing actually encouraging in them an awareness of their being as creative being? Is the primary value of this writing class for them intrinsic to the creative act of writing or is it just to avoid having to repeat the course? Is this truly a *creative* writing course?

These are troubling questions for me because in placing my fine abstractions against the reality of the classroom those abstractions come off looking out of place, uncomfortable, a little absurd. But I do believe that this is a creative writing course, or at least that it has that potential. Otherwise, I see no point in teaching it. We can't avoid the fact that creativity is a value issue that is critical to us and to our students. In its usual sense, creative writing is a value designation that pointedly devalues the writing my students do in that eight A.M. class and practically everywhere else in their lives.

The final step in this discussion of valuing writing, then, is to link the intrinsic value associated with archelogical creativity to writing, particularly the nonfiction writing students do in composition classes and elsewhere in the university. Of course, on one level this link is already implicit: in the last chapter I reconstructed writing—in contrast to scribing—as beginnings, and the bulk of this chapter has been given over to reconstructing creativity as beginnings. Conceptually, at least, writing and creativity are already identified with the other. But this identification is not enough: what does it really mean to say that the chief value of writing is located in the creativity associated with beginnings? I'll venture three possible (i.e., not definitive) responses to that question.

First, saying that writing is creative means that we need to rethink the role of invention in writing. In composition theory, the subject of creativity has traditionally been located under the aegis of invention. For example, in a recent overview of invention, Richard Young defines it as the particular form of creativity most often associated with nonfiction discourse, "the creative act as it manifests itself in rhetorical composition" (349–50). In our discipline, though, we have tended to limit this creative act by associating it primarily with formal heuristic procedures, an association that Worsham challenges in "The Question Concerning Invention" as the senseless technologizing of writing. The concept of invention we have brought to our teaching has presupposed an anemic and externalized conception of creativity, directed toward generating ready answers, finding something to say.

There is also the possibility for an understanding of invention that projects a much richer vision of creativity, a possibility that lies in the archelogical nature of invention itself, which we have tended to overlook. In an investigation of rhetoric and novelty, Carolyn R. Miller points out that in ancient Greek and Latin the word for "invent" means both gathering what is known and discovering what is new. This ambiguity, she says, was crystallized in the seventeenth century by Francis Bacon who drew out two separate forms of invention: the technical or scientific, which generates novelty, and the rhetorical, which recovers and manages knowledge that already exists. Miller argues that even though rhetorical invention had once encompassed both old and new knowledge, in the modern era the possibility for newness was seized by technology and science, leaving to rhetoric only the managerial function.

Richard McKeon makes a similar observation in his study of the relationship between the *topos,* or commonplace, and creativity. The sense of doubleness inherent in *topos* is illustrated for McKeon in the two arts of Cicero's rhetoric that depend on "places," invention and memory: the first a source for generating new ideas, the second a source for recollecting old ones. This distinction was lost, McKeon says, in later rhetorics in which all commonplaces came to be associated with the recovery of the previously known, as exemplified by the commonplace book (26–30). He locates the rediscovery of topics of novelty in the modern period, particularly in the work of Bacon, Leibniz, and Vico, who "transformed them into places for the perception, discovery, and explanation of the unknown" (31).

Miller and McKeon point toward an archelogical invention rooted in the doubleness and betweenness of the art. What would an art of invention as beginnings look like? For McKeon, the ambiguity that lies in both the commonplace and in creativity provides the key to a more fruitful understanding of both terms as the commonplace of creativity, which, he says,

> was expanded to the commonplace "known-unknown" and used to distinguish and merge the arts of invention and memory. As known-unknown, it retains an easy reversibility by which the known becomes unknown as well as the unknown known, and by which its inventive openness as a commonplace is preserved and the commonplaces derived from it provide structures for all philosophies in a pluralism of philosophies of invention and of varieties of creativity. (36)

For Miller, the spatial metaphor immanent in *topos* is especially rich because it offers a more complex way of understanding novelty, which "must occupy the border between the known and the unknown." A *topos,* she says, "is a region of productive uncertainty"; it "locates the borderline between the familiar and the unfamiliar, the known and the unknown" (141–42). The concept of *topos* is useful, then, because it situates novelty (141).[14]

Understood this way, *invention* denotes the threshold event of beginnings, the borderline between known and unknown, the point of openness at which the known is placed against the unknown and the unknown against the known. I see this as the same borderline that Desmond describes as the space between "nonknowing and knowing," fullness and lack, origin and creation; that process philosophers describe as the space between past and future, the given and the possible, the actual and the conceptual; that Prigogine in chaos theory describes as the space between order and disorder, stability and instability, linearity and nonlinearity. In fact, it is the same as described in the historical roots of invention by *stasis,* literally the space between two opposing movements.[15]

Invention, then, may be identified with an archelogical *topos,* the space marked off by contradictory forces, an "inventive openness," as McKeon puts it. To use Worsham's terminology, invention is not, therefore, a question concerning being but a question concerning Being. That is, it is not about finding answers, figuring out what to write about or supporting a thesis. Rather, it is about placing everything into question, the threshold between the unknown and the known, the familiar and the unfamiliar. As a threshold event, then, invention is marked by disruption, discontinuity, disorientation.

An archelogical invention provides a possible connection between archelogical creativity and archelogical writing. This possibility is strengthened considerably, I believe, by writing theorist Daniel J. Royer, who makes his own application of Whiteheadian metaphysics to composition:

> *Creativity* resides in the very structures of experience, in the welter of precognitive experience out of which consciousness, language, and thought emerge. *Invention* is best understood as a concrescence—a synthesis of contrasts that emerge as possibilities are entertained and anticipated against the backdrop of given experience. Invention must be understood, therefore, as the originality or creativity that emerges within, not as an addition to, *writing* experience. (175; my emphases)

Creativity, invention, writing—these are the key terms. Creativity, says Royer, is inherent in the very nature of experience as described by process philosophy, the experience of being creative. Invention is the point of concrescence in the Whiteheadian process of ongoing and (dis)continuous creation. Writing is an event through which we engage in the creative event of invention. Invention, then, is essential to the creative experience of writing as beginnings. It is not a step in a procedure, not an attachment or supplement to writing. Invention is how we conceive of creativity as utterly intrinsic to or, as Royer puts it, "emerg[ing] within, not as an addition to, writing experience."

Invention helps us comprehend archelogical creativity as intrinsic to writing, or at least as I am defining writing. One way of understanding this intrinsic relationship on a more practical level is to see creativity as embodying the textual act of writing itself. Royer describes invention in terms of the creative tension between two contradictory aspects of writing, the generative—the drive to explore meaning in greater and greater complexity—and the discursive—the drive to limit meaning in the precision and definiteness demanded by the text (172–74).[16] These contradictions hearken back to a couple of the composition theorists I mentioned in the introduction. Bruffee describes beginnings as the productive linguistic tension between what we have said and what we anticipate saying. Hilbert notes the tension in writing between the idealized version of what the writer wants to say and the troublesome materiality of the text.

The focus of the creative writing class, then, ought to be on that tension delineated by invention. As teachers, we can enhance the creative experience of writing by encouraging our students to extend their stay on the threshold formed by the generative and the discursive principles of writing. Invention is the act of questioning that juxtaposes the known against the unknown, the familiar against the familiar, and our role is to guide students in that questioning in such a way that no idea and no text is ever settled, complete, finished. Writing is disjunctive. The value of questioning, then, is not found in answers but in the act of questioning in and for itself. Invention focuses us not on making writing good but on the good of writing, the destabilizing experience of participating in beginnings. Writing is what happens in the creative space of the threshold. Invention is how we conceive of the good of writing as intrinsic to writing itself. And it is that good that we should keep before us as writing teachers.

A second way of conceiving of writing as creative is to look at the role that writing plays in making us aware of being in a state of being creative. As I've shown, the intrinsic value of creativity is intensified substantially in the mindfulness of creativity. In the terms that Suchocki employs, scribing may be seen as the equivalent in literate composition to rote consciousness—dominated by the givenness of past assumptions, characterized by the unreflective recapitulation of the actual—and writing as the equivalent to heightened consciousness—an awareness of the intense contrast played out on the borderline between what is given and the potential for newness. The value intrinsic to this heightened consciousness I've tried to express as awareness of enjoyment, firstness of experience, and metaphysical mindfulness of universal impermanence. As beginnings, then, writing is one of the most powerful and accessible ways we have of heightening our consciousness of being creative and thus becoming full participants in creation.

I believe that a writing course is ideally situated to encourage that participation in our students. One of the most basic elements of a writing course is that we focus our students' attention on writing *as* writing. Writing itself becomes the subject of the writing course, which is typically structured in such a way that students are encouraged to develop, at least for a while, a hyperawareness of writing. It is a course in metawriting. This intensified, and sometimes uncomfortable, awareness of writing as writing contributes substantially to an awareness of the experience of creativity itself. As beginnings, writing possesses the potential for making writers conscious of being on the threshold between doubting and believing, the personal and the public, the monological and the dialogical, conflict and accommodation, et cetera. This experience, in and for itself, defines the chief value of writing.

The creative writing course, therefore, may be thought of as promoting an awareness of being as creative being. It promotes an awareness of the radical openness of the universe, the extravagant freedom that comes of the ability of writing to (un)define each moment of creation. It promotes an awareness of the fullness of being, that is, the fullness of being creative and integrally connected to the possibility for invention that resides in writing. It promotes an awareness of the presentness of the present, the way writing intensifies the writer's experience of the creative moment. It promotes an awareness of the disruptive nature of creativity, the potential for newness in the unsettling nature of writing. It promotes an awareness of the againness of existence, the patterns of revision that mark the (dis)continuous character of beginnings.

Finally, understanding writing as creative means reconstructing the role that composition plays in the university. My argument that the chief value of writing is noninstrumental would appear to place in doubt any value a creative composition course could have in an academic setting. After all, if the value of a writing course is intrinsic to writing, what possible value is it to the university? It seems to me, though, that it is the intrinsic value of writing that makes a writing course integral to our students' academic lives.

Let me put this claim into perspective with a little historical context. The direct precursor of today's composition courses was "English A" at Harvard, which became a requirement in 1895 as a response to the widespread dismay at what was perceived as a major literacy crisis plaguing high schools and colleges. Reformers argued that a course was needed in the freshman year to bring students up to minimal standards of discourse before they entered their chosen course of studies. Soon, most colleges instituted freshman composition as their only requirement (Connors, "New" 4–5). The rationale behind the requirement, then, was that students needed remedial work in literate composition before they were able to perform the real work of their education. In this way, the value of the composition course was thought of as extrinsic to the academy. I would say that from the perspective of the university as a whole, these assumptions of remediation still determine the value of the course. Composition continues to be perceived as extraneous to the main work of the university.

All this changes, however, when we see the value of the course as intrinsic to creativity. In that shift of perspective, a creative writing course becomes central to the university, primarily because of the understanding of knowledge that it projects, which is also heavily influenced by our ideas of creation and creativity. Unfortunately, the conception of the creation of knowledge encouraged by our culture is dominated by the Creator tradition. As monolithic and unilateral, knowledge is complete, static, given, stable, possessed by the few who are deemed as experts in a field. Teaching-and-learning, then, is a one-way enterprise, moving from those who possess knowledge to those who do not. Learners are merely passive recipients in the creation and distribution of knowledge.

Look, however, at the way the knowledge game of the university changes in the paradigm shift from the Creator to the archelogical tradition. As universal and multilateral, the creation of knowledge is ongoing and (dis)continuous; knowledge is always incomplete, dynamic, emerging, mutable. Teaching-and-learning is no longer a one-way event because both teacher and learner are cocreators of knowledge, each participating fully as both teacher and learner. The knowledge game is a threshold experience: every class takes place at the borderline of the known and the unknown; every class imposes a question mark on knowledge for both teacher and students. Learning, then, is an active engagement in the creation of knowledge in the moment-by-moment possibility of the new.

Writing plays an integral role in the archelogical cocreation of knowledge at the university. Writing provides one of the most effective ways for teachers to generate the threshold event of learning. Let me take what may appear at first to be a trivial example. The standard academic lecture has a bad reputation as a knowledge delivery system that tends to pacify learners. But from a different perspective, it becomes an opportunity for the cocreation of knowledge, primarily through the students' note taking. Student notes are, as we know, not an exact re-creation of the lecture; indeed, they are often, from the professor's perspective, exasperatingly divergent from the lecture material. It seems to me, though, that it is this very divergence that captures the power of note taking as a learning event. Taking notes inevitably reshapes the knowledge presented in the lecture. For the lecturer, it is the opportunity, brought about by a new set of students, for the reinterpretation of knowledge in the re-presentation of it, always different in some ways from previous lectures. For the students, it is the opportunity to mold knowledge in their notes to meet their own needs and answer their own questions. Looked at this way, the lecture may be seen as taking place at the epistemic disjunction of the creative event of the classroom. Different genres of writing invite students to participate in the cocreation of knowledge in different ways, by reshaping it, interpreting it, and generating it.

Thus, a writing course, one that focuses on the cocreation of knowledge, is central to the real work of the university. No longer devalued by its focus on making writing good—the extrinsic value of rendering student writing grammatically and stylistically palatable to professors in other departments—the value of the course goes right to the source of the good of the university. We can understand the contribution the writing course makes to the good of the university in three ways. First, it sends a message to students about the participatory nature of knowledge, usurping the reigning Creator tradition. In this way, it helps to establish the expectations that students should bring to the teaching-and-learning opportunities they will find at the university. Second, a creative writing course provides the direct instruction and guided practice many students need to enable them to find the greatest benefit from these opportunities. If writing is at the heart of academic learning, then we can help students participate more effectively in their learning by focusing on the processes and genres of learning. Third, it can contribute to students' awareness of learning *as* learning, reinforcing the idea that the chief value of learning is not instrumental but intrinsic, in the event of learning itself. Learning, also, is beginnings. By heightening students' consciousness of learning we are endowing them with the capacity to value learning as full participants in that ongoing and (dis)continuous process of creating knowledge.

The relationship between writing and learning, then, is not merely instrumental. In the formal academic environment of the university, writing is not just a tool for learning, a value that lies outside writing; rather, writing is utterly integral to learning. An archelogical writing enables us to reconstruct an archelogical learning, which in turn provides a crucial justification for a writing course at the university.

Let me return now to my eight A.M. composition class and the essential question it imposes on this discussion: Is it truly a *creative* writing course? Thanks to these three ways of linking writing to archelogical creativity, the abstract concepts I have proposed may not seem quite so absurd placed against the backdrop of the classroom. It is creative if archelogical invention plays a prominent role in it. What this suggests to me is that the primary focus of my course should be not on producing acceptable student texts but on invention itself, encouraging students to sustain their experience at that disquieting but potentially productive threshold between the competing efforts of being generative and being discursive. In addition, my course is creative if it encourages an awareness of writing as writing and thus an awareness of creative being. It may be that such awareness best describes my most difficult students. They are the ones who struggle most with their writing, always trying to pin me down as to exactly what a paper should look like, unable to decide what to write on, having to go back again and again to revise their work. Perhaps they are the students who derive the greatest benefit from writing because writing is so difficult for them and they are so powerfully aware of writing. If this is the case, then my job ought to be to take their classmates—those who compose with such facility, hardly noticing what they do—and make writing more difficult for them, too. Last, it is creative if it contributes substantially to the work of the university, the cocreation of knowledge. This happens when I shape my course around that work, enabling students to become active participants in it by engaging them in the processes and genres that contribute to the creation of knowledge in this setting.

These are some of the features I can think of for a creative writing course. But the larger issue here is value, how we are to understand the value of writing not as instrumental but in and for itself. As archelogical, writing is creative; it has the power to connect us to the most essential force in the universe—creativity. That's the best answer I know to the question, Why write?

In part two, I have moved from a reconstruction of beginning to a reconstruction of writing itself, its being and value. Asking where writing begins has put me in the position of viewing writing through the lens of beginnings, which has sparked this reconstruction of writing.

I have framed part two as an argument, but as I look back over it, I find that it may be represented better not so much as an argument but as an invitation. It is an invitation addressed to those of us who profess writing to see writing differently. Writing is beginnings, which means that we could conceive of it not as a neutral term denoting any act of generating text but rather as that "something beyond the text" that involves the writer in the archelogical disjunction of productive contradictions. The value of writing may also be understood as beginnings, which means seeing the chief good of writing not as instrumental but as intrinsic to writing itself.

In part three, I will apply the destabilizing perspective of beginnings to the teaching of writing.

Part Three
Teaching Writing

8 Definition: Should Writing Be Taught?

> Can any one of my (even more open-minded) readers, therefore, imagine the National Council of Teachers of English or the College Composition and Communication Conference having as its conference theme the question Should writing be taught? . . . [I]f it were, indeed, asked and then acted on, it might very well put an end to the NCTE or the CCCC or at least change their ends radically. (The asking might bring with it insight and then disempower the field.)
>
> —Victor J. Vitanza, "Three Countertheses: Or, A Critical In(ter)vention into Composition Theories and Pedagogies"

I love teaching Vitanza's "Three Countertheses." I place it at the end of my graduate introduction to composition theory when we turn to postmodern rhetorics of writing. This is one article that never elicits a yawn from my students. They are perplexed by it, moved by it, fascinated by it, angered by it—sometimes all at once. It is by far the most challenging piece they read all semester, and not just because of the eccentric playfulness of the writing style or because of the multitude of references to difficult postmodern texts. Rather, it is because it challenges what is perhaps the most basic assumption of the field of composition, an assumption that remains unstated but is absolutely foundational in all the other articles we read throughout the course—that writing should be taught.

Vitanza starts out by announcing that this article has "the sole purpose of establishing the (postmodern) conditions for the possibilities of discourse in and about writing theory and pedagogy that, heretofore, the field of composition has had to disallow." We have disallowed, he says, such discourse because it would place into doubt all the presuppositions that underlie the discipline, "especially the revealed wisdom of even teaching students to write" (140). The three countertheses he proposes represent what he sees as necessary "counterresponses to the strong *will* of the field of composition; they are counterresponses to *(1)* the will to systematize (the) language (of composing), *(2)* the will to be its author(ity), and *(3)* the will to teach it to students" (140). It is by these three wills, which comprise the broader will to discipline writing, that Vitanza defines teaching writing.

One way of understanding this postmodern critique of composition, then, is in terms of definition. The problem for Vitanza is that in our drive to make writing teachable we have unjustifiably defined or constrained writing, establishing boundaries around it, determining and stabilizing it; making it definite and distinct, separate and knowable; presenting it as definitive, supplying final answers or solutions for it.

In short, teaching writing bends writing to the disciplinary will of composition, specifically by systemizing it, author(iz)ing it, and theorizing it (later in the article, the will to teach is associated with the will to theorize). To teach writing is to define writing; therefore, writing should not be taught. Vitanza's goal in "Three Countertheses," then, is to undefine or deconstruct the teaching of writing so as to loosen its grip on writing, reclaiming writing as undefined and undefinable. Thus unmoored from its defining will to teach, the discipline of composition will drift out to sea to its end, Vitanza hopes, utterly disempowered by his critique.

So what are we to do with this radical critique of our field? The answer is easy: ignore it. And to a large extent, that's just what we've done.[1] But I think that's a mistake. "Three Countertheses" is one of the most compelling critiques of composition in our literature—penetrating, perceptive, and on the whole, persuasive. Even though it was published more than a decade ago, it is still the richest encapsulation I know of the ludic postmodern in composition. In daring to ask the question, Should writing be taught? it demands that we cast a cold eye on the assumptions that found what we do as teachers and scholars of writing, that we question deeply our professional existence. If for no other reason than that, it is eminently worth our attention.

That's why Vitanza's impertinent question is so pertinent here. I believe that his radical skepticism of teaching writing is legitimate. I, also, am troubled by the presuppositions that his deconstruction of the field brings to the surface. And I can understand why those presuppositions would lead him to conclude that writing should not be taught and that, therefore, the discipline of writing should be undisciplined. But I draw a different conclusion. For me, this deconstruction is the first step, a necessary step, in a postmodern reconstruction of teaching writing. I agree with Vitanza that we should be "establishing the (postmodern) conditions" for a disciplinary discussion about writing and teaching writing. But I would like to take that discussion as an opportunity to redefine the discipline, what it means to teach writing.

Part three, then, continues the basic method I have used in parts one and two, though here I shift my attention to teaching writing, the third movement in the archelogical dialectic that has structured this book. The deconstruction and reconstruction of both beginning and writing have led me to this point. Asking where writing begins naturally raises certain questions about both beginning and writing, questions I've addressed in the previous chapters. In this part I will be working out an archelogical dialectic that involves a fresh interplay of writing and beginnings, as each has been reconstructed in terms of the other and can now be applied to *teaching* writing. It is about how we understand teaching writing in terms of beginnings, first an ontology and then an axiology of teaching writing. The present chapter offers a postmodern reconstruction of what it means to teach writing, the next chapter a postmodern reconstruction of an ethics (the value) of teaching writing.

Reconstructive Postmodernism

Back in chapter 2 I set up my treatment of ludic postmodernism by citing Theresa L. Ebert's distinction between ludic and resistance postmodernisms. From the perspective of the latter, ludic postmodernists, in their perpetual play of language, ignore the crucial role of emancipation from systems of exploitation. From the perspective of ludics, advocates of resistance are merely buying into the subjugating metanarrative of liberatory change.

This chapter, however, focuses on another way of parsing the postmodern: deconstructive and reconstructive postmodernisms. Obviously, *reconstruction* is a key term in this study and has already played an important role in it, though I have been using the term informally. I have reconstructed beginning and reconstructed what it means to write and the value of writing, in each case a response to a *deconstruction,* also used informally, of those concepts. At this point I want to formalize both concepts and their relationship to each other. Reconstructive postmodernism, also called constructive or Anglo-American postmodernism, represents the attempt by a number of different scholars working in diverse fields to build a framework for a positive worldview within postmodern indeterminacy. As Hans Bertans puts it in *The Idea of the Postmodern,* "Radical postmodern theory must be regarded as a transitional phenomenon, as instrumental in the creation of a more moderate new paradigm that is already building upon its achievements while ignoring its more excessive claims" (242–43). This is not a return to the premodern or to high modernism but an effort to establish the grounds for an entirely new perspective.

Though by no means a unified movement, reconstructive postmodernists tend to agree with the deconstructive critique of modernism but see deconstructive postmodernism largely as an extension of the modern and thus question its resistance to any and all foundations for new structures of thought. For example, in *Constructive Postmodernism: Toward Renewal in Cultural and Literary Studies,* Martin Schiralli offers an approach to cultural studies that "while clearly postmodern in its active embrace of uncertainty and the irreducible texture and complexity of human experience, is also quite distinct from the endemic ambivalences of deconstructionism" (44). His constructive alternative recasts philosophers like Toulmin, Dewey, and Wittgenstein within the context of postmodern uncertainty "to achieve plateaus of productive stability in our inquiries and hence to enhance the possibilities for cumulative and meaningful discourse in cultural studies" (46). Donald L. Gelpi, in *Varieties of Transcendental Experience: A Study in Constructive Postmod-*

ernism, acknowledges the validity of the deconstructive postmodern critique of the fallacies of Enlightenment metaphysics, particularly its ontology of *a priori* necessity and its epistemology of subject-object dualism. But he says that the deconstructive critique has, in effect, extended the same foundational fallacies to nominalism and relativism. Using the critique of modernism inherent in American transcendentalist philosophy and Peircean pragmatism, Gelpi argues for a constructive postmodernism that allows for metaphysical "working hypotheses" of reality.

Richard Harvey Brown's "Reconstructing Social Theory after the Postmodern Critique" explores the possibility of reinstating an ideology critique in the wake of the postmodern, generating "a politically constructive moment for an intellectually deconstructive critique" (17). He describes the possibility for a social theory that incorporates both a negative and a positive movement, both resistance and affirmation, turning the play of language toward the serious work of social transformation. In *Anglo-American Postmodernity: Philosophical Perspectives on Science, Religion, and Ethics,* Nancey Murphy embraces the deconstructive critique of postmodernism but seeks to stake a claim to a form of the postmodern that breaks with the modern while avoiding the excesses of the deconstructive postmodern. Her basis for this claim is her distinction between Continental and Anglo-American postmodernisms. She argues that the latter—best represented for her by Imre Lakotos, Theo Meyering, and Alastair MacIntyre—also developed out of a critique of modernism but without the radical relativism of the former.

Another type of reconstructive postmodernism is associated with theologian David Ray Griffin and a wide range of other scholars who have been influenced by Whiteheadian process philosophy. In chapter 5 I looked briefly at some of the implications of Whitehead's work for understanding archelogical dialectic, and in the previous chapter I made extensive use of process theology, an important movement from the late 1950s through the 1970s. Reconstructive postmodernism is, as it were, the third major incarnation of process thought, keeping Whitehead's work alive and relevant to this day. Though the influence of Whitehead predominates, reconstructive postmodernism is a broader philosophical movement that incorporates the work of Charles Sanders Peirce, William James, Henri Bergson, and Charles Hartshorne (Griffin et al.). Because I have already laid the foundation for this form of reconstructive postmodernism and because I find it a particularly rich source, I will rely on this process-based approach for the reconstruction of teaching writing in this chapter and the next.

The importance of Griffin and process reconstructive postmodernism to my own effort at reconstruction requires that I provide some context for it.[2] Perhaps the best way to understand Griffin's brand of postmodernism is to look at his response to Mark C. Taylor's *Erring: A Postmodern A/Theology.* Powerfully influenced by Derrida, Taylor's work begins by deconstructing four key foundations of Western thought: God, self, history, and text. In the void left by this deconstruction, he offers a deconstructive a/theology unfounded in writing, composed of nothing more than writing, indeterministic, ceaselessly displaced—an unending play of the word. In "Postmodern Theology and A/Theology: A Response to Mark C. Taylor," Griffin lays out the areas of agreement and disagreement with deconstructive postmodern thought.

According to Griffin, the idea of *re*construction is intended to denote two movements, *de*construction and *re*construction; a deconstruction is always implied in a reconstruction. In their deconstructive movements, then, both forms of postmodernism share a critique of modernity, an indictment of its errors. Griffin agrees with Taylor that the hub around which modernity moves is the death of the God of premodern Western tradition and the subsequent transfer of the attributes of that God to human beings and human society. The totality embodied by God was represented in the totalizing ideas of the individual self, of absolute truth and morality, and of a unified narrative of history. God—isolated, all-powerful, different in kind from the world, controlling the world—became the model for the modern human self ("Postmodern Theology" 31–32). Thus both forms of postmodernism portray modernity not as the norm for human society but as a historical aberration, ripe for critique.

The focus on *re*construction, however, points to crucial differences between the two. In its suspicion of any totalizing vision, deconstructive postmodernism eliminates any possible source of oneness: there is no truth (not just that we cannot know it); no unified self; no linguistic referents beyond language itself; no reality beyond interpretation; no aim, purpose, or meaning in history; no ultimate good or evil. However, as I've shown with the other versions of reconstructive postmodernism, the process-based approach, while it maintains a postmodern suspicion of modernist unities, offers at the same time the possibility for a postmodern worldview, a reconceived worldview, one that is reconstructed on the ashes of modernity. Thus the main difference between deconstructive and reconstructive postmodernism is the difference between a postmodern antiworldview and a postmodern worldview ("Postmodern Theology" 32–34; Griffin, "Introduction: Constructive" 1).

Another difference between these postmodernisms is their relationship to modernism, the way they interpret modernity and respond to its errors. On the one hand, the deconstructive works within the founding assumptions of modernism, seeking to deconstruct it from within by taking those assumptions to their extreme. Deconstructive postmodernists have succeeded in exposing the irrational nature of modernity but have stopped at that point: all that's left is the play of language. So deconstructive postmodernism may be seen as the (il)logical conclusion of modernism, an extrapolation of the antirationality of the modern into the absurd. On the other hand, the reconstructive alternative challenges the founding assumptions of modernism while at the same time recognizing some of the benefits of modernity, though without losing sight of the severe consequences brought by those benefits. Instead of stopping at the point of critique, this form of postmodernism seeks to reconstruct an entirely new way of understanding the world ("Postmodern Theology" 29; Griffin, Introd. to SUNY viii).

Griffin's postmodern alternative to the deconstructive comes largely out of his reading of Whitehead. It calls upon concepts such as panentheism and panexperientialism (that God is in all things and all things in God and that feelings and intrinsic worth are inherent in all things) and the ongoing creation of the universe in the process of concretion (which I described in the previous chapter). But is Whiteheadian postmodernism truly postmodern? According to John B. Cobb Jr. (friend of and coauthor with Griffin), the answer is yes. He points to many similarities between Whitehead's thought and deconstructive postmodernism and shows that, indeed, the term *postmodern* had been used by process theologians well before it was incorporated into French-influenced cultural and literary theory. Whereas deconstructive postmodernism continues to reside in the tradition of Kantian negativism, resisting any sort of orienting vision that would supply the grounding for a worldview, he says that the reconstructive postmodernism of Griffin and others follows Whitehead's objective of creating a wholly new cosmology on which to construct a new way of being in the world (164).

Some others, however, are not quite so sure about Griffin's reconstructive postmodernism. Theologian Graham Ward, for example, is concerned about its postmodern provenance. Though he places Griffin in a group of theologians he describes as "[u]ntil recently [1997] postmodern theology's most popular and well-known exponents in North America," he suggests that Griffin doesn't really belong there because he uses postmodernism simply to advance mainstream liberal theology and because the sources he calls upon in support of his postmodernism—such as Whitehead and Hartshorne—are not really postmodern thinkers. Ward says that Griffin's theology may be better understood as an animistic naturalistic theism—"in which everything in the world from rocks to human beings embodies creative energies"—than as postmodern theology (*Postmodern God* xl; "Postmodern Theology" 588).

Terrence W. Tilley and Craig Westman's critique of Griffin's vision for a new worldview focuses on its ecological and social agenda, which they describe as naturalistic, communal, affirmative, nondualistic, antianthropocentric, nonmechanistic, and anti-individualistic. Griffin's goal is no less than to change the world, and his reconstructive postmodernism provides the new ethics for achieving that goal. Tilley and Westman acknowledge that Griffin's understanding of the postmodern is unique to him and his followers, but is it really postmodern? They describe it instead as modern neoromanticism and question further how practical it is for serving as a foundation for radical change. In the end, they say, it offers an inspiring vision but one that may not have the power to change a culture so opposed to the ideals at its root.

Despite these more-postmodern-than-thou challenges to Griffin's credentials, it cannot be denied that his work has had a significant impact on the project of reconstructive postmodernism. His Center for a Postmodern World and the many publications from his SUNY Press series on Constructive Postmodern Thought have given him a prominent role in defining that project, which is especially apparent in the field of environmental ethics.[3] But I am basing my reconstruction of teaching writing on Griffin not because of his influence but because his conception of a postmodern worldview is so fresh and provides what I think is a valuable perspective on what we do as teachers and scholars of writing. Yes, the worldview he espouses demands a radical shift in our understanding of the other beings in the universe and our relationship with them. And yes, his sense of the postmodern is not steeped in what has become the canon of postmodern thought. But it is precisely these features of his work that make it so attractive: it offers what I take as a strikingly different vision for understanding both who we are and what we do as people who profess writing. Most important, this reconstructive postmodernism fits closely with beginnings. It is based on a cosmology in which the universe does indeed consist of an infinite and continuous stream of threshold events, ongoing creation, a universe (un)defined by unending beginnings. Furthermore, it uses beginnings, and the implications derived from beginnings, as the (non)foundation for a worldview.

So Griffin's version of reconstructive postmodernism provides for a philosophy of the between, located as it is between the two extremes of modernist foundationalism and deconstructive antifoundationalism (Griffin "Introduction: Constructive" 23–24). My method, then, is grounded in beginnings, an archelogical dialectic (like the one I described in chapter 5) creating a space between the doubt of antifoundationalism and the certainty of foundationalism, specifically between Vitanza's "Three Countertheses" and the modern discipline of composition he critiques so effectively.

Vitanza frames his countertheses appropriately—and very cleverly—by using Gorgias's "trilemma of negative propositions: 'Nothing exists'; 'If it does exist, it cannot be known'; and 'If it can be known, it cannot be communicated'" (144).[4] The three propositions of this trilemma correspond to the three representations of the will to discipline writing and together present a persuasive deconstruction of the modernist enterprise of teaching writing. As I read it, the first counterthesis deconstructs the ontological assumptions of composition theory and pedagogy, the second the epistemological assumptions, and the third the rhetorical assumptions. I accept each of these countertheses, but I follow them to a set of conclusions quite different from Vitanza's. My response is to propose a postmodern alternative to the definitions of teaching writing that Vitanza offers, redefinitions based on a reconstructed ontology, epistemology, and rhetoric of teaching writing.[5] Just as Vitanza has done for his countertheses, I will address the implications of my redefinitions in a subsection entitled "Relevance to Composition."[6]

Counterthesis 1

"*Nothing exists.*" Surely there is no claim more audacious than this, to present an apparently logical argument challenging our most basic ontological assumption, that something, anything, is. I like to imagine Gorgias performing this part of his speech just barely suppressing an impish grin at the brilliance of this surefire crowd pleaser. It is the ultimate rhetorical tour de force, to stand before an audience and dare to persuade them that—the witnesses of their physical senses to the contrary—nothing exists.[7]

To make Gorgias's statement more appropriate to today's philosophical environment, Vitanza amends it this way: "Nothing [of essence] exists." The bracketed addition emphasizes the antifoundationalism implicit in Gorgian and Sophistic ontology. The issue in this counterthesis, then, is whether what we know and do may be understood as "grounded either on some ontogenic theory (that is, on some universal law, or *physis*) or rhetorically on consensus theory (that is, on homology, or local *nomoi*)" (145). Is there any external, objective, universal grounding, an ultimate Being or Truth, that corresponds in any systematic way to our ideas or senses or language? Vitanza's answer is no. He challenges any attempt at foundationalism, both that which rests on some universal law or structure behind reality or that which disguises itself as antifoundationalism but is actually founded in consensual pragmatics, the assumption that consensus can be attained through universal structures of rationality, accountability, communication, or common sense (145–48). There is nothing essential "out there" that can serve as foundational Being.

Vitanza uses Lyotard to attack assumptions of foundationalism. First, all universal forms are impossible in the loss of grand narratives. Second, universalizing theories simply don't work; they inevitably collapse, overextended, into delegitimation. All that remains is paralogy—the radical resistance to oneness or correspondence between reason or language and reality—which Vitanza contrasts to "traditional or modern 'invention.'" Whereas invention is a means of understanding and controlling what we think and do based on a system or paradigm that allows for that control, Vitanza says that paralogy is (quoting Lyotard) "'discontinuous, catastrophic, nonrectifiable, and paradoxical.' It (re)turns—that is, radically tropes—against the system, or paradigm of knowledge" (147).

Given this deconstruction of modernist ontology, Vitanza concludes "either that there can no longer be or that ethically, micropolitically, there should not be any foundational principle or covering law or ontogenic model for composition theory and pedagogy" (148). Writing, therefore, cannot or should not be taught if by teaching writing we mean "the will to systemize (the) language (of composing)." In the wording of this definition, Vitanza adroitly sets up his argument: if language cannot be systemized, then neither can the composing of language nor language about composing language be systemized. Language itself disrupts and deauthorizes all attempts to discipline it with principles or models. They do nothing more than enslave students, Vitanza says, not guiding but *determining* what they write, the way they see the world (148–50). In making this claim, he casts into the seventh circle of doubt all of our efforts to teach writing, our assumptions that any one act of writing bears any discernible and describable and pedagogically productive relationship to any other writing act. Language cannot or should not be taught because language and the act of composing language and the language we use to talk about composing with our students and among ourselves—all are radically resistant to any order or procedure or structure outside language.

The message, I think, is loud and clear: if we eliminate all possibility of systemizing (the) language (of composing), that is, if we say that there is no correspondence between an act of writing and any ontological structure—principle or model or theory—outside that act, then we cannot and should not teach writing, at least not in any way that would probably be sanctioned by a university. Now I agree with Vitanza's deconstruction of modernist ontology and its problematic assumption that there is a Reality or a Truth that exists independent of individual contexts by which we can make sense of the world. The trouble is that he stops at that point, strongly resisting any pull toward an alternative worldview. We are left with two equally problematic choices for an ontology of composition: the modernist one, which enables us to render composition systematic and therefore teachable but at the cost of implicating us in highly questionable assumptions about reality; and the deconstructive postmodern one, which offers a more acceptable, to many of us, conception of being but at the cost of rendering writing unteachable in any acceptable form.

I want to make the case that there is an alternative ontology that does offer a postmodern worldview suitable for teaching writing. Process reconstructive postmodernism begins, Griffin says, by accepting the critical challenge to foundational ontology, an assumed correspondence between knowing and reality: "Critics of the idea of correspondence are rightly bothered by presumptuous and imperialistic claims by some people, whether religious, moral, scientific, aesthetic, or political fundamentalists, to have *achieved* correspondence." However, Griffin also questions the extreme position outlined by deconstructive postmodernists, arguing, "If we give up the notion that truth means correspondence, we give up the chief weapon of criticism" ("Introduction: Constructive" 25).

The archelogical method of this reconstructive postmodernism is to question the basic ontological assumptions that found *both* modernism and—because it accepts and then pushes modernity to the brink—deconstructive postmodernism. Griffin traces these assumptions back to the mind-matter problem that resulted from Descartes's dualism of subject and object, an experiencing being standing apart from a nonexperiencing reality. The premise that mind and body are ontologically different in kind became the starting point for the perennial modernist philosophical questions: What is the locus of reality, spirit or matter? and, What is the relationship between the two? These questions have been answered by various idealisms (emphasizing spirit) and materialisms (emphasizing matter) and persistent attempts to show how the mind can overcome its essential difference and attain some level of ontological correspondence with matter ("Introduction: Constructive" 4–7). Griffin, however, argues that this debate is one of the prime examples of the irrationality of modernist thought. The presumed ontological difference between mind and matter is a pure invention of the modern era, a made-up problem. A more rational approach, he counters, would be simply to question the premise: Is it based on a misunderstanding of mind or matter or both (5)?

The answer is both. Griffin grounds his process ontology in the premise of panexperientialism. In addition to the universality of creativity, which I discussed in the last chapter, Whitehead also suggests that all entities in the universe possess the capacity for experiencing reality and, through their creativity, the possibility for at least some degree of freedom. There are, thus, no essential ontological differences among entities; mind and matter, the apparent "in here" and the "out there" of modern thought, are at their root the same. Mind may possess more creative potential and thus greater opportunity for freedom, but this is a difference in degree not in essence. Therefore we are able to speak in a meaningful way about the correspondence between mind and matter because both are experiencing events, both subject and object ("Introduction: Constructive" 10–14.)

Another way of understanding the difference between these two ontologies is to think about them in cosmological terms. If you suppose that the universe existed before there were beings to experience it, then you would assume that reality is "out there" and exists apart from experiencing beings. On the basis of this premise, it follows either that reality exists as a criterion for ideas, reason, and language (modernism) or that the separation between mind and reality is so great there is no fundamental reality outside the mind (deconstructive postmodernism). However, if you suppose, as process philosophers do, that the universe is now and has forever been composed of experiencing beings, then you cannot accept any inherent separation between reality and the experience of reality, between being and the experience of being. Though beings that possess consciousness, the awareness of experience, may have arrived on the scene only very lately, that in no way marks a separation between being and the experience of being; rather, it marks the potential for a more complex and creative experience of being.

Process postmodernism, therefore, redefines the entire ontological issue of truth as correspondence. The premise of panexperientialism leads us to understand that all entities in the universe experience being. Thus, there is no essential ontological separation between being and the experience of being, no essential difference between the "out there" of being and the "in here" of experience, no mind-matter issue at all. So the problem with deconstructive postmodernism, as Griffin points out, is that instead of challenging the basic ontological dualism at the heart of modernism, it accepts it and then extrapolates it into the absurd in order to undermine the modern, a justification for claiming that there is no (essential) reality, that there is no possibility for any correspondence between idea and reality.

Rejecting the assumptions premised on the separation of mind and matter leads us to a different set of conclusions: there is no essential difference between ideas and reality, senses and reality, language and reality, reason and reality. The problem, therefore, is not about reality at all but about how we understand truth, or the *degree* of correspondence between ideas and reality, senses and reality, et cetera. Griffin says, though, that the issue of truth as correspondence is not about any claims of verification, as is implied in positivist notions and accepted by deconstructive postmodernism, but rather about what truth *means*. Truth cannot be the whole truth and nothing but the truth. The best we can hope for in this reconstructive ontology is a "working hypothesis" about reality, always partial, always tentative. The best we can hope for in language, for example, is that it "has the capacity to express and evoke modes of apprehending nonlinguistic reality that can more or less accurately correspond to particular features of that reality" ("Introduction: Constructive" 25–26). Such claims certainly fall short of modernist foundation-hope. But they also refuse to go to the other extreme in denying that anything of essence exists, that there is no reality beyond the constructs of language. Griffin's reconstructive postmodernism locates itself dialectically between the foundational and antifoundational extremes.

Relevance to Composition

For Vitanza, the key issue is language: language cannot be systemized and therefore neither can the composing of language nor language about composing language. There is nothing outside of language, no reality behind it, that allows us to order it, regularize it, control it in any way. Language itself works against this ordering by disrupting and delegitimizing it. To arrive at this conclusion about language, Vitanza accepts the modernist premise of the essential ontological difference between mind and matter. Upon dismissing any possibility of a connection between the "in here" and the "out there," he is left with no choice but to say that there is no essential "out there." All there is is language, free-flowing, undefined and undefinable by a reality "out there." It is this ontology of language that supports Vitanza's deep skepticism about teaching writing.

Process postmodernism, however, offers us a way to reconceive language from a completely different ontological perspective, as the following speculative ontology of composition suggests. Ontology is how we talk about the experience of being, and panexperientialism suggests that the experience of being is universal, an attribute of all entities in the universe. Experience of being is essential to being, defines being. There is, thus, no essential separation between being and the experience of being.

Language is one of the main ways in which human beings and other symbol-using beings experience being. There is, however, no essential difference between our experience of being and that of non-symbol-using entities. Language is certainly a more complex and creative form of experiencing being, providing us richer consciousness of being and thus enhancing our enjoyment of being. Language, then, is different but not different in kind from the forms of experience that characterize all other entities in the universe. As such, we are not separated from the rest of the universe by language, supposedly one of the distinguishing traits of humankind; rather, we are intimately connected to the rest of the world by language in that most essential of links, the ability to experience being. So Vitanza is right, to a certain extent, to conclude that all there is is language, but instead of undercutting our connection to the reality of being, language indeed connects us to that reality.

Beyond that essential connection, though, language does provide us some capacities not available to non-symbol-using beings. As I already said, it allows us to experience being in more complex and creative ways. It also gives us the capacity to experience the experience of being, including the capacity to experience language. Language provides us a way of ordering and shaping the experience of language through principles, models, or procedures. Not that any one of those principles, models, or procedures comprises the whole of language; rather, they are always partial, tentative, approximate, subject to change.

What Vitanza says about language is true: language cannot be systemized according to any foundational principles, models, or procedures that lie outside language. Language does indeed subvert any such attempts. But his grounding ontology is, I believe, wrong and thus leads him astray. It presupposes that language and reality are separate and that the existence of this separate reality would act as a justification for imposing a false order onto language. He then must conclude that language is utterly free-floating, loosed from reality. However, an ontology that assumes no separation between being and language as the experience of being frees us from totalizing ontogenic models of language. Language orders and shapes the experience of being and also, therefore, orders and shapes itself as the experience of being. This reconstructive ontology offers an alternative to the negative ontology of language of Gorgias and Vitanza without imposing a totalizing worldview. System does not come from some true reality outside language; system is inherent in the linguistic experience of being itself.

If language can be systemized in this way, then so can composing language and language about composing. Thus writing can and should be taught. What we do as teachers is to encourage student writers to bring language to bear on their experience of language. The goal in this case cannot be mastery, for such absolute control of language (in Vitanza's connotations of it) is out of the question. We can, however, help our students understand that their own experience of language is always under construction, help them to see the growth of their experience of language and how that growth contributes to their own growth as their experience of being becomes more complex and creative.

Vitanza defines teaching writing as the "will to systemize (the) language (of composing)." He takes this modernist definition as grounds for arguing that teaching writing unjustifiably defines writing by binding it to systems outside itself. I think he is right to resist dogmatic attempts to systemize language, to make foundational claims for principles, laws, and models of writing. No system can provide a full representation of writing; no assertion about writing can tell the whole truth about it. But that doesn't mean that no system can provide a partial representation of writing, that no assertion about writing can tell a partial truth about it. Dismissing foundational claims doesn't necessarily mean embracing antifoundational claims. Teaching writing within the reconstructive postmodern ontology I've described does allow us to systemize language but always in the recognition that such systems are tentative and approximate, working hypotheses.

Redefining writing as an experience of being allows me also to redefine teaching writing. Writing orders and shapes being, rendering being more complex and creative and thus enhancing the enjoyment of being. Teaching writing, then, is the desire to order and shape with others the experience of writing, rendering writing more complex and creative and thus enhancing the enjoyment of writing.

Counterthesis 2

"If [anything] does exist, it cannot be known." With this statement, Gorgias raises the issue of epistemology, shifting from Being to Knowing. He argues that concepts of the mind are not reality itself and that there is, thus, an absolute barrier between knowing and reality (if indeed reality does exist) (Freeman 129). Vitanza's emendation of Gorgias reads, "if anything exists, it cannot [should not/ought not to] be known" (152),

a way of stressing the ethical and political dimensions of knowing. For Vitanza, epistemology is largely an issue of authority. Knowing is an act of assuming authority over what is known, an authority that extends to language. So Gorgias's radical epistemology allows Vitanza to challenge what he sees as the drive to master language, "the will to be its author-(ity)" (144).

The critical question for this counterthesis is "Who speaks when something is spoken?" which Vitanza says is "a question of author(ship)" (152). In the modern humanist tradition, the answer to that question has been the speaking subject. The effect of this apparently obvious answer, however, has been to centralize authority in the speaker and to promote the illusion of the human subject as complete and autonomous and in control of reality (152–53).

Vitanza upsets this assumed natural authority of the speaking subject by citing Lyotard's assertion that such authority lies not in the addressor, who speaks, nor even in the addressee, who listens, but in "the addressee without an addressor or a receiver without a sender" (152). In other words, language is a "listening game": we don't control language as encoder or decoder; rather, we are *spoken by* language. There is no point of reference, no position of knowledge/authority, outside language. There is no speaker to whom language is subjected. An even more radical response to the question of Who speaks? is proposed by Deleuze and Guattari and Serres. They disrupt the authority of the speaker by asserting an "antispeaker, who is, in communications theory, sometimes called 'noise' (babel)" (154). Vitanza describes all of these "paratheorists" as aiming at "radical, noncodifiable (nonrational, minoritarian) ways of knowing or, in other words, to greater levels of noise" (155). They radically disperse the authority attached to speaking/knowing by placing it in language itself or in noise.

The answer to the question, Who speaks? has profound implications for the field of teaching writing. As Vitanza points out, we have tended to answer that question in one of two ways, both foundational and thus both suspect. The first way is that it is the subject who speaks, the subject as knower, the autonomous self as inventor, authoring the world; this answer is the basis for cognitive and expressivist schools of composition. The other answer shifts the locus of knowledge/authority from the subject to "the notion of the social bond" or "the community as inventor"; this answer provides the basis for social-epistemic theories of composition. Though Vitanza concedes that social theorists have done a great service to the field by dislodging the hegemony of the self, he accuses them of merely trading a romantic individuality for a "romantic socialism." Those who hold to social theories are not sufficiently suspicious of the grand narrative of emancipation that founds their teaching (156–57).

Vitanza's argument is that despite the fact that these two responses to Who speaks? offer quite different loci of mastery of writing, they are bound together by the foundationalist assumption that writing *can* be mastered. Whether the answer lies in the subjective or the social, we have steadfastly held to our assumption that language is authored and authorized by forces outside language. What's more, both groups are driven by metanarratives of power. Both talk of empowering students by providing them greater control over writing, but both, he says, end up further enslaving students: the first "places the self in bondage to the dominant-hegemonic discourse" and the second "places a bunch of already enslaved selves in an equally unacceptable—that is, nonemancipating—locus" (157).

The problem with the "paideia discourse of traditional-modern composition theory," Vitanza says, is that its "goals have been to control/master language and knowledge or, in other words, to 'totalize.' . . . As Nietzsche says, the will to knowledge is the will to power or the will to critical mastery, which leads to political disaster and violence" (153). Here, then, is the link between the will to be the author(ity) of writing and the will to knowledge: it is the will to power. As writing teachers, we have typically described our purpose as to encourage authorship in our students; and yes, authorship does imply a sense of authority or power over writing, a greater understanding and control of writing. We have convinced ourselves that this act empowers our students.

But the illusion that writing can be known and thus mastered—totalized—supports the illusion that the world can be known and mastered, the will to power over the world, which, as Vitanza points out, can have dire political consequences. This illusion of mastery, however, actually masks an enslavement to the language game of knowledge. Vitanza prefers a different sort of language game,

> whose sole purpose is not faithfulness to the story of knowledge (i.e., to the dictum "ye shall seek knowledge and it shall set you free!") but to "just gaming" or to hamming it up or cutting up (i.e., to Foucault's idea "ye shall free yourself from knowledge by cutting up"). (158)

Such gaming undermines the will to knowledge, as well as the will to mastery that supports the teaching of writing. If teaching writing is defined by the will to be its author(ity), then writing should not be taught.

What we are presented with, then, are two untenable epistemologies of composition. The modernist one has been thoroughly and, I think, convincingly undermined by Vitanza as the will to power. The deconstructive alternative, however, is so radical that it cannot be taught in any fashion we would recognize as teaching.

As it did for ontology, process reconstructive postmodernism describes an epistemology that allows me to argue that composition both can and should be taught. Griffin gets at the problem of epistemology by focusing on the role played by the senses in knowing. Foundationalists tend to assume an empiricist epistemology: that the only reliable means of knowing is through the direct apprehension of the senses (or those senses as they are extended by technology) and, more important, "that sensory perception includes a noninterpreted element in experience that is simply given" ("Introduction: Constructive" 18). This epistemology runs directly counter to Gorgias's, relying on the existence of a knowable external reality and the presumption that the senses provide a largely unmediated opening to that reality (18–19). In this epistemology, reality is subject, at least in part, to mastery of the knower.

Deconstructive postmodern antifoundationalists reject this theory, arguing that there is no such thing as unmediated reception of sensory data; instead, all knowing is interpretation because all knowledge from sense-data is constructed by the human perceiver. There can be no external given in the experience of sensory perception and thus no basis for making any firm knowledge claims about reality (19). It is utterly unmasterable, radically resistant to the authority of the knower.

Griffin counters by saying that there are significant problems with both positions. On the one hand, the foundationalist claim of givenness is problematic because it puts all its emphasis on sense perception; if sense perception were the only source of information about external reality, then all we can know is what is given in the present experience with no knowledge of actualities beyond that experience—a built-in solipsism. On the other hand, if there is nothing beyond interpretation, then all our knowledge of the world is ultimately arbitrary. The problem with deconstructive epistemology, then, is that it takes the implied solipsism of modernism to its (il)logical conclusion, arguing that all knowledge is purely constructed, having absolutely no grounding in reality: even if reality does exist, there is no way we could know it. Each position, however, seems to have an important truth on its side. Certainly, our day-to-day practice is based on the assumed existence of an external world that is present outside our interpretation. Yet it is also true that sense-data are actively constructed to create what we construe as knowledge (19–20).

Griffin's reconstructive postmodernism offers a way out of this dilemma: "we can fully admit—indeed, insist upon—the constructed character of sense-data, without concluding that nothing is given to perceptual experience as such" (20). Just as in the ontological move, Griffin opens with a critique of modernist assumptions of epistemology, specifically placing into doubt the assumption that sensory perception provides the only source of knowledge of the world. The reconstructive position challenges not only that assumption but also the assumption that it is even the *primary* source of data. One argument supporting that conclusion is *a priori*, reasoning deductively from Whiteheadian panexperientialism:

> If all individuals, not just those with sensory organs, experience, there must be a nonsensory mode of perception; and if

> sensory perception has evolved out of nonsensory perception, it is likely that creatures with this derivative form of perception still retain the more basic form as well. (14–15)

Because all entities in the universe are "experiencing events," whether they possess sensory organs or not, those beings that do have sensory organs must have evolved from those without. Therefore, this reasoning runs, sensory perception is itself a secondary mode of perception, having evolved out of other modes of perception, other modes of knowing the world ("Postmodern Theology" 45). So the entire modernist epistemological structure, founded as it is on the primacy of sense perception and thus the assumption that there is a direct connection between a given reality and our senses, is questioned. Also questioned is deconstructive postmodernism, which extrapolates modernist assumptions to absurd lengths. By reasoning that there are other ways of knowing that are not based on the senses, Griffin points to a postmodern epistemology that escapes radical, antifoundationalist solipsism: it doesn't matter to what degree knowledge from the senses is constructed; deeper structures of knowing allow us to make tentative knowledge claims about reality.

One important component of this reconstructive epistemology is its challenge to the modernist self—or mind or soul or subject—as knower. According to process thought, the self is not "monological" but "dialogical"; "we are constituted just as much by others as we are by ourselves . . . an ever-changing unity of personal events intimately related to all other events" (Gier 56–57). There is, then, no isolated, enduring self, no individual to experience actual occasions more than once. Each actual entity comes into being only in the formative moment of each occasion (Griffin, "Postmodern Theology" 42–44).[8] Knowledge of an external world cannot, therefore, be tied to the persistence of an individual knower. The radical connectedness to past occasions and other actualities combined with the radical dissolution of the unchanging and independent self indicates that the locus of knowledge/authority cannot reside in the self.

That doesn't mean, however, that reality cannot be known. In Whitehead's philosophy, there are two ways of achieving conscious prehension of actualities in the external world. First, we have direct knowledge of our bodies as actualities beyond our immediate experience, and this direct knowledge that there is *anything at all* beyond an immediate experience serves as the basis for an analogy by which we can ground assumptions that there are other knowable physical actualities beyond our bodies. In addition to analogy, a second way of perceiving the real world is "that, by prehending our bodies, we thereby indirectly apprehend actualities beyond our bodies *insofar as those actualities beyond our bodies are present within the actualities comprising our bodies*" (22). According to process thought, each individual entity participates in "occasions of experience" by prehending previous occasions and thus absorbing into itself aspects of the actualities of prior existences. (I am referring here to Whitehead's moment-by-moment process of concretion I described earlier, in which the "objective aim," the diverse realities of past actual occasions, are taken into and become one in each actual occasion of the present moment.) In prehending the actualities of other occasions, each of us is profoundly related to, indeed quite literally composed of, those actualities. All entities share the essence of experience and, through these shared essences, have nonsensory experience of other actualities beyond themselves (22).[9]

There are, then, two general modes of perception in human and other beings with well-developed sense organs and the ability to process sense-data. One is sense perception, but this form provides data only of the moment, isolated and thus solipsistic. The other mode of perception is, as Griffin describes it, "primordial," that which we share with all other entities in the universe, past and present. This latter form provides the basis on which we can know anything of an actual world beyond the limitations of our senses ("Postmodern Theology" 45–46).

This reconstructive epistemology occupies the archelogical middle between the negativism of deconstructive postmodernism and the positivism of modernist foundationalism. Both of these other epistemologies, however, fall into the same error, the assumption that knower and known, that which experiences being and being, are essentially different. Modernism projects a whole and autonomous subject that possesses a passive object, colonizes it. Deconstructive postmodernism projects a knower that has no direct knowledge of reality and therefore must construct what passes for reality.

All this changes with an epistemology of shared essences. In contrast to modernist epistemology, knowing cannot be imperialistic, a power relationship between wholly different entities. First, there is no real distinction between subject and object. There are no whole and enduring subjects; all entities in the universe experience the intermingling of subjectivity and objectivity in each actual occasion. Second, because all entities experience the reality of other beings, then all entities possess the ability on some level to know that reality. Process postmodernism offers an epistemology of shared essences in the shared occasions of actual experience. Each entity in the universe knows other entities through the experience of the many becoming the one, fully interwoven in each actual occasion. There is no essential difference between knower and known.

And in contrast to deconstructive epistemology, we human beings *can* know reality, but not through a form of knowing limited to the senses. There are also primordial forms of knowing, which we share with all other entities and by which we share the essential experience of being. It is a knowledge of the world that comes of *being* the world, a knowledge based on shared essences with other actualities. What we have, then, is an epistemology of the between: both nonsensory and sensory perception, both constructed and given, both antifoundational (the dissolution of loci of mastery) and foundational (shared essences).

Relevance to Composition

In "Three Countertheses," Vitanza defines the modernist enterprise of teaching writing according to the will to be the author(ity) of writing, the will to power, which is associated with the will to knowledge. Teaching writing is implicated in this will to knowledge through its goal of mastery of writing. To escape the ethical and political consequences of this will to power, he undefines and thus deauthor(ize)s composition, saying that writing should not be taught because knowing is nothing but noise, which leaves us with no authority over reality or language. Reconstructive postmodern philosophy shifts the epistemological ground considerably, offering what I think is a viable alternative to both modern and deconstructive postmodern ways of knowing. I'm going to sketch out some possible implications of this reconstructed epistemology for teaching writing.

Process postmodern philosophy enables me to redefine teaching writing through its redefinition of authority. As writing teachers, we encourage authorship in our students, a form of knowing that is indeed implicated in authority. But instead of vesting authority in either of the loci of mastery associated with the subject or the community and instead of deconstructing authority by dispersing it into language, this reconstructive postmodernism locates the will to knowledge in the shared essences that bind all entities of the universe together in being and knowing. Looked at this way, authorship does not denote a mastery over a passive reality; it is not an imperialistic form of knowing. As I suggested in the last section, language is different but not different in kind from the forms of experience that characterize all other entities in the universe. As such, we are connected to the rest of the world by the ability to experience the actual; language is one of the ways in which we human beings experience the being of other beings. Language provides a complex and creative form of knowing.

Thus, the authority vested in authorship resides not in a will to power but in shared essences, an essential connectedness to reality. This is not a colonizing of language and reality, an authority based on the essential difference between experiencing subjects and nonexperiencing objects. Rather, it is an authority that comes of being one with reality. We know the world because we are literally *of* the world. All knowing is, thus, a mutual experience (as Desmond's philosophy of the middle also describes it), an intimacy of entities that comprise each other and each other's reality. As authors of language, we share in this universal being and knowing—a very different sense of being its author(ity). This is not a form of authority that is in any way external, imposing. It is the very essence of what it means both to be and to experience (to know) the world. As teachers, we should promote this kind of authorship, an enhanced act of knowing.

As teachers we should also encourage in our students an authorship that leads to a greater authority in writing. Process thought portrays the enjoyment of human and any other conscious beings as different though not different in kind from the enjoyment of nonconscious entities. The key distinction is the capacity of *awareness* of enjoyment, the ability to participate in enjoyment more fully. I think that it may be useful to understand language in a similar fashion. Consciousness of language allows for a more intense and sustained enjoyment of the experience of being; it also allows for a certain authority concerning language. As beings who possess an awareness of language as language, we possess an authority that is represented in our ability to play with language, to construct it, mold it, enjoy it, talk about it, learn about it, and teach it.

So I agree with Vitanza's initial claim that teaching writing has been defined by the will to be its author and its authority, and I agree that, as a rule in our discipline, this authority has been associated with the will to knowledge and the will to power. But the reconstructive postmodern epistemology of teaching writing I have described here challenges the necessary association of knowledge of reality and language with power over reality and language. It is an authority that resides not outside language but in language itself. Teaching writing, then, is the desire to heighten others' consciousness of language as language and as a way of participating in more complex and creative ways in the shared essence of being.

Counterthesis 3

"If [anything] can be known, it cannot be communicated." Gorgias completes his philosophy of negation by adding to the ontology and epistemology a rhetoric. The substance of his argument is that language is not the same as reality (even if reality does exist and is knowable) because reality is different in essence from language. Language is nothing but language, refers only to itself; therefore, the linguistic representation of a reality outside language is impossible. But I think that Gorgias taps into an even richer philosophical vein in this argument. The broader implication is that it is language itself that perpetuates the illusion of a unified and knowable reality (Freeman 129). This rhetoric is not, then, an afterthought to his previous ontology and epistemology; rather, it is the linchpin that holds the whole philosophy together.

Vitanza's application of Gorgias to teaching composition is captured in this restatement: "if 'it' could be known, it cannot and should not be communicated (that is, taught)." For Vitanza, the link between communication and teaching writing resides in theory, "that theory as a game of knowledge cannot help as a resource [in composition], because theory of this sort resists finally being theorized, totalized" (159). Just as writing perpetuates the illusion of a unified and knowable reality, composition theory perpetuates the illusion of writing itself as unified and knowable and, therefore, teachable.

Vitanza points out that composition theory itself is undone by two paradoxes, each concerned with the relationship between theory and practice. The first is that our drive to turn theory into practice—to render writing as "'teachable, generalizable and highly responsive to systemization'" (Paul de Man qtd. in Vitanza 160)—is overmatched only by theory's resistance to be known and applied. Theory, by its very nature, disrupts all theorizing, particularly the desire to apply theory as a guide to practice. The second is "that (critical) theory paradoxically can, but cannot, be employed to critique and to found theoretical practice" (160). The discipline of composition has misinterpreted theory as a source for unity, a vain "theory hope" for a cogent and coherent approach to teaching. In composition this theory hope is driven by the powerful sense of a pedagogical imperative Vitanza labels "pedagogy hope," the sustaining belief that improved teaching can have an improving effect on students (160–61). But he insists that theory resists any form of unity, any sort of overarching model or principle or codification—any "totalitarian knowing-doing-making" (160). The paradox of "can, but cannot" signifies the way theory both undercuts, fragments, and destabilizes the will to pedagogy and also points toward the possibility for a postpedagogy that itself undercuts, fragments, and destabilizes writing and the teaching of writing (161–66).

Composition, then, has been built on the fault line of theory–not theory and can–cannot teach. This fault line has exposed two important problems in the discipline. One is that though we have assumed otherwise, there is no viable and productive relationship between writing theory and writing practice.[10] The main problem here is that theorizing practice has the reverse effect of defining theory, of limiting and domesticating it. Practice is essentially different from theory, and theorizing practice reduces theory to a unifying model or principle. Instead of theory defining practice, it is practice that defines, and therefore inappropriately grounds, theory. In our rush to define a writing that submits to teaching, we have ignored the inherent disjunctions between theory and pedagogy (161–63).

Another problem is that even if there were a viable and productive relationship between theory and practice, theory cannot be communicated. Any attempt at theory-talk involves us in what Vitanza disdains as "the language of the game of the profession of composition (i.e., the language game of knowledge)" (161). This game of knowledge is characterized by the attempt to totalize writing, to apply uniform and unitary concepts to that which radically resists the uniform and unitary. Theory-talk is no more than the blind submission to the hegemonic grand narratives of theory hope and pedagogy hope. Vitanza prefers instead the ludic "radical multiplicities" and "paralinkages" "which attempt to keep knowledge from being realized as a system, as categories, as generic, as *techne,* as political 'linking'—and more so, as 'teachable'" (163). Writing is, thus, incommunicable; writing cannot be taught. Dispensing with both theory-talk and the assumed relationship between theory and pedagogy "leave[s] no room for us to teach writing," Vitanza says, "and, after all, we are a teaching profession, not purely a contemplative profession" (162).

Again, we have what I think are two unacceptable modes of conceiving the relationship between theory and practice, two unacceptable rhetorics of composition. The modernist rhetoric espouses a productive relationship in which theory defines writing practice in such a way that it is made communicable, unified and sensible, susceptible to teaching. As Vitanza points out, however, this productive relationship comes with a heavy price: writing becomes domesticated to the will to teach, and theory itself becomes illegitimately grounded in practice. This critique strikes at the very root of our disciplinary assumptions concerning theory and practice, but as radical as it is, I think Vitanza makes a good point. We have not been sufficiently suspicious of our assumptions about theory and practice. But these suspicions, taken to an extreme in Vitanza's deconstructive rhetoric of composition, have the effect of undercutting any possibility for communicating theory or practice. As before, however, process postmodernism offers a way to claim a postmodern rhetoric of composition that is also teachable.

Griffin, too, challenges the basic assumptions of modernism, in this case, the residual Oneness left over from the death of God. Two of the ways this assumption of unity has presented itself are in the drive for unified and unifying theories and in the hegemony of theory over practice. Both forms are founded on the privileged nature of theorizing: first, that any theory that possesses greater powers of unity is privileged over other theories and over other ways of knowing; and second, that theory is always superior to practice, which is viewed as merely supplemental to theory ("Postmodern Theology" 40–41). Thus, both reconstruction and deconstruction launch a critique of modernist assumptions of unity related to theorizing. They differ substantially, however, in the direction this critique leads them. "Perhaps the most fundamental difference between the two types of postmodernism," Griffin says, "involves their respective attitudes about theory and practice" ("Postmodern Theology" 40). The problem with the deconstructive position is, as we've seen before, that its critique is based on the acceptance of modernist premises of Oneness, which it takes to an extreme ("Introduction: Constructive" 29). Vitanza, for example, continues to emphasize the modernist unity of theory and the assumption that theory is superior to practice but makes the case that because modernist concepts of theory cannot justify such a privileged position they should be denied in favor of a radically dispersed conception of theory that disallows any possibility of theorizing, or communicating, a practice of writing.

Reconstructive postmodernism offers an alternative to both modernist and deconstructive postmodernist assumptions about the role of theory, redefining the link between theory and practice. It does this by establishing the possibility for a set of privileged beliefs, or theories, though not privileged as in foundational—certain, existing without presupposition. "The beliefs in question are those that we inevitably presuppose in practice even if we deny them verbally" (27; emphasis removed). In other words, some beliefs are privileged over other beliefs insofar as the former come closer to representing what Griffin calls "hard-core commonsense notions": commonsense because they are common to most people and hard-core because they are not necessarily verbalized *as* beliefs by most people; indeed, they rarely are. However, they function as the assumptions on which most human practice is based ("Postmodern Theology" 35).

This idea of a set of privileged beliefs based on what people assume in practice, even if they deny them verbally, comes out of the pragmatism of Henry James and Charles Sanders Peirce and is applied in process philosophy by Whitehead and Charles Hartshorne. In contrast to the deconstructive approach, this reconstruction accepts certain base-level concepts common to most people, but at the same time it subverts modernist notions by questioning the role that language plays in theorizing that reality. Any verbalization of these bottom-layer beliefs will always and inevitably be vague, tentative, and incomplete. There can be no unified and unifying theoretical statement concerning the presuppositions that found practice because these presuppositions are but intuitions on the edge of our consciousness. They are privileged as beliefs because we are prepared to act on them, but they are not beliefs in the usual sense of verifiable propositions ("Introduction: Constructive" 27–28).

So instead of denying the possibility of any foundation and thus the possibility for any privileged belief or theory, this reconstructive position proposes a foundation for privileged beliefs in the essential substratum of that which cannot be contradicted in practice. And instead of eliminating the possibility of theory-talk, or communication about theory, as doomed to failure because theory resists the unifying pull of communicating a practice, process postmodernists celebrate the conversation of theory-talk. Theory is communicable, but because of the nature of hard-core commonsense beliefs, no single attempt to account for it can ever succeed. The bottom layer of experience may be prevalent among human beings, but trying to communicate it, to put it in words, is by necessity an ongoing, ever incomplete, cooperative effort among people who offer many different perspectives on it ("Introduction: Constructive" 28–29).

Relevance to Composition

Let me return to the two critiques found in Vitanza's skeptical rhetoric of composition: *(1)* there is no viable, productive relationship between theory and practice, that is, theory does not submit to the practice of writing; and *(2)* even if there were such a relationship, theory could not be communicated, that is, it could not be taught. As to the first issue, I have, so far, described three possible relationships between theory and practice. One is that theory defines practice, the hegemonic relationship associated with modernism. This idea privileges theory over practice, theory as that which unifies practice and makes it logical. The second is that practice defines theory, which is the unintended consequence Vitanza uses as an argument against the modernist notion of theory: practice unacceptably limits theory, making it definite and unified. The third relationship is one in which theory exists apart from practice, free-floating and disruptive—Vitanza's position. Like modernism, then, deconstructive postmodernism also argues for a privileged place for theory; it must be unshackled from pedestrian practice.

The reconstructive alternative offers a fourth possibility, one in which theory and practice are mutually definable, each defining the other. Griffin's idea of the hard-core commonsense beliefs that are presupposed in practice shows how practice is embedded in theory and theory in practice. What we do tends to make sense, and not just idiosyncratic sense or sense within cultural mores but sense that runs broader and deeper than that. Such theories are what we stake our day-to-day actions on, typically without even knowing it; they resist verbalization and in most circumstances cannot be contradicted in practice. In this way, theories define practice, render practice sensible. But it is also true that the only way such theories can be recognized is through practice or tested against practice. And I think it is probably true that these beliefs emerged from practice in the first place. So practice also defines theory. Theory is not, then, completely loosed from practice, running rogue. Theory and practice are each animated and illuminated by the other.

Given this reconstructed understanding of theory and practice, we can see that neither is superior to the other and, indeed, that neither makes any sense separated from the other. This perspective lends credence to what we in composition have recognized for a long time: practice is important. We are, as Vitanza points out, a field grounded in practice. We have no basis for theorizing in a way that is divorced from practice. Our focus on practice may diminish us in the eyes of many of our professional colleagues whose fields seem to be ruled by free-floating theorizing, but those fields are missing something essential, the productive bond between theory and practice, each driving and nurturing the other. It may seem to some that theory is sullied by practice, especially student practice, but I believe, rather, that it is practice that gives life to and sustains theory.

Now I turn to the second issue, communicating theory. Vitanza is right to say that theory resists communication and that therefore theory and practice are both ultimately incommunicable. But this is a limited idea of communication that is tied to totalization, the language game of knowledge. Reconstructive postmodernism concedes that theory cannot be fully known and communicated, always incomplete, exploratory, hypothetical, speculative, fragmentary. But instead of a liability, a reason to dismiss theory-talk as it relates to practice, our limited access to theory is the primary impetus and justification for theory-talk. The speculative and partial nature of our understanding of writing invites communication about it, in both teaching and scholarship.

This relationship between theory-talk and practice means that teaching writing is by necessity a cooperative enterprise, the ongoing cocreation of knowledge about writing. Students bring their own experience of practice, we bring ours, and we all negotiate theories of practice. Theory is communicable, teachable, not in terms of imposing an external theoretical structure on students' writing but in terms of seeing the writing class as an occasion for collaboratively constructing theories about writing, a shared conversation about what works in practice and in theory and why. Theory is communicable because our necessarily partial and tentative understanding of writing provides an impetus for theory-talk as a way of enriching that understanding.

Scholarship is another venue in which writing theory may be communicated. The effort to understand the diverse and multiple nature of writing creates the need for community, diverse and multiple perspectives on writing. It is *because* we cannot achieve any ultimate, unified expression of writing theory that we continue to talk about writing. Indeed, I would suggest that it is the inherent inability of language to theorize fully a base-level practice that invites and sustains theory-talk. It is, thus, a conversation that has no end (in either sense of the term). The discipline of writing is where we make our inevitably exploratory attempts to put theories about writing into words and practice. Different perspectives on writing represent different attempts at describing our essentially incommunicable common experience of writing and teaching writing; no theory is *ultimately* superior to any other. It is the essaying that makes the conversation both interesting and worthwhile.

Vitanza defines the teaching of writing according to the will to theorize, the will to communicate or teach writing. He, of course, applies that will to an argument that writing cannot and thus should not be theorized and therefore cannot and should not be taught. But I have used process postmodern philosophy as a source for redefining the teaching of writing by reconstructing the will to theorize: theory has a mutual and productive relationship with practice, and theory can be communicated, though always tentatively and approximately. Teaching writing, then, is the desire to participate in theory-talk, conversations about the shared but ultimately incommunicable practice of writing.

Conclusion

Should writing be taught? I wonder what would happen to our profession if we started each semester we teach and each article we write by questioning our founding premise, that writing should be taught. Well, we probably wouldn't want to take it quite that far, but I do think that asking Vitanza's question could be beneficial for the discipline because it encourages us to take a profoundly critical view of what we do and why we do it. In a field like ours, with no founding subject matter to ground us and little evidence that teaching writing actually improves writing,[11] all we really *have* is the assumption that writing should be taught.

Vitanza's answer is no, writing should not be taught, and I think his arguments are, to a large degree, persuasive. He says that teaching writing has been defined by the powerful will to discipline writing, manifested in the will to systemize writing, the will to be its author(ity), and the will to theorize writing. His greatest concern is what the discipline of writing as a teaching profession has done to writing: submitting writing to teaching has defined writing, limited it, made it definite, definitive, subject to mastery. Vitanza, then, takes it upon himself to undefine the teaching of writing by deconstructing its modernist foundations.

As I have said, this critique of composition is one of the most compelling I have found in our literature. Vitanza's deconstruction of the basic assumptions of our field is valuable for what it reveals to us about the way we have defined teaching writing. But in this chapter I have offered reconstructive postmodern countertheses to each of Vitanza's countertheses. I have redefined an ontology, an epistemology, and a rhetoric of teaching writing based on an archelogical dialectic between the certainty of modernism and the doubt of deconstructive postmodernism. I don't intend these definitions to be definitive, ultimate, but rather a part of the ongoing cocreation of knowledge of our field.

The way I see it, teaching writing itself is beginnings. Teaching writing takes place on that threshold between certainty and doubt, between ontogenic models and paralogy, between totalizing knowledge and just gaming, between unifying theory hope and the resistance of theory to being theorized. It is an act of faith that being does exist, that we can experience being, and that we can communicate about and through the experience of being. It is this act of faith that shields us from the unwarranted pride of certainty while keeping us from sliding into the despair of doubt.

9 Value: A Heretical Ethics of Teaching Writing

> The Prophet is he who has *completed* a world-view; thus the word *heresy* in Arabic is synonymous with the verb "to innovate" or "to begin."
>
> —Edward Said, *Beginnings*

Anyone who has studied classical Greek rhetoric is likely to be familiar with the controversy over teaching *aretê*, or virtue. Evidently, many of the Sophists of the late fifth and early fourth centuries B.C.E. lured paying students with exaggerated promises of the ethical worthiness to be attained through instruction in disputation. In "Against the Sophists," Isocrates pokes fun at these claims by pointing to a telling contradiction in their application: the Sophists insisted on receiving their payments in advance, demonstrating a distrust of the very people they pledged to make virtuous (49). And in *Gorgias*, Socrates baits his trap for that eminent Sophist with the assumption that, as Polus puts it, "the rhetorician knows what is just and noble and good, and will himself teach these to anyone who comes to him without knowing them" (70). Gorgias takes the bait and gets strung up in his own contradiction: his claim to teach virtue is countered by his own defense of teachers whose students use rhetoric unvirtuously (67–69). In these cases, the idea that teachers can inculcate moral goodness in students is used as a source of ridicule and doubt aimed at the Sophists.

It may seem strange, however, that this challenge to teaching virtue is associated with three of the most respected and influential teachers in Western civilization—Socrates, Isocrates, and Plato. But the issue of teaching virtue is not as simple as it appears. At the end of the extant fragment of "Against the Sophists," Isocrates ventures a more qualified claim to teaching virtue. Though he admits that sobriety and justice cannot be rooted in a depraved person, he does contend that the study of political discourse "can help more than any other thing to stimulate and form such qualities of character" (49), a position he maintains in the later *Antidosis* (52–54).[1] And Socrates' paean to virtue at the end of *Gorgias* makes it clear that it is not through learning rhetoric but through learning philosophy that one finds the path to moral goodness, thus providing his own lure to paying students. The issue, then, is not whether teaching can or cannot generate virtue in students; rather, the issue is the degree to which it may be taught and what kind of teaching leads to virtue.

There is another issue, hidden but assumed, in this controversy: an argument for the teaching of virtue is also an argument for the virtue of teaching. In each of these cases, there is a direct link between the moral good students derive from teaching and the moral good of the teaching itself. Isocrates and Plato's explicit challenge to the Sophists' claim to teach virtue is an implicit challenge to the virtue of sophistic teaching. But Isocrates and Plato cannot categorically deny the possibility of teaching of virtue because that would challenge the virtue of their own teaching.

Moreover, I think it is significant that this whole discussion about teaching and virtue is associated with language instruction. The Sophists were teaching eristics and forensic discourse. Isocrates staked his claim to the more ennobling political discourse. And Plato's Academy was dedicated to dialectics, which, as Aristotle pointed out, is the counterpart to rhetoric, both arts of language having no particular subject matter and involved in generating opposing arguments (*Rhetoric* 154). In *Gorgias,* Plato heightens the distinction between the language arts and other arts: the manual arts, medicine and gymnastics, for example, do include some speech about their particular subjects, but rhetoric, Gorgias maintains, is concerned only with speech itself and no such working with the hands (62–63). Of course, the same can be said of dialectic.

Here we find what may be at the core of this ancient controversy. There is no need to argue the virtue of teaching gymnastics or medicine or armory or shipbuilding or any of the other manual arts. Teaching these arts is virtuous because of the clear good that these arts bring to the society. Their virtue is a given; they meet a common need. The issues of teaching virtue and the virtue of teaching seem to arise only with the arts of language beyond basic literacy. It was simply not clear what virtue was associated with those arts. This is why the Sophists had to rely on exaggerated claims about the moral goodness their students would attain. This is why Isocrates ended up making similar claims but in a qualified form. And this is why Plato tells his fable of the final judgment at the end of *Gorgias,* an argument that the truest path to virtue is "by inquiry into the truth," dialectical philosophy (111). They are making competing claims for teaching virtue because that is the only justification they have for the virtue of teaching the arts of language. How else can they attract students?

For most of us who teach composition today, attracting students is not the problem; the problem is how to handle the hordes required to take our courses. Yet we are still haunted by the same need to justify what we do, and for many of the same reasons. We teach an art of language, an art that has no apparent subject matter yet claims to encompass all subjects, an art that can provide little evidence of tangible benefits for the students who are forced to study it. The traditional justification that we can improve students' general writing skills has, to my knowledge, never been convincingly demonstrated, a case made by the contributors to *Reconceiving Writing, Rethinking Writing Instruction,* edited by Joseph Petraglia. This inconsistency comes to most of us as no surprise, evidenced by our attempts to find other justifications to buttress the virtue of our teaching.

In this chapter, I return to the issue of value as it is framed by the virtue, or ethical value, of teaching writing. In chapter 7 I addressed the issue of the value of writing—the good or worth of writing—in terms of process theology. I argued that the greatest value of writing is intrinsic to writing itself: it engages the writer in the larger creative process that underlies the universe. Writing is an act of creativity, one of the most accessible and most powerful ways of participating in creativity, the act of beginnings.

I believe it is possible to understand *teaching* writing as possessing similar intrinsic value. Teaching writing is an act of beginnings, but in a somewhat different sense from writing itself. Teaching writing is a form of creativity, the teacher stimulating, guiding, and participating in the creativity of others. As such, it is valuable, in and of itself, for the teacher. It is also valuable in that it enhances the enjoyment of writing for both students and teacher. In process theology, enjoyment is enhanced by the awareness of creativity that is peculiar to conscious beings. If writing is an act of creativity, then one of the chief functions of the writing teacher is to enhance the students' awareness of writing as beginnings, enhancing the enjoyment of participating in beginnings. Of course, the teacher is enhancing his or her own enjoyment as well, becoming conscious of creativity in an act of metawriting: teaching writing becomes, in a way, a writing of writing.

I would very much like to stop writing this chapter at this point. I think this is a rich and productive way of understanding the good of teaching writing. But it is also idealistic, perhaps to the point of blindness. What I am portraying here is a utopia in which a group of people gather voluntarily to write under the guidance of a teacher-writer. The object of such a gathering is to write for its own sake, for the enjoyment of it, enjoyment in both the usual and the process senses of the term. This, I believe, has been the hope of many writing teachers, one of the dreams that keeps us going. Sometimes we manage to achieve that ideal, at least for a moment, when writing for its own sake, a freshly discovered enjoyment in writing generated by a greater consciousness of it, overcomes the competing goals of the classroom.

These competing goals, however, almost always smother the ideal. The very act of *teaching* writing alters our understanding of writing, requiring that we consider the question of its ethical value within its institutional setting. It's typically a required course. The primary sponsors of the requirement—parents, faculty in other departments, university administrators, legislators—support it because they still believe in the myth of general writing skills instruction, a myth we haven't rushed to dispel. It's often seen as having a gatekeeping function, keeping weaker students out of the real courses of the university. The pall of remediation continues to hang over it. It is, as a rule, taught by an underpaid, overworked cadre of adjuncts and graduate students. How can we possibly argue for the virtue or ethical value of teaching composition? Vitanza is, as expected, even more pointed in his criticism: he associates composition pedagogy with pederasty and composition teachers with pederasts (161–62). Can we defend ourselves from such accusations?

The teaching of writing requires that we look at writing from an ethical perspective, teaching virtue and the virtue of teaching. Can the teaching of writing be justified as a moral good? Like language teachers of old, we can't rely on the implicit virtue of what we teach to make a case for the virtue of our teaching. We have to face that issue directly. And all the other ethical problems associated with our field only create a greater urgency for an ethics of teaching writing. The issue then is what, if anything, can we claim as the locus for such an ethics.

What I will do in this chapter is look at the way we have addressed the problem of ethics in the instruction of advanced arts of language. I will frame my discussion with a consideration of the debate in composition about the source of ethical value in teaching writing: is it located in the ends or the means, the universal or the local? As before, I will take the postmodern deconstruction of our ethical assumptions as an opportunity for an archelogical reconstruction of an ethics of teaching writing, based on reconstructive postmodernism.

The Value of Teaching Writing: Ends Versus Means

In "Diversity, Ideology, and Teaching Writing," Maxine Hairston launched a well-known attack on left ideologues in composition, arguing that they should keep ideology out of the writing classroom. Though it's certainly tempting to dismiss this article as ideologically naive, as many of its critics did,[2] or as mere nostalgia for those Edenic days when "The Winds of Change" were sweeping across composition, I think there is much more to it than that.

Missed in all the wrangling over ideology was Hairston's focus on the issue of intrinsic and instrumental value. Referring to her chair's address in 1985, she says,

> I asserted that we teach writing for its own sake, as a primary intellectual activity that is at the heart of a college education. I insisted that writing courses must not be viewed as service courses. Writing courses, especially required freshman

> courses, should not be *for* anything or *about* anything other than writing itself, and how one uses it to learn and think and communicate. (179)

She then accuses left ideologues of subverting that model by turning composition classes into "vehicles for social reform." "It's a model that doesn't take freshman English seriously in its own right but conceives of it as a tool, something to be used" (180). That is, its value is located in purposes outside writing itself, which makes the composition class merely a "vehicle" or "tool" for other ends. Thus, the issue here, as Hairston frames it, is not so much the role of ideology in the classroom as it is the source of value in writing and teaching writing: is composition a means to an end external to the writing class or is it an end in itself; is teaching writing to be valued as a instrument or for its own sake?[3]

As evidence that ideology itself is not really the issue, Hairston declares her alignment with the overall aims of the left. Admitting that "we all know the terrible inequities and contradictions of our society," she further acknowledges common hopes for the world: "we'd all like to bring about a fairer, more compassionate society. But I fear that we are in real danger of being co-opted by the radical left, coerced into acquiescing to methods that we abhor because, in the abstract, we have some mutual goals" (187). The disagreement, then, is not about broad political and social ends; it is, at least from her perspective, over the means to those ends, methods of teaching writing. To demonstrate this point, Hairston describes how to "create a culturally inclusive curriculum in our writing classes," not by making diversity the explicit aim of the course—dominating what students read and write about—but by allowing students to focus on their own cultural experiences and sharing them with other students (190–91). In an open, democratic, student-centered classroom, absent a political agenda, writing happens. And in the classroom she describes, real diversity and understanding and acceptance of differences happen because writing happens. This method, she contends, "makes the teacher a midwife, an agent for change rather than a transmitter of fixed knowledge" (192).

Though I suspect that Hairston and the left pedagogues she criticizes may have somewhat different views of what it means to be "an agent for change," what is at stake here, as I have said, is not so much ideology but the locus of value in teaching writing—in writing itself or in ends extrinsic to writing for which teaching writing serves as an instrument. To put it another way, is teaching writing an ideologically neutral act or is it, following the leftist aphorism that how we teach is what we teach, always and inevitably ideologically instrumental?

This is a question that Patricia Bizzell takes up in her work, heightening the differences between the intrinsic and the instrumental in composition. One of the people specifically identified by Hairston as guilty of "asserting that they have not only the right, but the duty, to put ideology and radical politics at the center of their teaching" (180), Bizzell does indeed recommend that composition teachers "be more forthright about the ideologies we support as well as those we attack, and . . . articulate a positive program legitimated by an authority that is nevertheless non-foundational" ("Beyond Anti-Foundationalism" 271). She says that we can accomplish this, in part, via "positionality," declaring in the classroom our ideological positions and political goals for students and making the positions and goals key features in the rhetoric and rhetorical values of the classroom (271–75).

What is important to me about her position in this article is her critique of the pedagogies of other leftist compositionists for not being instrumental enough in attaining their ideological ends, again a question of means and ends. For example, Bizzell points to a curriculum developed by James Berlin that "asks students to deconstruct the dominant ideologies" of sexism and capitalism, a pedagogical stance she describes as "trying to be value-neutral and anti-authoritarian" (269; 272). By not making the ideological goals of the class explicit, Berlin's curriculum relies on the rhetorical process itself to accomplish his goals. The idea is that creating an antifoundational classroom—open, pluralistic, democratic—will encourage students to write in a way that interacts critically with the ideological formations of their world and take action to change them. But Bizzell suggests that a very different result is more likely, a value vacuum that encourages students to stiffen their defense of old value systems or to fall into a skepticism of all value systems (269).

It is useful to consider Bizzell's position in "Beyond Anti-Foundationalism" in the context of her introduction to *Academic Discourse and Critical Consciousness,* an introduction that lies somewhere between confessional and academic *Bildungsroman.*[4] From the beginning of her teaching career, her work in the classroom was influenced by her "left-liberal values." She describes her well-known focus on the direct teaching of academic discourse to basic writers as founded on the assumption, supported by the work of Paulo Freire, that engaging students in the method of academic thought, characterized as it is by objective detachment and inquiry, would in turn encourage critical consciousness in her students, which would inspire them "to work not just for reform, but for radical change in American society" (3–8).

Her radically instrumentalist stance in "Beyond Anti-Foundationalism," however, emerged out of a crisis of confidence caused by a growing distrust of this founding assumption. For one thing, the idea that students would automatically develop the insight and then the praxis of critical consciousness was not borne out in her experience. Also, she realized that Freire's pedagogical methods were not objective and value-free as she had believed; rather, they were founded in the value system of Roman Catholic liberation theology, which would have been assumed by Freire's followers and student-peasants (18–22). In other words, there was a specific instrumental end—determined by the goals of liberation theology—implied in the pedagogical means (25–26). The problem, then, is that simply engaging students in the process of critical thinking without also providing an explicit ethical and political program for acting on that critique is likely to generate not critical consciousness but a negative skepticism or political quietism or even resistance to critical thinking.

From this perspective, the way that both she and Berlin were teaching was not really instrumental at all. Indeed, it placed just as much faith in the process itself, the pedagogical and writing process, as Hairston's ideal class. The instrumental nature of a classroom is not, Bizzell argues, a function merely of the instructor's political intentions. The way we teach is *not necessarily* what we teach. Rather, the instrumental classroom is defined by an explicit statement of the ideological goals of the class and a course design that provides a way for students to achieve those goals.[5]

A different take on the ethical issue of ends and means may be found in Jeff Smith's "Students' Goals, Gatekeeping, and Some Questions of Ethics." Like Bizzell, he looks at the teaching of left ideologues and finds a confusion of means and ends, "the belief that the means must *always* and *immediately* enact the ends" (310). Smith also questions the assumption that creating a nurturing, nonhierarchical, student-centered classroom somehow automatically serves the *telos* of social transformation. But unlike Bizzell, his ideological position is oriented to the right.

For Smith, teaching writing is ethical only to the extent that it explicitly reflects the values imposed upon it by the university and the social order in which it exists. As people who have voluntarily taken a job in the university, composition teachers are a part of a value system determined to a very large degree by the values of our students and their parents and by the values of the institution. Smith points out that these students are here, for the most part, because they believe that the university experience will help them become members of an overclass of professionals and managers.

> Students attend college as a means to an end. We can labor mightily to make it an end in itself; we can try to make each task intrinsically valuable, and sometimes we will. But no matter what sort of personal discovery or empowerment or ideological reorientation a given assignment offers, it is self-deluding to think that students will do it . . . for those reasons. (316)

Smith says that when we see our students as people who bring a set of values to the university and whose eventual work as managers and professionals will have tangible ethical effects, this confusion of ends and means becomes problematic. As composition teachers, we work for others' ends, not our own. Our work is ethical only to the extent that we provide effective means to those ends. We should not, therefore, set ourselves up as people who determine the *ends* of education. "The only thing we are certainly justified in imposing on students is our judgment of *means:* Here, in my expert opinion, is the best way to learn this thing that you and I have agreed should be taught" (317).

I have used Hairston, Bizzell, and Smith to set up what I think is a crucial issue in our understanding of the virtue or ethical value of teaching writing. For Hairston, the primary source of value is intrinsic to the process of writing: *teaching writing is ethical insofar as it focuses on writing itself as an open, democratic, critical act that enables students to achieve unstated but assumed progressive aims.* Composition is ethical only as a means; any explicit attention to an external end is indoctrination and therefore unethical. For Bizzell, the primary source of value is extrinsic to writing: *teaching writing is ethical insofar as it is explicitly instrumental in encouraging students to apply a critical perspective to dominant ideologies and to work toward social justice for all.* This ethics focuses on the *telos* of teaching, so composition is ethical to the extent that it is instrumental to that end. From Bizzell's perspective, noninstrumental left ideologues share Hairston's locus of value in the process or means. And for Smith, the primary source of value is also extrinsic to writing: *teaching writing is ethical insofar as it adheres to the capitalist ends that students and their parents expect of an investment in a college education, helping students to attain the professional credentials that pave the way to economic prosperity.* Because the ends are dictated to us by the system we work within, our chief contribution is to apply our expertise in writing to provide the most effective means to those ends.

Whether the locus of ethical value is intrinsic or instrumental, focused on writing as an end or as a means to an end, there is in all three positions a strong belief that teaching writing participates in a larger "story" that provides a sense of purpose that extends beyond the writing itself.

Postmodern Ethics: Universal Versus Local

The natural reliance on a "story" to undergird an ethics of teaching writing has been radically challenged by postmodern compositionists. Once again, it is Vitanza who establishes the position most vividly. He readily acknowledges "the dangers of the capitalistic consumer 'game of knowledge'" and the insidious way that composition textbook authors openly justify their texts "in economic-capitalistic terms." However, he is equally critical of "socialist rationalism" and its "narrations of emancipation" (142). Vitanza describes himself as "still unequivocally contra to these social-consensual theory-hopeful rationalists, who through social reengineering and instrumental reason . . . want to cure society and make the world into a great, good place" (143). The problem, he argues, is that this left-wing orientation in composition represents merely another form of foundationalism and is, thus, all the more worthy of suspicion because it works under the guise of antifoundationalism (143). Any positive program, any attempt to provide guiding principles for ethical action, smacks of foundationalist thinking. Vitanza's suspicion of ideology, left or right, in the classroom reflects a postmodern suspicion of *all* ideology—*all* grand narratives, *all* worldviews, *all* value systems.

Though Vitanza celebrates the erasure of grand narratives from the composition classroom, for most of the rest of us his position presents an ethical dilemma, the consequences of which are expressed in Lee Ann Carroll's "Pomo Blues: Stories from First-Year Composition."[6] Carroll looks at the way postmodernism has influenced our understanding of both students and teachers, not as autonomous individuals but as people telling stories authored by the cultural, political, and institutional contexts that surround us, stories that are inevitably decentered, multivoiced, provisional. "The dilemma of postmodernism," Carroll says, "is that all discourses are limited, and there is no outside place to stand to judge what is harmful or what is good" (930). What you can accomplish in teaching a composition class is, thus, very modest; since we cannot adjudicate among stories, all we as writing teachers can do is "consider what kinds of stories it is possible for us to tell in English I, what it means to tell such stories 'effectively,' and what is at stake in playing different variations of the same tune" (918). Carroll fully accepts these modest goals for the postmodern classroom, but they leave her reflecting on the point of teaching writing.

> I wonder why I am standing in front of the classroom. I cannot make romantic claims for the particular consequences of any one story, and I am skeptical of others who say they are able both to represent students' experience and to change their lives during a few months of Freshman Comp. (932)

And that leaves her singing another refrain of the Pomo Blues.

What kind of ethics can we maintain in this pluralism of stories? This is what Lester Faigley, in *Fragments of Rationality*, calls the "impasse" of postmodern theory. Faigley points to Bizzell's statement in "Beyond Anti-Foundationalism" that what is required is an authoritative stance that is also nonfoundational, but the question, he says, is, how can we have it both ways (20)? In its radical suspicion of grand narratives, postmodernism may provide a powerful critical method, but it offers no position of authority for redressing the ethical and political problems exposed by that critique.

Faigley offers what he sees as a way out of this "impasse," relying particularly on Iris Young and Jean-François Lyotard to outline the possibility for a postmodern ethics of composition. About justice, Lyotard asserts that we cannot depend on any sort of preexisting ideal or authority because it is constantly being undermined by differends, the fissures or conflicts or linkages that represent the incommensurability of all language games. He advocates instead a concept of justice that is always local and kairotic. Faigley uses this idea of the differend to argue against the traditional ends-means view that ethical value exists first as the ends and rhetoric serves as the means for gaining acceptance for that value. Rather, ethical value lies in the rhetorical act itself. The rhetorical subject (writer, speaker) is Young's "urban subject," constructed in the linkages present in crossing the boundaries of personal experience and multiple competing discourses. As such the rhetorical subject is conscious of differends and, in that moment of awareness, engages in the ethical questioning prompted by a particular set of linkages. So for Faigley, the ethical value of writing is found not in the universal but in the local, in that moment of awareness at the juncture of competing discourses when a writer must ask ethical questions raised by a particular set of discourses and must make a judgment based on a conditional sense of what is right in that situation (230–39).

This solution is similar to James E. Porter's postmodern ethics of composing, which he describes as "a model that accommodates the postmodern critique of traditional ethics while at the same time resisting the traditional ethicists' charge of 'relativism'" ("Developing" 216). A postmodern ethics is distinguished by its rejection of any preexisting set of principles, laws, or moral codes that are derived from outside and exist apart from immediate behavior and procedure. Indeed, it must be located at the critical junctures of competing principles, laws, and moral codes, in the indeterminate act of questioning and negotiating among these competing standards (215–19). This postmodern ethics finds a ready companion in the act of composing, which is itself an act of negotiating principles and methods from various sites, questioning the dynamic relationships among these competing domains and responding with judgments and decisions based on a critical understanding of that dynamic relationship (221). An ethics of composing, then, is located in the act itself, particularly, Porter points out, in that every rhetorical act has as its aim some idea of the good for that occasion. "Ethics in this sense is not an answer but is more a critical inquiry into how the writer determines what is good and desirable. Such inquiry ultimately leads toward a judgment about what is good or desirable for a given situation" (223).

In "Ethics in the Writing Classroom: A Nondistributive Approach," Christy Friend also asks the question, "How is it possible to negotiate ethical issues productively and humanely in the postmodern classroom?" (549). For her answer, she, like Faigley, applies the work of Iris Young. In *Justice and the Politics of Difference,* Young proposes a nondistributive theory of ethics, based not on the more typical "end-state" of the good, which derives its sense of justice from the equal distribution of the goods of society to individuals, but rather on a group-centered ethics that derives its sense of the good from the delineation of "common interests."

It is an ethics that rests not on a universal end point but on local processes that lend themselves to change and variability (Friend 549–52). Friend describes a pedagogy that emerges from this nondistributive ethics as one that lies in the tension between separation and identity, conflict and consensus. Such a pedagogy creates open forums for students to debate and write about ethical issues, offering ways for them to encounter difference and making sure that there are no "right" answers to the issues that are raised (562–66). Thus, the ethical value of teaching writing resides not in any end-state of justice it may achieve but in the local processes of negotiating the tensions and common interests that exist in the differences within which we live, an ethics not of having—accomplishing or achieving an end—but of doing.[7]

Faigley, Porter, and Friend seek to define a postmodern ethics of composing whose value is located not in any extrinsic, broadly accepted story of the good (modernist ethics) but in the fissures, the conflicts, the disjunctions inherent in the competing discourses that surround us. One of the interesting aspects of this ethics is its position on the intrinsic-instrumental value continuum I have set up. These postmodernists have located themselves on the intrinsic side of that continuum, placing value in the process of writing itself. An illustration of this postmodern tendency toward intrinsic value may be found in the odd alliance between D. Diane Davis and Hairston. Davis takes Hairston's declaration that writing courses should be about nothing but "writing itself" as a starting point for her own radical postmodern pedagogy based on a rhetoric of laughter, though she admits that "it is unlikely she [Hairston] would approve of our interpretation of this passage" (231).

Despite the anti-instrumental stance of postmodern rhetorics, their foregrounding of the issue of local versus universal pushes the idea of intrinsic value far beyond anything recognizable by process compositionists who, as Hairston shows, tend to assume a story of progressive values underlying their teaching. In contrast to this vision of process, postmodernists argue that there is *nothing but* process, radically local and contingent, a reflection of the multiple and provisional nature of the postmodern experience. Perhaps a postmodern ethics of composition could be summarized this way: *teaching writing is ethical insofar as it engages the student writer in the postmodern experience of negotiating among competing discourses and having to respond in a way that reflects the writer's best understanding of the good at that moment.* The source of value for this ethics lies neither in the ends nor the means, which is defined by the ends. Rather, it deconstructs modernist assumptions of ends *and* means by banishing all ends and radicalizing the means.

I admit that I find myself attracted to this postmodern ethics, in large part because I see in it the positive potential of beginnings. I find particularly appealing Faigley's description of the moment of awareness at the disjuncture of differends at which the writer engages in the ethical questioning stimulated by that disjuncture. This sounds to me very much like the threshold experience of beginnings. However, I cannot fully embrace this ethics for reasons that are apparent in the critiques of it mounted by some left ideologues. In the afterword to *Academic Discourse and Critical Consciousness,* Bizzell observes that under the influence of postmodern scholarship we have become so successful in explaining away values in terms of historical and social forces that we now see the profession of values in the classroom as an academic form of "false prophesy" (277–78). To be postmodern is to be suspicious of values, but Bizzell says that this position makes her uncomfortable: "[I]f I am honest I must say that what I really care about is what my students believe, how they will conduct their lives, and not just whether they have learned to analyze beliefs or lives in correct postmodern fashion" (279). The only solution that postmodernism offers for avoiding "'vulgar politicization'" is "to install a debunking or deconstructive method in place of persuasive efforts on behalf of my world view" (285).

Ebert's "For a Red Pedagogy: Feminism, Desire, and Need" makes a pointed challenge to the application of ludic postmodern feminism in the classroom. She charges ludic feminism with being "an accomplice of capitalism," arguing that its continual mystification of social relations disables a critique of capitalism (805). The problem is that critique demands an objectifying distance, which ludics claim is merely a nostalgia for modernism, the belief that one could station oneself outside the moment and find a basis for critique. "Critique, in other words, is seen as a product of modernity that is . . . an act of totalization" (809). But there *is* an outside, Ebert contends, located in the objective reality of the Marxist understanding of surplus labor and the class antagonisms sparked by that surplus (809). The immanent critique of postmodernism, focusing as it does on the play of differences in texts, serves only to obscure the true differences that underlie capitalism and thus reinforce the status quo (813).

In a review, John Trimbur provides a neo-Marxist perspective on postprocess pedagogy. Trimbur begins by noting the irony that exists in process pedagogy: that in its attempt to help students find individual, authentic voices within an oppressive institution, it only created another kind of oppression in the writing class, "reinstitut[ing] the rhetoric of the belletristic tradition at the center of the writing classroom" ("Taking" 110). He says that a similar problem is now afflicting the postmodern movement in composition. For example, a book by Knoblauch and Brannon offers a pedagogy of "stories." "But the now fashionable postmodernist suspicion of the 'terrorism' of metanarratives leaves Knoblauch & Brannon unwilling to argue for their beliefs, to attempt to persuade their students" (112). Kurt Spellmeyer garners a similar criticism, focused on his hope that reading and writing in the essayistic tradition will provide a way for students to attain the language and the institutional control of authoritative academic genres through the "common ground" found in the essay genre. Trimbur, however, contends that the essay is just another authoritative form. He casts doubt on "the belief that a particular kind of discourse . . . can be privileged as the means to liberate or empower its practitioners." Like the process movement before it, the postmodern, postprocess faith in writing itself is, Trimbur says, merely the installation of yet another institutional form of domination, what he calls "text-based determinism" (118).[8]

One of the interesting features of this leftist critique of postmodern ethics is the accusation that it is characterized by a fixed and completed worldview (reminiscent of Hairston's description of left pedagogy as "a transmitter of fixed knowledge" ["Diversity" 192]). On the surface, it would seem that postmodernists, with their suspicion of grand narratives, would have the advantage in this debate. But that suspicion, as the leftist critics have suggested, may veil a dogmatism sheltering within. In demanding an authority for no authority, the postmodern classroom offers students no positive values to act upon, leading to a political quietism or skepticism that does nothing but support the ideological status quo.

At what point does the suspicion of grand narratives itself become a grand narrative? This question is raised by Nancy Welch's "Resisting the Faith: Conversion, Resistance, and the Training of Teachers," a description of a teacher-training seminar at what she calls University B. This seminar prepared teaching assistants to teach composition according to one interpretation of postmodern Foucaultian theory. The problem with this approach, according to Welch, was not so much the theory but the way it was approached by the directors of the program. Both the seminar and the composition class the TAs were being trained to teach were based on a confrontational pedagogy that demanded a conversion experience to this particular worldview. In such an environment she felt that active, productive debate was outlawed. "Doubting, debating, questioning, revising: these are the activities of so-called heretics and prodigal sons and daughters who recognize their familial/institutional histories but who also see heterodox and critically conscious readings of those histories" (400).

I think Welch uses just the right label for this issue. It's all about heresy. In the epigraph to this chapter, Said associates the Arabic word for *heresy* with the verb "to begin," the opposite of a completed worldview. The issue, then, is who represents orthodoxy—a fixed and completed worldview that limits possibilities—and who represents heterodoxy—an open, pluralistic worldview that encourages possibilities. In this larger discussion about the value of teaching writing, each side claims the higher ground of heterodoxy. The virtue of teaching writing is, ironically, located in heresy.

So what we find in our discourse on the ethics of teaching writing is a complex set of contrasts that have become more extreme as postmodern compositionists have pushed process to the limits. The intrinsic value of writing is set against the instrumental; the local, indeterminate, and transitory is set against the universal, definite, and fixed. Postmodern compositionists have created an ethics that effectively deconstructs the ethics of teaching writing by tarring all other ethics with the same modernist brush. But I believe that this postmodern ethics of teaching writing does not provide a sound ethics for our field. Thus we end up back at Faigley's postmodern "impasse," how to establish ethical authority in an antifoundational environment. We need to find a position that embraces both intrinsic and instrumental value, both the local and the universal—in other words, both the doubt associated with the postmodern and the certainty of modernism. This dilemma, the prelude to an archelogical dialectic, is, by now, familiar in this book. Using that dialectic, I will argue for a reconstructed postmodern virtue of teaching writing. And the key to this argument is heresy. What I propose, following Said, is a heretical ethics of beginnings. Indeed, an archelogical ethics lies *in* beginnings itself, in the very heresy of beginnings.

A Heretical God

To understand the role of orthodoxy and heterodoxy in modernity and postmodernity, it is helpful to look again, as I did in the previous chapter, at the work of David Ray Griffin and others who are attempting to reconstruct postmodernism on the basis of Whiteheadian philosophy and process theology. As a reminder, Griffin argues that modernity itself is defined by the death of the premodern, supernatural God, a God that was all-powerful, all-knowing, self-constituted, independent, deterministic, removed from the natural world. But in the reigning paradox of modernity, the attributes of this premodern God were taken on by the human self. The highly attenuated self of premodern ages became the God-like Self of modernity: the human Self as all-powerful, all-knowing, self-constituted, independent, et cetera. The sovereign God as conceptual center of the universe was displaced by the sovereign Self.

Postmodernism, for Griffin, is a justifiable and much needed reaction to the contradictions and unethical excesses of modernity. He acknowledges that many people are attracted to deconstructive postmodernism out of a moral outrage, particularly at the destructive consequences of modernism's totalizing worldview. As I discussed in the previous chapter, however, Griffin portrays ludic or deconstructive postmodernism not as a rejection of the modern, and thus a viable alternative to it; rather, he says that deconstructive postmodernism accepts the basic assumptions of modernism only to take these assumptions to their natural and absurd conclusions—the deconstruction of modernity. Therein, for Griffin, lies the problem. In their revulsion at the evils of modernity, deconstructive postmodernists have, in effect, thrown out the baby with the bathwater. Their distrust of the conceptual center at the core of modernity has been extended unreasonably to *all* conceptual centers. Thus, the irony of deconstructive postmodernism: in its drive to eliminate the evils associated with totalizing worldviews, it has also eliminated any firm distinction between good and evil, the basis for a moral stand *against* totalizing worldviews. There is nothing in deconstructive postmodernism that could be put into practice for positive personal and institutional change. Griffin says, "I cannot see how the effects of [deconstructive] postmodernism, were it to become a widespread outlook, could do anything to overcome totalitarian tendencies. It would probably only make things worse" ("Postmodern Theology" 39).

So how do we conceive of a postmodern world that possesses a moral center? I believe the key to finding that elusive balance lies in Griffin's characterization of modernity and deconstructive postmodernity. Because they are ruled by the same set of assumptions, there is no heresy in either. The orthodoxy outlined in the premodern, supernatural God is retained in modernism, though in the paradox-riven form characteristic of that worldview: the death of that God clears the field for the apotheosis of the Self. In accepting the assumptions of modernity, particularly the death of God and the consequences that ensue from that death, deconstructive postmodernity also retains that orthodoxy, though it does so in a way that exposes the paradoxes at the root of modernity: its disciples of doubt implicitly support modernist orthodoxy by offering no viable alternative to it.

Where's the heresy? Heresy must call into question the assumptions of orthodoxy. In this case, it must challenge the fixed and complete God that has founded the modern Self and has been taken to absurd extremes in deconstructive postmodernism. It must propose an alternative God, an unorthodox God, a heretical God. This is what process postmodernism does, and in doing so, it delineates what I think is a viable route around the postmodern dilemma: an unfixed and incomplete God that forms the conceptual core of a heterodox ethics.

Before I continue, though, I want to acknowledge that all this talk about God in the context of a scholarly discussion of teaching writing is bound to offend some readers, perhaps even most. To some it may represent a sacrilege in its application of the sacred to the profane. To others it may represent an unwarranted breach of academic integrity by ignoring the traditional separation between religion and our secular profession. I am sensitive to those accusations, and I apologize for any offense I give.

In my defense, however, I cite the precedent of Kenneth Burke's *The Rhetoric of Religion: Studies in Logology,* a work he describes as "concerned not directly with religion, but rather with the terminology of religion; not directly with man's relations to God, but rather with his relationship to the word 'God'" (v). For Burke, theology, or "'words about "God,"'" provides the ultimate case for "'studies in words-about-words,'" or logology (vi). For me, words about God provide a way of understanding words about the good, specifically the good of teaching writing. I have come to believe that any serious treatment of the good depends in important ways on conceptions of God. The two are intimately connected. Ethical value is a function of how we conceptualize the world and, as Griffin points out, how we conceptualize the world is influenced to a large extent by how we, implicitly or explicitly, conceptualize God—the premodern God, the modern God as Self, the postmodern death of God and Self. Griffin also observes that one of the problems that has plagued modernity is that it has attempted to construct its ethics without due consideration given to conceptions of God ("Introduction" 29). I want to challenge that modernist approach to ethics.

These words about God, then, are not an argument for any particular religion or religious orthodoxy. Indeed, that's the point: I am arguing for a heterodox way of understanding the good, a postmodern ethics that provides a basis for positive, authoritative values.

Process reconstructive postmodernism addresses the issue of the good directly by presupposing a sacred center of existence, a God, but not the premodern, supernatural God that has exerted such a negative influence on modernism. Griffin says that both deconstructive and reconstructive postmodernists agree that if such a God is not dead then it should be. "Both types of postmodernism find it repugnant to call upon this being, imagined to be the exception to all principles applying to things within the world, to patch up the holes in our account of these principles" ("Postmodern Theology" 48). But the similarities in the two postmodernisms' conception of God ends there. Instead of stopping at the deconstruction of the premodern-modern God, process postmodernists reconstruct a postmodern God.

Reconstructive postmodernism influenced by process philosophy describes a God that is, in contrast to the premodern supernatural God, a naturalistic God. The God of postmodern theology is not removed from the world but is in the world and of the world and is, thus, continuously being created *by* the world, by all the entities in the world. This is clearly not the premodern, supernatural God on which the modernist conception of Self is modeled. This postmodern God is forever unfixed and incomplete, which leads to the inevitable conclusion that the human self—and all other entities in the world as well as the world itself—is forever unfixed and incomplete ("Postmodern Theology" 48–49).

This heretical God is an insult to those who hold to the all-powerful Creator-God of Western orthodoxy and to the modernist Self modeled on that Creator-God. The naturalistic God of postmodern theology is limited, incomplete, nondeterministic, of the world and in the world and constantly subject to change as the world changes. It is a God that projects a world that is radically open, free of defining ends and thus the controlling vectors of history that are determined by those ends. It is a

God that shares with all the entities of the world the most important power of all, the power that in the orthodox tradition only God possesses—creativity. It is heresy to propose such a God.

The postmodern God is heretical also because it challenges the orthodoxy of deconstructive postmodernism. This latter accepts the basic modernist assumption of the death of God as an absence at the center of the universe, but instead of filling that absence with the Self as modernism has done, it extrapolates that absence to the Self as well as to any other candidate that would occupy the center. It therefore projects a fragmented self in a fragmented world. But I would argue that this is a worldview that is also fixed and completed; its orthodoxy of fragmentation offers no direction and no ethical force for positive change and growth. In denying the possibility of a totalizing center, fragmentation itself occupies the center, becomes a totalizing force. In contrast, reconstructive postmodernism proposes not only a center of the universe but, to add to the insult, a *sacred* center. It offers a heretical alternative to both the worldview of fragmentation and the worldview of totality. It offers a worldview based not on the beginning but on beginnings.

Naming and Knowing the Good: An Ethical God

This heretical God of beginnings also has significant bearing on the primary issue at hand, our understanding of the ethical value of teaching writing. Before I can address this value, however, I need to establish a reconstructed postmodern ethics on which to reconstruct an ethics of teaching writing, an archelogical ethics that is both and between the certainty of modernism and the doubt of deconstructive postmodernism. There are two important and related topics that ground arguments about ethics: one is what is the good and how can we know it, and the other is how the good may be enacted. Reconstructive postmodern theology offers its own approach to these topics. In this section, I will explore the first topic, the problem of naming and knowing the good.

The premodern solution to that problem depends on a supernatural understanding of the good as embodied in an all-powerful God; thus, the good can be known but it is always extrinsic to the natural world, subject to divine revelation. The modernist solution posits a universal good that centers not in God but in philosophical premises that have the same effect as God, premises usually residing in some form of utilitarianism; thus, the good can be known but it resides in external standards constructed by the Self. The deconstructive postmodern solution has been to deny any conception of a universal good altogether; thus, the good cannot be known because it is intrinsic to the little narratives of each situation, always local and transitory, ultimately relativistic.

Process postmodern theory offers a different solution to the problem of the good, what it is and how it can be known. It projects *(1)* a God that embodies the good and thus provides a moral center for the universe;

(2) a God that characterizes a good that is knowable by natural means; *(3)* a God that depicts a good that is both local and universal; and *(4)* a God that represents a good that is both intrinsic and instrumental. I will consider the implications of each of these statements in turn.

First, how can this postmodern God be both heretical *and* the moral center of the universe? A God that embodies the good would appear to be a reversion to the premodern God. But the whole idea of the good changes with the postmodern God. Whitehead conceived of the good not as moralistic dictates—commandments, laws, rules of behavior—but as an aesthetic quality captured in the process idea of enjoyment or enriched experience. "What the Divine Eros favors," says Griffin, "is intrinsically valuable experience—delight in existence" ("Postmodern Theology" 51). For process theologian Lewis S. Ford, the good is captured in the sense of beauty that is engendered in the harmony and intensity of experience. Harmony arises out of the adaptation of a selection of all previous creative moments that become one in each present actualization of self-creation; intensity is a product of variety and contrast inherent in God's initial aim for each moment, the possibility of new creation. "In effect, then, actuality is good insofar as it occasions an intrinsic experience of harmonious intensity" (L. Ford, "Divine Persuasion" 294).[9]

Thus, the ultimate good in the process universe is not moral but aesthetic. All there is is God's preference for enjoyment and God's aim at increasing the complexity of the universe, primarily because complexity leads to a greater awareness and thus an enhancement of enjoyment. The good, therefore, is that which maximizes the harmony and intensity of experience. In contrast to most philosophies and religions, the aesthetic in process thought is primary to the ethical. An act is ethical to the extent that it promotes the broader aesthetic good.[10]

The second consideration in this treatment of the good is how it may be known. The good is not invested in a supernatural God and thus knowable only through the vagaries of divine revelation. It is not represented in projections of the Self in supposedly external philosophies and thus knowable only as philosophical Gnosticism. And it is not strictly relativistic, local and transitory, and therefore not knowable at all. Instead, the good, as embodied by God, may be apprehended in completely natural ways. According to the reconstructive postmodern epistemology I discussed in the previous chapter, knowing is not limited to sensory perception. All that we know is based on experience, both direct and indirect, of actual entities. Thus, even things that do not possess sensory presence can be known, things like the good. We cannot, of course, perceive moral values directly, but we can and do perceive God directly in the initial aim for each actual occasion. "Moral values must be derived by perceiving another actuality, one who entertains these moral values favorably" (Griffin, "Postmodern Theology" 49). This is God, the actual existing embodiment of those values. Because the naturalistic God postulated by process postmodernists is an active and intimate participant in the natural world, God is actual, real, and fully experienced by all entities in every moment of existence. God as the embodiment of the good implies both that the good is knowable and that the good is one, not relativistic. Griffin does acknowledge that because moral values are derived from a direct experience of the good, there are multiple perspectives and interpretations of the good. The fact remains, though, that all entities experience the same embodiment of the good, so our appeals to what is ethical may be made on the assumption that the good is universally knowable even if it is not universally understood in the same way (49–50).

The third feature of a reconstructed sense of the good is that it is both local and universal. God is the source of value in the universe, but as Lewis Ford points out, this value is complex:

> For God thus serves as a dynamic source of value, personally responding anew to the concrete situation confronting each creature in turn, and providing it individually with its own particular initial aim. Through this ever ongoing activity God becomes the ultimate source for all value, though not one which is static and impersonal like Plato's Form of the Good. ("Divine Persuasion" 293)

The good, then, is both dynamic and ultimate. It is dynamic in the sense that it is always local, interpreted by God for each entity on each occasion, the ideal outcome for that occasion projected in God's initial aim. Like God, the ethical good is unfixed and incomplete, unique to the situation, each moment of existence self-creating, independent, indeterministic, its outcome dependent on a negotiation among the forces that mark the occasion.[11] God, however, is also the *ultimate* source of value and in this way redeems this localized ethics from the cynicism associated with radical relativism. The heretical God is, after all, still God, implying a oneness that deconstructive postmodernists would find suspicious, though it is by no means a totalizing oneness. It is in this oneness that a positive, postmodern ethics is possible.[12]

God, even this postmodern God, implies a good that transcends the local. As moral center, God has preferences for the universe, preferences that Griffin says "are identical with the preferences of an omniscient, all-inclusive, sympathetic participant, which is the best definition of the very meaning of our moral terms *good* and *right*" ("Postmodern Theology" 50). Process theologians, as I have shown, have attempted to describe these preferences in terms of enjoyment—complexity, intensity, and harmony; the good is that which enhances the aesthetic quality of enjoyment of each occasion and also increases the complexity of the universe. This ultimate good may be universal, but it is redeemed from the absolute and totalizing good of the Platonic Forms and other totalizing ethics by the very nature of both the heretical God and the universe, each unfixed and incomplete. The initial aim for each moment is an instantiation of a broad aesthetic good, unique to that moment but grounded in a good that transcends it.

Last, a reconstructed postmodern good is both intrinsic and instrumental. Each occasion is marked by the intrinsic enjoyment of self-creation, but this mode of enjoyment is only the first mode of the creative occasion. "As soon as this act of self-creation is completed, creativity swings over into its other mode, which is other-creation, efficient causation, or 'transition' (transitive or transuent causation)" (Griffin, "Postmodern Theology" 42). It is this second mode that holds more traditional moral implications, for in every moment of creation we and all other entities have the power to influence future moments of creation for better or worse. Because each act of self-creation is influenced by the many acts of creation of the past, those acts exert a power for good or ill on that self-creation; thus, each self-creation also has the potential to influence for good or ill future moments of creation, into infinity. It is in this way also that the good in reconstructive postmodernism may be interpreted as both intrinsic and instrumental, according to the two modes of creativity. Griffin points out, though, that the two "are not disjoined, because anticipation of contributing to future satisfactions increases the satisfaction of the present. . . . The divine aim is always for the present to be intrinsically satisfying, as well as a ground for a better future" (51).

What is the good and how can we know it? The heretical God of this reconstructive postmodernism embodies a good that is naturalistically knowable. This reconstructed ethics, then, offers a complex understanding of the good. As embodied by a heretical God, the good takes on the archelogical characteristics of that God. It is a good that is both one and infinitely variable, both divine and heretical, both local and universal, both intrinsic and instrumental. Thus, each pulse in the beginningless and endless existence of the universe forms itself in the dynamic intersection of the many and the one, of the orthodox and the heterodox, of the immediate and transitory and the fixed and complete, and of the immanent and the transcendent. It is at this intersection that a postmodern ethics may be reconstructed.

Enacting the Good: A Rhetorical God

The second issue that must be addressed in this reconstructive postmodern ethics is how the good is to be put into action: what does it mean to act in an ethical manner? Once again, the answer to that question depends to a large extent on the character of God. A heretical God is not only the embodiment of good but is also the model for how to enact the good. Unlike the supernatural God—isolated Subject, controller of destinies, enforcer of laws, demander of obedience, the God of premodern theology and the basis for the modernist Self—this reconstructed postmodern God is of the natural world and is thus a God whose participation in that world is limited by the nature of that world. God is, therefore, not omnipotent, not a controlling and deterministic power in the world. So how can such a God act for good and right in the world? "God acts by persuasion only," says Griffin, "and cannot do otherwise" ("Postmodern Theory" 49).

The concept of divine persuasion is crucial to an ethics based on process thought. In *Adventures of Ideas,* Whitehead says that divine persuasion, whose Western philosophical origin he attributes to Plato, is one of the most important intellectual advancements in the history of religion, "by reason of which ideals are effective in the world and forms of order evolve." The divine persuader exists in telling contrast to the typical Western conception of God or gods as all-powerful, imperial, ruling the world through coercion—obedience or else (213–14). In *Process and Reality,* Whitehead represents persuasion as the lure of God, "the eternal urge of desire" (522). Instead of the wrathful God of thunder, Whitehead describes God as "the poet of the world, with tender patience leading it by his vision of truth, beauty, and goodness" (526). Divine persuasion has continued to play an important role in process philosophy and theology.[13]

God is rhetor. Divine persuasion, then, is a way of understanding how a limited, naturalistic God, a God that depends on the individual processes of the world for God's own completion, has any influence at all in the world. As Lewis Ford points out, the power represented by divine persuasion, as opposed to coercion, is always indirect. The outcome of the persuasive acts of God inevitably depends on the degree to which any entity of the world actualizes God's persuasive aims ("Divine Persuasion" 288–90). The persuasive powers of God may be summed up this way: "God creates by persuading the world to create itself" (289).

As rhetor, God models for us what it means to act ethically in the world. This rhetorical God is an appropriate model because we are, like God, of limited power and exist in a world defined by the freedom inherent in self-creation. The only form of action available to God, the only force God can exert on the world for the good, is persuasive action. We human beings have the alternative of coercion, but process thought demonstrates that such action is always and inevitably futile because it runs against the nature of the universe, against the principle of self-creativity and thus the freedom that marks each moment, and against the principle of enjoyment, the principal vector of the universe. As modeled by God, persuasion represents the only mode of action available to us that corresponds to the nature of the universe. And as modeled by God, persuasion also represents what it means to act ethically in the world, that is, to influence the future for the good. Thus, divine persuasion not only forms a sound basis for understanding what it means to act ethically in the world but also provides the crucial link to an ethics of writing and, as I will discuss in the next section, an ethics of teaching writing.

God is rhetor. And as model for effective and ethical persuasion, God is rhetorician. It is important, then, to understand how God enacts the good through persuasion. The first movement in divine persuasion is the point at which the initial aim is projected against the objective content, the ideal against the actual. God begins each occasion by delineating God's desire for that occasion, the outcome that best enhances its enjoyment. This point, this contrastive movement, marks each actual occasion by establishing what is possible for that occasion, the hope, the potential for newness, both as a guide and a standard. The second movement in divine persuasion is the act of God in seeking to make the initial aim desirable. Whitehead, as I mentioned before, describes God as "leading it [the world] by his vision of truth, beauty, and goodness" (*Process* 526). For Cobb and Griffin, this movement is rendered as "a primordial envisagement of the pure possibilities. They are envisaged with the appetition that they be actualized in the world" (28). Lewis Ford turns to another Whiteheadian concept, Appearance. Though our culture seems to prefer Reality to Appearance, it is through Appearance that God creates desire for the ideal ("Divine Persuasion" 300–301). These images—vision, envisagement, and Appearance—provide an appropriate way to understand this second movement. It is because the ideal doesn't (yet and may never) exist that the difference between the ideal and the actual must be made desirable as a vision, what could be but isn't. This vision of possibility completes God's act of persuasion.

Divine persuasion works on a scale that is unimaginable to human beings. God participates actively in the being of every entity in the universe at every moment of an infinite existence. God experiences with each entity the objective content of each occasion and shares the all-too-prevalent disappointment at the difference between the ideal projected by the initial aim and the outcome of the occasion (L. Ford, "Divine Persuasion" 299). Human persuasion, of course, exists on a vastly smaller scale. But despite their dramatic differences, divine persuasion provides a powerful model for human persuasion, a way of understanding what it means to enact the good. I contend that one version of this model is already familiar to rhetoricians. We call it epideictic rhetoric.

After many years of being relegated to the dustbin of rhetorical history—despised for being impractical and mindlessly showy, an acute embarrassment to its more industrious siblings, deliberative and forensic rhetorics—epideictic has recently enjoyed a significant elevation in reputation.[14] This elevation is based largely on a fresh understanding of the role of epideictic in shaping ethical values of a community.[15] However, even this focus on epideictic as a source of value would seem to undermine the argument that it represents divine persuasion because epideictic has traditionally been seen as a *conservative* source of value, upholding or reinforcing shared values, defined by situations in which the audience and speaker begin and end with similar sets of values. This conservative role of epideictic within rhetorical tradition certainly does not appear to jibe with the potential for radical newness that characterizes the persuasion of a rhetorical God.

But it may be that our understanding of value in epideictic is incomplete. In "The Public Value of Epideictic Rhetoric," Cynthia Miecznikowski Sheard makes a convincing case for the revolutionary possibilities of epideictic, its ability to challenge values and generate change in ways that are remarkably similar to divine persuasion. Sheard acknowledges that epideictic has typically been portrayed as conservative, promoting adherence to currently shared values. She argues, however, that epideictic can also be revolutionary: "[I]t can be an instrument for addressing private and public 'dis-ease,' discomfort with the status quo" (766), "for overthrowing orthodoxies" (777), "for altering realities and for inspiring change for the better" (783).

I see in Sheard's treatment of revolutionary epideictic two rhetorical movements similar to divine persuasion. "Ultimately," she says, "the epideictic 'moment' is one of dis-ease" (790), which I see as related to the contrastive movement in God's initial aim. Epideictic can respond to situations of dis-ease that need to be restabilized, the goal of rhetorical forms such as the eulogy. But more important, epideictic can also serve to destabilize a situation in which dis-ease is deemed necessary, a prelude to change. Sheard says of epideictic that it not only

> participates in reality at critical moments in time but that it interprets and represents one reality for the purpose of positing and inspiring a new one. We could say that epideictic's relation to the world is reciprocal because such discourse both responds to and creates "opportune" or "critical" moments in time *(kairos)* that warrant critical attention and corrective action. (790)

These kairotic moments are a crucial part of epideictic, captured in the opposing ideas of praise and blame. Sheard rehabilitates this seemingly trivial traditional aim of epideictic by describing the power inherent in the tension implied in praise and blame. Of course, this contrastive moment has played an important role in rhetorical theory as *stasis,* the point at which the opposing movements of accusation and denial are brought into productive proximity, and more recently in Lloyd Bitzer's concept of exigence, "an imperfection marked by urgency . . . a defect, an obstacle, something wanting to be done, a thing which is other than it should be" (6). Exigence, like Sheard's epideictic contrast, is a rhetorical dis-ease, a strong sense of the difference between what is and what could be.

"But critique is only part of the story," says Sheard. "Ultimately, the critique leads to a vision that the audience is not only invited to share but exhorted to help actualize" (779–80). This vision is parallel to making the good desirable in divine persuasion. I think that what is especially interesting about Sheard's interpretation of epideictic is that she shows how the traditional liabilities of that rhetorical form—such as its tendencies toward poetic excesses at the expense of sober prose, exaggeration at the expense of the truth, and aesthetic delight at the expense of *logos*—are actually among the sources of its revolutionary power. Sheard says that epideictic can spark change by joining the real with the imaginary, the historical with the fictional in such a way that it "allows speaker and audience to envision possible, new, or at least different worlds" (770).[16] Rhetors can also take advantage of the linguistic possibilities in poetry and exaggeration and aesthetic delight to create forceful visions both of worlds that should be and worlds that should not be. For example, Sheard points out that "epideictic's questionable relationship to the truth" does not serve to diminish its value but is, rather, "the source of the imaginative, visionary potency" that many ancient rhetoricians referred to (774).

The challenge is to "make the vision appear as a viable and worthy possibility for the entire audience. Such epideictic discourse necessarily fuses the empirical and doxastic with the fictional and imaginary to accomplish its rhetorical aims" (780). Poetic figures serve to intensify the rhetoric, helping to create a vision that motivates the audience to make that vision a reality (780–81). Thus, epideictic rhetoric makes full use of the resources of language to make the good desirable: it "moves its audience toward a process of critical reflection that goes beyond evaluation toward envisioning and *actualizing* alternative realities, possible worlds" (787); "epideictic can be seen not only as an invitation and an opportunity for participation and engagement . . . but as a means of envisioning and urging change for the better" (788).

So what does it mean to enact the good? It means following the model of the rhetorical God. To show that this idea is not so far-fetched, I have used Sheard's excellent treatment of the revolutionary potential in epideictic rhetoric, which, as I see it, follows a pattern similar to that of the two rhetorical movements of divine persuasion. Persuasion is ethical insofar as it projects a contrastive vision that is grounded in the good, the ideal for the situation, against the actual; and insofar as it seeks to make the vision desirable by creating an intensity and vividness for that vision: family stories, folktales, gossip, jokes, signifyin', advice, informal logic, songs, sayings, rap, et cetera. Divine persuasion is key to an ethical rhetoric. Human beings have the consciousness to model a divine persuasion, to use it and theorize it. In the next section, I will discuss the ethical value of teaching writing as defined by divine persuasion.

Reconstructing a Postmodern Ethics of Teaching Writing

Let me return now to the controversy over the ethical value of teaching writing that has driven this exploration of reconstructive postmodern ethics. I started off by using Hairston, Bizzell, and Smith to outline the ethical dilemma found in ends versus means: first, that ethical value is intrinsic to writing, that is, the good of teaching writing lies in the process of writing as an end in itself; and second, that ethical value is instrumental, that is, the good of teaching writing is located in standards or principles external to writing for which the process of writing is a means to those ends. This dilemma has been radicalized by compositionists seeking a postmodern ethics of teaching writing, an ethics that deconstructs both ends and means as sources of ethical value by pointing out that each is invested in modernist "stories" or universal narratives. According to postmodern ethics, teaching writing is ethical to the extent that it reflects the nature of the postmodern interpretation of reality, values that are radically contingent, local, indeterminate, and transitory.

Though there is much that I find attractive in this postmodern ethics, I am also swayed by the leftist critique of that ethics, that in its suspicion of all worldviews, it denies the possibility of positive action on the basis of its critique and thus ends up supporting the status quo—if not making things worse. This problem led me to search for a source of ethical value somewhere between the deconstructive postmodern and the modern and thus to the God of process postmodernism. This heretical God is the moral center of the universe, which allows for the deconstruction of premises at the root of both modernism and deconstructive postmodernism and thus the reconstruction of new postmodern ethical premises. Now I will sketch out a reconstructive postmodern ethics of teaching writing based on a premise and three propositions that flow from that premise.

Premise: The ethical value of teaching writing is established in and defined by the divine persuasion of a postmodern God. A rhetorical God is more than a rhetor-God, a divine persuader; a rhetorical God is also a rhetorician-God, one that encourages and guides persuasion in beings of relatively complex consciousness. In other words, God is not only a persuader but also a persuader of persuaders, seeking to influence the future for the good by also modeling ethical persuasion. It is in this way that the postmodern God provides a model for writing teachers. We are also persuaders of persuaders. Our awareness of divine persuasion *as* persuasion allows us to "theorize" a human rhetoric modeled after our interpretation of a rhetorical God.

The first two propositions derived from this premise are based on the direct intervention of God in persuading persuaders, the two rhetorical movements of divine persuasion: placing the good at the center of each actual occasion in the contrastive moment of the initial aim and creating an appetite for the good, making it desirable. We can think of these as the two teachable moments in writing with the greatest ethical potential. The third proposition reflects the indirect effect of God on human persuasion, the writing teacher as rhetorical model for ethical persuasion.

Let me quickly add, however, that the application of these propositions to the classroom is by no means intended to be definitive and complete. All I can do here is rough out a few of the many possible implications of each proposition for a reconstructed postmodern writing class. These propositions are not meant to be exhaustive but generative.

Proposition 1: Teaching writing is ethical insofar as it encourages students to place the good at the center of their writing.

God places the good at the center of divine persuasion through the initial aim for each occasion. It is in this contrastive moment that God creates a threshold at each pulse of the universe, an openness to new possibilities. Without this particularized projection of the good, each occasion is destined to be but an iteration of previous occasions. This projection of the good generates the rhetorical moment and marks off the potential for ethical persuasion, for influencing the future for the good. It is this sense of the good that provides the ethical end or *telos* for writing, an end that is both and between the local and the universal.

Proposition 1 suggests that teaching writing is ethical to the extent that we writing teachers guide our students in making the good the focus of their writing. I try to establish the conceptual ground for this proposition by helping students grasp the idea that what they do, the decisions they make and the way they act, does indeed have a potential influence on the future, their own and others'. This concept may be difficult for those who have a highly deterministic understanding of the world, but I have found that most of my students see that such a worldview allows for no valid ethical action at all, only a despairing impotence. The main reason that writing is worth studying, I suggest to them, is that it is one of the most effective means we have for influencing the future.

Once students grasp this essential rhetorical concept and its importance in the study of writing, I can bring up the issue of the good: what we do is ethical insofar as we seek to influence the future for the good. Most students readily accede to this proposition. If what we do has a potential influence on the future, then that influence ought to be for the good. Of course the problem of naming and knowing the good is not easy. I place the good at the center of my writing course by approaching the good from both the local and the universal perspectives.

For the local perspective, I take my cues from *kairos, stasis,* and exigence, all leavened with Sheard's sense of the ethical value framed in the epideictic moment of dis-ease. I seek to show students that what drives a writing situation is the archelogical moment of the threshold marked by the contrast between what is and what could be and should be and that, furthermore, students have the ability to create these potent situations by generating this threshold event for themselves and for others. We analyze every writing situation we encounter in class, as well as others that are brought in for discussion, in terms of its exigence, the contrast between the objective content, that which is given, and the good that is possible for that particular situation. The point is to guide students in apprehending these moments of dis-ease that give writing its persuasive potential and ethical validity.

Following in the ancient rhetorical tradition of *stasis,* I encourage students to describe every writing situation by naming the contrastive elements that spark that situation, identifying the rhetorical nature of the good itself.[17] This contrast is what Sheard is getting at in her treatment of the epideictic moment in rhetoric, a moment of dis-ease initiated by some sense of the good and how it can be applied to make a specific situation better. This is also a version of the good that ludic postmodernists would not be terribly uncomfortable with. It is a good that is implicated in the process, in the particular situation, a good that is local, that both defines and is defined by the situation. Certainly, this view reflects one aspect of a postmodern sense of the good.

There is another aspect of the good that can play a role in the writing class: in process thought, the good that is applied locally is a reflection of a broader aesthetic good. Thus, the other means of placing the good at the center of our teaching is by addressing a universal sense of the good and its impact on our students' writing. This perspective is, of course, more difficult to deal with in the classroom. The local nature of the good is rendered teachable by the pragmatic or technical rhetorical tradition and its application in Sheard's understanding of epideictic. But the idea of a universal good, embodied best in Plato's understanding of rhetoric, represents a greater challenge to writing teachers. The idea of the universal good in process reconstructive postmodernism is complex, especially given the nature of God and the aesthetic nature of the good itself. As embodied by God, the good is both one and knowable but subject to many different interpretations by human beings. Thus, reconstructive postmodern theory makes it clear that we should not seek to impose any one conception of the good on our students; according to process principles, such imposition is coercion and thus betrays the essentially persuasive nature of the universe.

This does not mean, however, that we should give up trying to help our students think through the issue of the good and the way that good is instantiated in particular rhetorical situations. I do that by focusing on two issues that the students and I consider together at critical points during the course: whether there is a universal good; and whether there is a general direction for the world implied in this universal good. It's not unusual for students in the class to respond in ways that range from fundamentalism to anarchy. The point, though, is not to arrive at a consensus but to allow students to give voice to their conceptions of the good. One benefit is that they typically discover just how complicated ethics is, which enables them to see their own ideas of the good within the complex of many others. Another benefit is that as they discuss different and often conflicting conceptions of the good, they come to understand the absolute limits of coercion on the basis of their own sense of the good; all they have is persuasion. My primary goal, however, is to help them see that what they do in their writing is related to a sense of the good, that the way they define the good on a local level is typically a reflection of that broader sense of the good. All the writing they do has an influence on the future. What I hope they gain from our discussion of the good is an understanding of the ethical potential for their writing and the source of that ethical potential in both a local and a universal good.

Proposition 2: Teaching writing is ethical insofar as it guides students in making the good desirable.

For writing teachers, the issue of making the good desirable focuses largely on language. It is one of the most powerful means we human beings have at our disposal for enacting the good, making it desirable. Our relatively complex consciousness gives us the capacity to use language in sophisticated ways, a capacity that brings to our persuasion so much potential for good but also so much potential for ill. It is our responsibility, then, to counsel students in using language effectively to make the good persuasive. This effective use of language is, of course, ground that we are very familiar with, those so-called "niceties" of rhetoric.[18] We understand quite a bit about how to use language in such a way that it makes what we are saying attractive, focusing on the linguistic issues of structure, syntax and diction, and grammar and mechanics, as well as broader rhetorical issues of audience appropriateness, generating ideas, and informal reasoning. It is important, though, that we teach these linguistic and rhetorical forms within the context of the good that they are to make persuasive. Without this context, they lose their ethical import; they really do become mere niceties.

This position takes us beyond the ends-means arguments I looked at earlier to an ethics of language that is intrinsic to language itself, an ethics that places us writing teachers on more uncomfortable ground. Because language can be used unethically, even in the service of the good, it demands its own intrinsic ethical standards. The reconstructive postmodern ethics I described suggests that the most important standard is that language ought to be used as truly persuasive, as opposed to coercive. We don't have to look far to see how great the coercive potential of human language is. Language can be used to manipulate an audience, appealing to greed or fear; it can easily take advantage of selfishness or lack of self-esteem; it can be used for purposes of narcissism or exploitation. In short, language in and of itself can be ruled by the coercive will to power.

It is, unfortunately, very easy to fall into such abuses of language, justifying them as being in service of the good, the ends justifying the means. However, the model of divine persuasion suggests a good that is much more complicated than that: as persuasion, the means may be understood as an end in itself and thus have value in and of itself. Language has an intrinsic ethical dimension. As modeled by divine persuasion, human persuasion is unethical to the extent that it seeks to make the good attractive by using language as the will to power.

Acceptance of this message is very difficult for our students. When they believe they know the good for a particular situation, they want to use all the means of language at their disposal to lead the audience to that good. They find this approach modeled so powerfully and ubiquitously in advertising, political campaigns, product packaging, and so forth. They also want to be effective, to achieve their persuasive ends. We need to teach that achieving the good is not the only source of ethical value, that the way one makes the good attractive has ethical value in itself, ethical value that, I would argue, supersedes the former.

The model of divine persuasion suggests that writers enact the good in such a way that the enacting *is* the good. For writers, this means using language in such a way that it represents not the will to power but rather the ultimate powerlessness of coercive language, a reflection of the very nature of the universe. Writers' language should show that they recognize the freedom of the audience to create itself and indeed celebrate that freedom. It should reflect an empathy for the audience, a real attempt to understand its objective content, the influences that have brought it to this occasion. It should represent the essential interrelatedness of all beings, not separation. It should project the hope of persuasive openness, not the closed and rigid necessity of coercion.[19]

To be ethical, then, our teaching must seek a balance between using language to make the good as end state attractive and the possibility for good that resides in using language itself ethically. Both are ways of making the good desirable, and an ethics of teaching writing is both and between those two approaches. It is an archelogical solution that encompasses and seeks to find an ethical balance between instrumental and intrinsic value.

Proposition 3: Teaching writing is ethical insofar as writing teachers model persuasion by following the model of divine persuasion.

Proposition 3 offers a perspective on the ethical value of teaching writing that is different from the first two. Propositions 1 and 2 may be understood as relatively instrumental: both propositions presented the ethical values of teaching writing in terms of students, the objects of teaching. Value in these propositions tended to be extrinsic, ethical value located outside the act of teaching writing itself, that is, in the ends or the effects this teaching can have on students. This approach has been modeled on the direct interaction of God in the world via the initial aim.

But God, as I have argued, also acts to influence the world for the good *indirectly* by modeling ethical persuasion. God enacts the good most powerfully by modeling the good, what it means to be persuasive. Divine persuasion, then, is ethical not just in terms of what it does in encouraging greater intensity and harmony in the world; it is ethical also simply for what it is: it is how God acts in the world, a model for ethical action. It is in this role as model that God also teaches, simply by being persuasive, a persuader of persuaders.

Thus, in addition to the ethical value located in the instrumental effects we may have on our students, our teaching also possesses ethical value that is intrinsic, ethical in and of itself—insofar as we follow the model of divine persuasion. The effect of such teaching is inevitably indirect, but I believe we have a potent influence on our students' persuasion simply by the way we conduct ourselves as teachers-persuaders. We model persuasion for their imitation, much as the teacher-persuader–God models ethical persuasion. Teaching writing is the persuasion of persuaders. From this perspective, teaching writing is ethical insofar as it *is* ethical, a model for ethical persuasion.

One way to understand what it means to model ethical persuasion is to consider the two ethical moments of process thought—projecting the good and making the good desirable. The first suggests that to be a model of ethical persuasion, we need to place the good at the center of our own teaching. God models ethical persuasion in the act of projecting a particularized good for each actual occasion, a projection of an ideal that both defines and guides the occasion; the good is always what is best for that occasion. We can do something similar in our writing classes. One way of projecting the good is through the purpose of the course, which I see as a crucial expression of its ethical value. If we are to follow divine persuasion, this statement of value ought to reflect the ideal for that situation, what is best for the students in this particular context. It should be an ideal that is persuasive for the students. Indeed, one approach is to enlist the participation of the students in defining the purpose for the course. If they are not persuaded by the ideal, then the course becomes an act of coercion.

In my own first-year writing classes, I define the good this way: the purpose of this class is to help students to make the best of the formal learning situations they will encounter at college. My students readily see that most of these learning situations revolve around writing, from taking lecture notes to writing reports for major design projects. One of the chief ways their professors generate learning opportunities is by creating writing situations. Students can take better advantage of those learning opportunities by enhancing their understanding of the writing situations they will meet at college, what it is that creates and defines those situations and how to respond to them in ways that increase their learning potential. In our writing class, then, the good is defined by learning, the larger good of the university experience.[20] All the course decisions flow from that sense of the good for the students. For example, one result is that the writing course I teach is focused on the specific academic genres students are most likely to encounter at our university. My students and I start by addressing the value of the course, the good at its center, and return to that value throughout the course, with every writing occasion and with every evaluation of their writing. As a writing teacher, my best teaching strategy is to model ethical persuasion. And I do that in part by demonstrating for the students what it looks like to place the good, their good, at the center of my own teaching.

The other primary element in modeling divine persuasion is making the good desirable. We teach our students to make the good persuasive, but we can also have a potent indirect effect on our students by modeling this aspect of divine persuasion. At its most basic, such modeling means that we should approach our courses as an act of persuasion, seeking to avoid the coercion represented in the pedagogical will to power. What we do as teachers of persuasion is to try to make the good desirable, and we need to do so in ways that follow the model of the divine persuader so as to offer a suitable model for our students.

One way in which we can enact the good in our classes is to identify the moments of coercion that presently exist in our teaching and try to turn them into moments of ethical persuasion. Let me suggest a few possibilities. We could reconceive of our course as revolving around writing occasions rather than writing assignments, relying less on the threat of what happens if students don't participate in them and more on the positive potential in doing so. We could allow students to have a voice in creating course policies. We could involve our students more in the evaluation process by allowing them to establish criteria and engage in evaluation. We could stop attaching grades to our evaluations of students' writing, given that reward and punishment are associated with the will to power. We could approach our students' writing from the broader perspective of the value of the course, not enforcing a futile obsession with perfecting individual papers, which turns writing into mere performance. We can demonstrate to our students that we really do understand what it feels like to fall short of the ideal in a writing situation and help them see the benefit of anticipating the possibilities of future situations rather than dwelling on past failures. These possibilities represent only a handful of instances of the way we might conduct ourselves more closely to the model of divine persuasion.

Everything we do in the classroom to make the good desirable has a potential effect on our students. It's clear to me, however, that one of the biggest impediments in our attempts to ground our teaching in divine persuasion is inherent in the way writing classes have been institutionalized by colleges and universities. I am referring to the fact that most first-year writing courses are required for graduation, the overwhelmingly dominant moment of coercion in teaching writing. Thus, no matter what we do in the course itself, the very fact that students are given no choice but to take it tends to undercut our efforts at teaching the course in an ethical way. Because we cannot expect to model ethical persuasion for a captive audience, we ought to abolish the requirement.

This requirement has become a hotly debated issue among compositionists these days, as it has been off and on since its instatement back in 1885.[21] I want to make it clear, however, that I am not arguing for the abolition of writing courses but only for the abolition of the requirement. Indeed, I believe that doing away with the requirement could have great benefits for the first-year writing course. Without it, we would be obliged to make the course so good that students would be *persuaded* to take it, just as they are persuaded in various ways to take other non-required courses. We would have to design courses that are clearly guided by the students' best interests, in which the value for students is paramount. We would have to reach out to faculty in other disciplines and encourage them to participate in making the course so good they would advise their students to take it. As persuaders of persuaders, our teaching has intrinsic value insofar as it reflects divine persuasion and thus avoids the will to power. Requiring students to take our writing courses is unethical and therefore becomes an argument itself against the ethical value of the course.

The purpose of this part of chapter 9 has been to outline a reconstructive postmodern ethics of teaching writing, an application of a broader ethics based on the ethical and rhetorical nature of a heretical God. This ethics has been reconstructed by means of archelogical dialectic, between the unreasonable certainty of modernism and the debilitating doubt of deconstructive postmodernism. This reconstructed ethics places the moral good at the center of what we do as writing teachers. It provides a way out of the postmodern dilemma, achieving an authoritative ethical stance in an antifoundational reality by balancing the universal good against the local. It demonstrates that our teaching consists of both instrumental value and intrinsic value and suggests ways to guide students toward each form of value. It furnishes us with focal points for addressing ethics in the writing classroom, the two ethical movements that define both our teaching and our students' writing: the contrastive movement of projecting the good against the actual and the demonstrative movement of making the good desirable. And it shows us how to understand the productive relationship between teaching virtue and the virtue of teaching.

Conclusion

The ethics of teaching writing that I have proposed here means no less than that we be God-like as teachers of writing. What's more, it means that we seek to make our students God-like as well. Now I realize that on its surface, the import of these two statements probably surpasses even the ancient Sophists for extravagance in claims for teaching virtue and the virtue of teaching. As I've been saying, however, everything in this ethics of teaching writing depends on our understanding of God.

In the premodern and modern traditions and in the postmodern deconstruction of those traditions, being God-like means being supernatural, all-powerful, removed from the world, master of all there is, fixed and complete. What I'm proposing, however, is a *heretical* ethics of teaching writing based on the heretical God of process postmodernism. Being God-like, then, means being subject to the natural order of the world, limited in power to persuasion, in and of the world, and dependent on it for the cocreation of the world, forever unfixed and incomplete. *God-like* in this instance implies not an overblown sense of the self—in other words, the modernist Self—but a diminished sense of the self, one that is utterly integrated into and dependent upon all the entities of the universe.

What is the ethical advantage to being God-like? This heretical God still provides a moral center for the universe, a source of ethical value. Like the orthodox God, the heterodox God embodies and enacts the good. But whereas the orthodox God embodies the good as monolithic and subject to revelation, the heretical God embodies the good as both universal and local and also naturalistically knowable. And whereas the orthodox God enacts the good unilaterally, modeling a form of coercion, the heretical God enacts the good multilaterally, modeling a form of persuasion.

Thus, when I say that we as writing teachers should be God-like and should seek to make our students God-like, I mean something far different from the usual connotations of that term. For our students, to be God-like means that they would learn to be more aware of the good and of the power of writing to promote the good for themselves and others, creating dis-ease by projecting the good against the actual to generate a rhetorical and ethical situation. It means learning to use language with a consciousness of both the instrumental goal of enacting the good and the intrinsic good located in using language ethically. For us to be God-like means encouraging students directly to be ethical in their persuasion but also indirectly by modeling ethical persuasion for our students.

This ethics gives us a different sense of what it means to teach virtue and a different sense of the virtue of teaching. The key lies in the rhetorical God. Any act is ethical insofar as it follows the model of divine persuasion to influence the future for the good. In this way, a reconstructed postmodern ethics is essentially a rhetoric. I suggested earlier that one of the reasons teachers of advanced arts of language have had to struggle so to justify the virtue of teaching is that such arts have seemed remote from the apparently more obvious ethical value of other arts, from ancient shipbuilding to nuclear engineering. The ethical value of teaching those other arts seems incontestable because of the clear value they possess for the community. From the perspective of reconstructive postmodernism, however, it is the ethics of teaching persuasion that is incontestable because it is so closely associated with the rhetorical nature of ethics. As teachers of writing, the virtue of our teaching—along with its ethical impact and responsibility—is heightened considerably by the fact that we are teaching persuasion, we are persuaders of persuaders. Persuasion is at the core of this ethics. So the virtue of our teaching depends on our teaching virtue and teaching it virtuously.

This heretical ethics of teaching writing is an ethics of beginnings. It is an ethics of beginnings because it is formed in the archelogical dialectic of the modern and the deconstructive postmodern, of the instrumental and the intrinsic, of the universal and the local. It is an ethics of beginnings also because it depends not on a God of the beginning but on a God of beginnings. The fixed and completed universe of orthodoxy, with its definite beginning and end, projects a limitless God, one that need not rely on persuasion. But a limitless universe with no beginning and no end, only an infinitude of beginnings, projects a limited God, a heretical God. It is an ethics of beginnings finally because it is contingent upon the assumption that each instant of the universe is a threshold event generated in the contrastive moment at which the past is brought into disjunction with the future, the actual with the ideal for that instant. It is a universe in which each beginning holds the potential for persuasion that can lead to a new reality. This heretical ethics make sense only in a universe of beginnings.

Postface

Where does writing begin? Perhaps a more appropriate question at this point in the book would be, Where does writing end? or, How do you end a book on beginnings? I am reminded of Robert Denoon Cumming's remark about existentialists and endings: "Indeed, the difficulty we face with existentialism is to reach a conclusion that would be as warranted as an introduction" (399). Introductions are so full of possibility. Conclusions are so, well, conclusive; they bear the burden of all that possibility, the great expectations, all the suspects gathered in the drawing room in anticipation of the brilliant deduction, the song-and-dance finale that brings the crowd to its feet, the ultimate word on what it all means. Endings are hard, too. But it's not my job here to understand endings. Besides, it may indeed be true that the best ending is a return to the beginning.

Which is why I'm returning to the question of where writing begins. Clearly this book has been much occupied with beginnings. One way of understanding the role of beginnings here is to think of it in the context of the other key term, besides *writing* and *beginning*, in my initiating question—*where*. Asking *when* writing begins makes the question unalterably temporal and, by my lights, unanswerable. But asking *where* allows for a certain ambiguity in the question, which permits me to take advantage of the implications of "place" in *where*. Beginnings, then, may be conceived as a *topos*, a generative "place" from which to explore something.

Like any *topos*, beginnings describes a particular way of seeing, in this case a way of seeing that encompasses both deconstruction and reconstruction. Beginning is a double-faced, threshold experience; the principle of beginnings consists of a destabilizing movement and a movement toward a new stability that contains within itself the seeds of its own destabilization. Beginnings is a way of describing these contradictory though complementary movements and the ongoing potential for newness inherent in them. As a *topos,* beginnings brings this pattern into focus.

Applying this archelogical *topos* to writing has allowed me to take advantage of the deconstructive postmodern critique of composition to destabilize writing and teaching writing and thus to seize on the potential in that deconstruction for reconstruction. The *topos* of beginnings has permitted me to refigure writing as beyond the definiteness of text and recast the value of writing as intrinsic to writing itself, creativity understood as the mindfulness of being on the threshold of the known and unknown, the familiar and unfamiliar. In addition, the *topos* structures a reconception of teaching writing, a revised ontology, epistemology, and rhetoric as well as a heretical ethics. Writing is beginnings.

Asking where writing begins is a fruitful question in its own right, but I find it particularly intriguing in light of the broader question I mentioned at the opening of the preface: What is writing? I took that question from Sidney I. Dobrin, who uses it to frame his argument that we in the field of composition, we who claim to profess writing, have actually neglected writing itself. Though the shift of emphasis in our field from pedagogy to theory has certainly been beneficial, says Dobrin,

> [f]urther shifts are needed. . . . That is, our conversations need to shift from discussing ideas like public and private discourse to discussions of writing and rhetoric, not as representative of those discourses nor as something more nor less than those discourses, but as something independent of those discourses, as the thing itself of writing. (8)

It is time, Dobrin says, to turn our attention to theorizing writing, not writing as something else but writing as writing.

I agree with Dobrin. In addition to being pedagogical, we are a knowledge-making field, and we should focus our efforts on generating knowledge of that which most defines the field—writing itself. But how do we theorize writing? One approach, the one I've attempted here, is to ask questions about writing that have the effect of defamiliarizing it, that challenge our assumptions about it and thus provide the ground for reconstructing it. Asking where writing begins has done just that, has led me to resee writing from the *topos* of beginnings.

Theorizing writing need not be limited to knowledge making for its own sake. It can also be applied to pedagogy. In composition, it has long been our tradition to import guiding concepts for teaching from outside sources, from cognitive psychology, from social linguistics, from cultural studies, and so forth. But it may also be possible to project teaching strategies from within writing itself. In part 3, though I tried to keep my discussion of teaching writing from veering into *how* to teach writing, I lapsed at the end of the last chapter, addressing some implications of my ethics of teaching writing for pedagogy. Theorizing writing may provide the impetus for finding pedagogies derived from the study of writing itself.

We may also find that writing itself is such a richly inventive concept that it could be used to theorize other concepts. This usage would be a reversal of the usual vectors in composition that Dobrin describes. For example, instead of looking to theories of cultural (re)production to provide a basis for theorizing writing, we could apply theories of writing to question, revise, reinterpret cultural (re)production. We may very well find that writing itself provides a powerful lens through which we, and perhaps even scholars outside our field, could understand other concepts.

But there I go again, yielding to the urge to philosophize, putting on the ludicrously somber tones of one who knows, taking it all too seriously. This is, after all, a comedy. I suppose I should admit here at the end that one of my goals for this book has been to keep from looking completely ridiculous as I have tried to carry off the comedy of philosophizing with all the dignity I could muster. Indeed, I did end up playing all three of the comic characters implicit in Stephen North's rather derisive description of philosophizing I described in the preface—the accidental philosopher, the far-ranging forager, and the polemicizing preacher.

As I also said in the preface, however, comedy seems to me an appropriate overall methodology for this study of beginnings. It traditionally consists of a series of disruptions that ends with a wedding, a new beginning. Comedy portrays life as perpetual beginnings and its characters as perpetual beginners, caught up in a play of confused identities, of deconstructions and reconstructions. Comedy—like beginnings, like writing—undoes us. Perhaps this is where writing begins.

> What we call the beginning is often the end
> And to make an end is to make a beginning.
> The end is where we start from.
>
> —T. S. Eliot, "Little Giddings"

Appendix
Notes
Works Cited
Index

Appendix

Textbooks with No Explicit Mention of Beginnings

Bartholomae, David, and Anthony Petrosky. *Ways of Reading.* 2nd ed. Boston: St Martin's, 1990.
Carroll, Jeffrey. *Dialogs: Reading and Writing in the Disciplines.* New York: Macmillan, 1992.
Clippinger, Erle E. *Written and Spoken English.* Boston: Silver, Burdett, 1917.
Comley, Nancy R., David Hamilton, Carl H. Klaus, Robert Scholes, and Nancy Sommers. *Fields of Writing: Readings Across the Disciplines.* 3rd ed. New York: St. Martin's, 1990.
Daniel, Robert W. *A Contemporary Rhetoric.* Boston: Little, 1967.
Eastman, Richard M. *Style: Writing and Reading as the Discovery of Outlook.* 2nd ed. New York: Oxford UP, 1978.
Gilbert, Marilyn B. *Clear Writing.* New York: Wiley, 1972.
Giltrow, Janet. *Academic Writing.* Peterborough, ON: Broadview, 1991.
Gunning, Robert. *The Technique of Clear Writing.* 2nd ed. New York: McGraw, 1968.
Hardison, O. B. *Practical Rhetoric.* New York: Appleton, 1966.
Hartwell, Patrick [with Robert H. Bentley]. *Open to Language.* New York: Oxford UP, 1982.
Howard, C. Jeriel, and Richard Francis Tracz. *Each and All: Reading, Thinking, Writing.* Boston: Allyn, 1992.
Kiniry, Malcolm, and Mike Rose. *Critical Strategies for Academic Writing.* Boston: St. Martin's, 1990.
Neufeld, Jacqueline, Teresa Gaudiot, Mary Nevill, Terence Wiley, and Heide Wrigley. *It's Academic: A Multi-Skill Approach to College Writing.* New York: Holt, 1986.
Schuster, Charles I., and William V. Van Pelt. *Speculations: Readings in Culture, Identity, and Values.* Englewood Cliffs, NJ: Prentice, 1993.
Seyler, Dorothy U. *Read, Reason, Write.* 3rd ed. New York: McGraw, 1991.
Winterowd, W. Ross, and Geoffrey R. Winterowd. *The Critical Reader, Thinker, and Writer.* Mountain View, CA: Mayfield, 1992.
Zinsser, William. *On Writing Well.* 3rd ed. New York: Harper, 1985.

Textbooks Whose Beginnings Depend on Choosing and/or Limiting a Subject

Anderson, Thayle, and Kent Forrester. *Reading, Then Writing.* New York: McGraw, 1992.

Axelrod, Rise B., and Charles R. Cooper. *Reading Critically, Writing Well.* 2nd ed. New York: St Martin's, 1990.

Batteiger, Richard P. *Issues and Perspectives: Reading and Writing in Communities.* Boston: Allyn, 1992.

Behrens, Laurence, and Leonard J. Rosen. *Writing and Reading Across the Curriculum.* 4th ed. New York: Harper, 1991.

Berke, Jacqueline. *Twenty Questions for the Writer.* 2nd ed. New York: Harcourt, 1976.

Brooks, Terri. *Words' Worth: A Handbook on Writing and Selling Nonfiction.* New York: St. Martin's, 1989.

Calderonello, Alice Heim, and Bruce L. Edwards. *Rough Drafts.* Boston: Houghton, 1986.

Cooley, Thomas. *The Norton Guide to Writing.* Shorter ed. New York: Norton, 1992.

Cowan, Gregory, and Elisabeth McPherson. *Plain English: Rhetoric and Reader.* 3rd ed. New York: Random, 1982.

D'Angelo, Frank J. *Process and Thought in Composition.* 2nd ed. Cambridge, MA: Winthrop, 1980.

Dougherty, Barbey Nyce. *Composing Choices for Writers.* New York: McGraw, 1985.

Duncan, Jeffrey L. *Writing from Start to Finish.* San Diego: Harcourt, 1985.

Egleson, Janet Frank. *Design for Writing.* Beverly Hills: Glencoe, 1970.

Fencl, Shirley Crum, and Susan G. Jager. *The Two R's: Paragraph to Essay.* New York: Wiley, 1979.

Fulwiler, Toby. *College Writing: A Personal Approach to Academic Writing.* Portsmouth, NH: Boynton, 1991.

Fulwiler, Toby, and Arthur W. Biddle, eds. *A Community of Voices.* New York: Macmillan, 1992.

Garrison, Roger. *How a Writer Works.* Rev. ed.. New York: Harper, 1985.

Gefvert, Constance J. *The Confident Writer.* New York: Norton, 1985.

Genung, John F. *Outlines of Rhetoric.* Boston: Ginn, 1895.

Greenberg, Karen L. *Effective Writing.* 2nd ed. New York: St. Martin's, 1992.

Hall, Lawrence Sargent. *How Thinking Is Written.* Boston: Heath, 1963.

Heffernan, James A., and John E. Lincoln. *Writing: A College Handbook.* 2nd ed. New York: Norton, 1986.

Herrick, Robert, and Lindsay Todd Damon. *Composition and Rhetoric for the Schools.* Chicago: Scott, 1902.

Hoover, Merle M., and Henry Fisk Carlton. *Learning to Write.* New York: Ronald, 1929.

Kinneavy, James L., William J. McCleary, and Neil Nakadate. *Writing in the Liberal Arts Tradition.* 2nd ed.. New York: Harper, 1990.

McCrimmon, James M. *Writing with a Purpose.* 3rd ed. New York: Houghton, 1963.

Parker, John F. *The Independent Writer.* San Diego: Harcourt, 1986.

Proffitt, Edward. *The Organized Writer.* Mountain View, CA: Mayfield, 1992.

Ruggiero, Vincent Ryan. *Composition: The Creative Response.* Belmont, CA: Wadsworth, 1985.

Schenck, Mary Jane. *Read, Write, Revise: A Guide to Academic Writing.* New York: St. Martin's, 1988.

Scholes, Robert, and Nancy R. Comley. *The Practice of Writing.* 3rd ed. New York: St. Martin's, 1989.

Stevens, Martin, and Jeffrey Kluewer. *In Print: Critical Reading and Writing.* New York: Longman, 1983.
Stoval, Sidney T., Virginia B. Mathis, Linda C. Craven, G. Mitchell Hagler, and Mary A. Poole. *Composition: Skills and Models.* Atlanta: Houghton, 1973.
Tanner, William M. *Composition and Rhetoric.* Boston: Ginn, 1922.

Textbooks that Depend on Finding a Purpose

Bazerman, Charles. *The Informed Writer.* 4th ed. Boston: Houghton, 1992.
Bensel-Myers, L. *Rhetoric for Academic Reasoning.* New York: Harper, 1992.
Davidson, Donald. *American Composition and Rhetoric.* 5th ed. New York: Scribner's, 1968.
Dietrich, Julia, and Marjorie M. Kaiser. *Writing: Self-Expression and Communication.* San Diego: Harcourt, 1986.
Driskill, L. P., and Margaret Simpson. *Decisive Writing.* New York: Oxford UP, 1978.
Dutwin, Phyllis, and Harriet Diamond. *Writing the Easy Way.* 2nd ed. New York: Barron's, 1991.
Ede, Lisa. *Work in Progress.* New York: St. Martin's, 1989.
Flower, Linda. *Problem-Solving Strategies for Writing.* 3rd ed. San Diego: Harcourt, 1989.
Hunt, Douglas. *The Riverside Guide to Writing.* Boston: Houghton, 1991.
Jones, Alexander E., and Claude W. Faulkner. *Writing Good Prose.* 4th ed. New York: Scribner's, 1977.
Jones, Lois B., and Jane L. Evanson. *The Write Stuff: Writing for a Purpose.* Chicago: Contemporary, 1985.
Lutz, William, and Harry Brent. *The Critical Reader: Responding Through Writing.* New York: Harper, 1990.
McCuen, Jo Ray, and Anthony C. Winkler. *From Idea to Essay.* 4th ed. Chicago: SRA, 1986.
Schmidt, Gary D., and William J. Vande Kopple. *Communities of Discourse: A Rhetoric of the Disciplines.* Englewood Cliffs, NJ: Prentice, 1993.

Textbooks Whose Beginnings Depend on Discerning a Dissonance

Lauer, Janice M., Gene Montague, Andrea Lunsford, and Janet Emig. *Four Worlds of Writing.* 2nd ed. Cambridge, MA: Harper, 1985.
Young, Richard E., Alton L. Becker, and Kenneth L. Pike. *Rhetoric: Discovery and Change.* New York: Harcourt, 1970.

Textbooks Whose Beginnings Depend on Observation

Hairston, Maxine C. *Successful Writing.* 2nd ed. New York: Norton, 1986.
Hall, Donald. *Writing Well.* Boston: Little, 1973.
Hammond, Eugene R. *Informative Writing.* New York: McGraw, 1985.
Kane, Thomas S. *The Oxford Guide to Writing.* New York: Oxford UP, 1983.
Laib, Nevin K. *Rhetoric and Style.* Englewood Cliffs, NJ: Prentice, 1993.
Murray, Donald M. *Writing to Learn.* New York: Holt, 1984.
Paull, Michael, and Jack Klingerman. *Invention: A Course in Pre-Writing and Composition.* Cambridge, MA: Winthrop, 1973.

Notes

Preface

1. I am leaving out one of North's characteristics, his third, "Making Argument(s): The Communal Dialectic" (105–11). This one seems to me to be more a description of what he calls "The Great debate" than a particular feature of a philosophical argument.

Introduction: Beginnings

1. In fact, "Writing Assignments" may be seen as a direct precursor to "Inventing the University." The former uses the phrase that became the title of the latter. Referring to a student writer, Bartholomae says, "He must invent the university when he sits down to write" (300). I think it is significant that it was his exploration of beginnings that led Bartholomae to his larger understanding of student writing as inventing the university.
2. In the original, all of this quotation was italicized as a way of marking it as a significant definition of beginnings.
3. It is no accident, then, that Foucault's "The Order of Discourse" plays an important role in Said's broader argument. See especially Said 297–313. His argument concerning structuralism and poststructuralism is most directly articulated on pages 315–43.
4. The source for this material about Janus is the *Encyclopedia Britannica*. The two-faced image of Janus has proved a useful metaphor for contemporary thinkers. For example, Arthur Koestler presents what he calls the Janus principle, a way of understanding the units of a social organization as looking in both directions, facing downward and upward, composed of smaller units but part of a larger unit. This characteristic gives these units two opposing tendencies, both integrative and self-assertive (*Janus: A Summing Up* and *The Act of Creation*). Albert Rothenberg uses "janusian thinking," conceiving of two or more opposing thoughts simultaneously, as one of the characteristics of creativity ("Creative Contradictions"). Neither Koestler nor Rothenberg, however, uses Janus as a reference to beginnings.

1. At the Beginning: Starting Point

1. This classification is not pure, of course. It suffers from the problems endemic to all classification—imposing an order on material that is not inherently ordered. In addition, there is diversity within some of the categories.

2. Erle E. Clippinger's 1917 classic *Written and Spoken English* is an early example of this sort, with its focus exclusively on correct written presentation and correct grammar. See also Gunning and Hardison, similar approaches from the same era. More recent examples are Robert W. Daniel's *A Contemporary Rhetoric* (1967) and William Zinsser's *On Writing Well.* Rounding out the formalist texts with no treatment of beginnings is a set of workbooks composed of exercises that claim to heighten the student's awareness of the formal properties of written discourse (e.g., Gilbert; Neufeld et al.)
3. Bartholomae and Petrosky; Carroll; Comley et al.; Eastman; Giltrow; Howard and Tracz; Kiniry and Rose; Schuster and Van Pelt; Seyler; Winterowd and Winterowd.
4. William M. Tanner's *Composition and Rhetoric* (1922) offers these criteria: The subject should have personal interest for the writer and should be specific enough to allow the writer to write well and forcibly on it (68–69). Similarly, *How Thinking Is Written,* by Lawrence Sargent Hall, advises writers to choose subjects that are singular, unified, and limited (170–73).
5. See Herrick and Damon 27–31; Berke 15–16; D'Angelo 6–14.
6. See Duncan; Heffernan and Lincoln. Of all the strategies recommended for finding a subject, unfocused freewriting is the one mentioned most often. See also Calderonello and Edwards 23–25; Cooley 46–47; Greenberg 21; Stevens and Kluewer 4–9.
7. See Dougherty 19–33; Fencl and Jager 246–48; Heffernan and Lincoln 16–28; Proffitt 21–24; Stoval et al. 5–9. Several other books in my survey, beyond those mentioned above, treat the beginning of writing as choosing and/or narrowing the subject. Some mentioned it only briefly: Brooks; Cowan and McPherson; Egleson; Kinneavy et al. Others were rather vague about it: Fulwiler; Schenck. I have discussed McCrimmon's place in this category above.
8. In *American Composition and Rhetoric,* for example, Donald Davidson advises students to decide "*before you begin to write,* exactly what your guiding purpose is. It is best to state it briefly in written form, so that it stands before your eyes. This statement of the guiding purpose is often called the thesis sentence" (21).
9. See Dietrich and Kaiser; McCuen and Winkler 4–7; Jones and Evanson 2.
10. Many other examples of texts use this purpose-oriented approach to begin writing. Charles Bazerman's *The Informed Writer* begins with an analysis of the writing problem. The real problem of writing, he says, "is knowing why you are writing—that is, *knowing what you wish to accomplish with your readers in each particular situation*" (11). See also Ede 50, 96; Driskill and Simpson 1–15, 34; Dutwin and Diamond 1–9; Hunt 64; Lutz and Brent; Schmidt and Vande Kopple 6–20, 35–46.
11. In *Four Worlds of Writing* Lauer et al. follow in the footsteps of Young, Becker, and Pike by providing students with an explicit heuristic strategy for analyzing dissonances. Good writing, they say, begins with questions that emerge out of

    > a sense of discomfort or with feelings of exhilaration that arise when your expectations are either met or are exceeded, when your values are challenged by some situation, event, or experience, when your image of the world in which you grew up does not fit the world in which you find yourself. (24)

    Somewhat weaker forms of dissonance strategies may be found in Gefvert 28–30; Greenberg 21.
12. For a fuller treatment of this difference, see Carter, "Problem Solving."
13. Thomas Cooley also advises student writers to "embrace [their] preconscious selves"; he recommends a number of strategies: freewriting, looping, creating a topics pentad, and writing from reading (46–60). Other texts that rely to some degree on observation as a starting point are Hairston 29–30; Hall 180–81; Hammond 148–50; Kane 24–25; Laib 8.

14. In this article, Coe says that students should be taught both focusing strategies, to find and to narrow a contradiction, arguing that sometimes one is preferable to the other and that at other times students may need to use both in the same writing project. His strong criticism of the narrowing strategy is a response to its being used to the exclusion of the other strategy.
15. Though it is outside the boundaries of this survey of textbooks, another perspective on dissonance is one influenced by cultural studies. One example is a composition course described by James A. Berlin whose purpose is to help students become aware of the competing cultural codes that surround them, all of which are ideologically invested, and to encourage students to resist and negotiate those codes. Students begin by looking at their own experience but not just gazing in a general way at that experience. They search for the various ways that they have been defined by cultural codes and "then locate points of conflict and dissonance in the cultural codes" ("Poststructuralism" 30). These points of conflict, these contradictions, lead students to problematize their experience and then to deal with those problems in their writing, resisting or negotiating among these conflicting ideological determinations of the self ("Composition" 50–52; "Poststructuralism" 25–32). If inquiry may be loosely defined as a questioning that grows out of a perceived conflict, then the cultural studies approach may also be understood as the encouragement of inquiry, the act of questioning indicating an awareness of contradictory cultural codes and resistance to and negotiation of those codes. The point is to invite students, through writing, to enter into a critical engagement with their experience. Writing, then, is defined in terms of that critical engagement sparked by the writer's encounter with dissonance.
16. This argument is, of course, very familiar to us now in composition theory. It has been made effectively in, for example, James Porter's treatment of intertextuality ("Intertextuality") and Marilyn Cooper's model of an ecology of writing.
17. One of my favorite stories (perhaps apocryphal) about Einstein helps to illustrate the complexity of space-time. Einstein's wife was having a tea for some women students at Princeton, and they prevailed on him to explain his general theory of relativity. He said it could be summed up this way: If you drop a ball to the ground, you have no way of knowing whether the ball is moving toward the Earth or whether the Earth is moving toward the ball. One of the coeds pressed Einstein on this matter. She wanted to know what would happen if two balls were dropped at the same time on opposite sides of the Earth. Wouldn't that indicate that both were moving toward the Earth? Einstein didn't have a ready answer for her and said he would think about it. After the tea, he sought out the woman who had challenged him and said that he had the solution to the problem she put to him: there is no such thing as the same time in two different places.

2. In the "Pre-beginning": Origin

1. I am using *Webster's Third New International Dictionary.*
2. As I mentioned in the introduction, one of Said's central arguments is the distinction between origins and beginnings. The former is defined by continuity and linearity, the latter by discontinuity and nonlinearity.
3. For example, see Aristotle's treatment of the premise in the enthymeme in *Rhetoric* (154–57) and Toulmin's use of the warrant in *The Uses of Argument* (1110–17).
4. See Berlin, "Contemporary"; Faigley, "Competing"; and Berlin, "Rhetoric."
5. Flynn does acknowledge, however, that Bartholomae never labels his position or Elbow's. She applies the postmodern label to Bartholomae herself.
6. See "'Difference,'" "Ludic Feminism," and *Ludic Feminism and After.*
7. Despite these challenges to the resistance-ludic dichotomy, I think that the

distinction these labels describe still holds, providing a valuable way of understanding the postmodern in composition. Rouzie, for example, while taking an otherwise conciliatory tone in his article, reserves his harshest criticism for Vitanza and others on the ludic fringe: "Extreme forms of ludic postmodernism in composition studies—such as Victor Vitanza's 'third sophistic rhetoric'— . . . challenge the existence of or at least any access to material realities, making activist intervention ineffective and, more seriously, making them complicitous with dominant hegemonic thought structures" (647). Davis refers to Ebert's dichotomy as "a distinction in which many American feminisms operate (even if they don't accept Ebert's terminology or her brand of materialist feminism)" (19). Moreover, it is highly doubtful that Ebert and other "red" postmodernists would find Davis's ludic brand of politics an acceptable alternative to their own.

8. Kent's *Paralogic Rhetoric* provides a rich context for the postprocess theory of composition described in his introduction to *Post-Process Theory: Beyond the Writing-Process Paradigm*.
9. In addition to representing the ludic in composition, these three have closer connections, Worsham and Davis having studied with Vitanza at the University of Texas at Arlington. I hesitate, however, to portray them as a school of thought. Though obviously influenced by Vitanza, Worsham and Davis bring to their scholarship their own unique and engaging perspectives on the postmodern in composition.
10. See Barrow and Tipler 27–122; Hurlbutt; Dennett 23–84. Dennett's *Darwin's Dangerous Idea* provides a full-scale argument against natural theology. However, John Polkinghorne's *Belief in God in an Age of Science* makes an interesting case for the validity of a new conception of natural theology, one that is influenced by contemporary science (1–23).
11. The second is that even if something essential does exist, we cannot know it. And the third is that even if we can know it, we cannot communicate it (Freeman 128–29). These pronouncements support Vitanza's second and third countertheses.
12. Some of the work in axiology has sought to establish taxonomies for sources of value; for a broad overview, see Frankena. Many axiologists, however, have argued for intrinsic value or extrinsic value. Examples of arguments for intrinsic good may be found in Garnett; Parker; Neville, *Reconstruction* 94–100. Examples for extrinsic value are Dewey; Pepper.

3. In the Beginning

1. In his commentary on *bereshit,* Ramban is contesting another understanding of the term associated with the eleventh-century commentator Rashi. Rashi argued that the first line of the Torah was not about the beginning at all. As evidence, he cites a midrashic interpretation of *reshit* as referring to the Torah or Israel, creating a very different sense of the Hebrew: "'For the sake of that which is *reshit* [Torah and Israel] G-d created'" (*Ramban* 20).
2. For a description of the typical interpretation of this passage as a theodicy and a persuasive argument against that interpretation, see Brueggemann 40–44.
3. A number of books probe the links between the Genesis story and big bang theory. See, for instance, Hyers; Jaki; Monsma; Polkinghorne, *Science and Creation;* and Schroeder.
4. Rozental's theory was more fully developed by another Russian physicist, M. A. Markov, who proposed a mathematical model for a perpetually oscillating cycle of universes with no ultimate beginning.
5. In the laboratory, when certain particles align they create a cylindrical magnetic field that attracts other particles and creates a dynamic vortex that generates an electromagnetic field. This field results in a pattern of plasma ropes or filaments. In the last several years, accumulated data suggest that our solar system, our

galaxy, our supercluster of galaxies, and clusters of superclusters are aligned in a similar filamentary pattern, indicating that similar electromagnetic forces are responsible for shaping our universe (Lerner 39–52, 214–80).

6. A small sample of recent challenges to the necessity of a big bang include a thermodynamic cosmology that dismisses gravity as the major physical principle for understanding the universe (Criss and Hofmeister); a universe that is spatially flat and emerges not out of a singularity but out of empty space (Saa et al.); and mathematical models for a five-dimensional universe that supports the big-bounce theory (Liu and Wesson).

7. For information about responses to the big bang theory, see Rhook and Zangari. Regarding the revival of steady state theory, see also Balashov; Mitchell.

8. This translation is from the New International Version (Grand Rapids: Sondervan, 1986).

9. This particular translation heightens the ambiguity further in a note that says that a possible reading of the beginning of verse 2 is, "Now the earth *became* formless and empty." This is a significantly different understanding of creation from that suggested by the verb *was*. See Drees 257–58.

10. Both of these versions are influenced by Rashi's reading of *bereshit* (see note 1). Rashi claimed that the primary purpose of this passage was not to describe the order of creation (*Torah* 18).

11. For a description of these early Christian dualistic heresies, see Drees 264; L. Ford, "Contrasting Conceptions" 98.

12. Thomas Aquinas offers an interesting solution to the problem of the beginning in time, one that balances religion and philosophy. He often dealt with the issue of the beginning in his writings, even producing a special treatise on it, *De aeternitate mundi (On the Eternity of the World)*. Profoundly influenced by Aristotle, Aquinas's argument, simply put, was that the world was indeed created *ex nihilo* but that such an act of creation did not necessarily mean that it was created *in time* and *literally out of nothing*. Creation, as Aristotle reckoned it, implied change. For Aquinas, creation is more a representation of a relationship, a one-sided dependence on God the Creator who caused the existence of the creature. There is no need, logically, for such a relationship to require a beginning in time. If creation is about the creature's absolute dependence on the Creator, this dependence, Aquinas said, is just as strong whether or not there is an absolute beginning. A universe without a beginning must still have a divine First Cause. Though he does admit that biblical revelation inclines one toward belief in an absolute beginning, he says that such a belief rests on faith alone; there can be no rational demonstration of a beginning of the world (Vollert 13–17). Thus Aquinas offers what William Lane Craig calls a third way, an alternative to the medieval dichotomy between theology and philosophy: "*creatio ex nihilo* does not, in Aquinas' view, entail a temporal beginning of the universe" (476).

13. For example, Karl Barth in his massive *Church Dogmatics* argues for an ontological, as opposed to temporal, interpretation of creation. His position is that the various cosmologies that are described in the Bible are always a reflection of the myths appropriate to the time and place of their origin and therefore are part of a worldview that is alien to Christian faith. Thus, stories of creation must be understood as having nothing to say, either directly or indirectly, about the nature of the cosmos (6–11). The significance of creation stories for Barth lies in their dual structure, the relationship between heaven and earth, the divine and the human, a relationship of dependence, mercy and goodness, and love and praise (11–19). "Thus," says Barth, "we lose nothing and gain everything if we resolutely refuse to make the doctrine of the creature a doctrine of the universe, a cosmology" (19). The creation stories in the Bible are not about the physical nature of the universe but about humankind and its relationship with God.

Paul Tillich says, "The doctrine of creation is not the story of an event which took place 'once upon a time.' It is the basic description of the relation between God and the world" (qtd. in N. Young 107). That relationship is one of continuity between Creator and creature. Creation is about God's originating, sustaining, and directing creativity in the lives of human beings (N. Young 107–13). In Rudolf Bultmann's existentialist theology, it is necessary that all statements must be concerned with people's lives, their existence. "Statements which speak of God's actions as cosmic events are illegitimate. The affirmation that God is creator cannot be a theoretical statement about God as *creator mundi* in a general sense. The affirmation can only be a personal confession that I understand myself to be a creature which owes its existence to God" (qtd. in N. Young 130). The narrative of creation, then, is not about the beginning of the cosmos but about the present existence of humankind (128–33). Wolfhart Pannenberg also dismisses the creation story of Genesis 1 as "basically a *mythological* concept." In myths of creation, the cosmos is considered to be fully ordered at the beginning. This view is antithetical, he says, to Christian theology: "The continuous activity of God in the world, then, is not only conservation and government of what was created in the beginning, but should be envisioned in terms of a *continuous creative activity,* corresponding to the unity of one single, eternal act of creation that comprises the entire history of the universe" (Pannenberg 301–2).

14. For example, William Barclay says that referring to Jesus as being of the house and lineage of David would be meaningless to most of this Greek audience, having no idea who David was or why any familial relationship between Jesus and David would be of significance (xxi).

15. For example, *Harper's Bible Commentary,* Sloyan, and *The Interpreter's Bible* note the connection to Genesis 1.1. Barclay and Filson leap over *archê* to *logos.*

16. The Septuagint does, however, translate *bereshit* as *en archê.* I'm not sure why Ehrhardt doesn't mention that parallel. Certainly, John's Greek audience would probably not have seen the parallel; there would have been little opportunity or desire for them to have read the sacred texts of the Jews, even though they were available in Greek. Perhaps John meant to use a term that would resonate with both a Jewish audience familiar with the Septuagint and a Greek audience who was not.

17. After Aristotle, Ehrhardt says, *archê* as a philosophical issue became much less important. It continued, however, to be prominent in medicine, which explored the link between the generation of both the cosmos and the fetus (161–62); in Greek apocalyptic literature (162–71); in the mysticism associated with revivals of Pythagoreanism and Orphism (172–73); and in the magical incantations of various mystery religions that sought to create links between the worlds of the empirical and the transcendental by using various ritualistic accounts of creation myths (175–89). The need to find solace in mysticism and mythology, Ehrhardt notes, was a result of the political and economic difficulties in the Greek world during the last generations of the millennium. The mysticism and mythology, he points out, were founded on beliefs concerning the beginning that were supported by their deep roots in the ancient philosophical issues. "The solution of the spiritual problems which faced men of that time could only lie, it was felt, at the 'beginning'" (190).

18. Ehrhardt's major insight is interesting, though not crucial to my study. He looks at the opposing theories of *archê* in first-century Jewish theology. The school of Alexandria, as represented by Philo, tended to interpret *archê* in a neo-Platonic way, with the emphasis on the infinite world. The Palestinian Jews, such as Paul of Tarsus, meanwhile, saw *archê* more in the Aristotelian way, as a causal principle with emphasis on the empirical world. Both of these perspectives grew out of Greek philosophy. Ehrhardt says that much Western religious thought has been given over, unsuccessfully, to trying to reconcile the two positions, the other-worldly and the this-worldly (199–205).

19. I am using the plural form *beginnings* but conceive of it as singular and use it with the singular form of the verb. Beginnings denotes the principle of *archê.*

20. Theologian Paul Tillich captures this sense of *archê* in his use of *kairos,* an important concept in his understanding of the influence of God in history. Tillich describes instances of *kairos* associated with Christ as "the times in which the eternal breaks into the temporal" (164). I think this parallel between *archê* and *kairos* is more than coincidental. *Kairos* also may be defined as the creative potential generated by the intersection of opposing worlds (see my "*Kairos* and *Stasis*" for a full treatment of these features of *kairos*). I think there is an intimate connection between these two concepts: *kairos* is an archelogical principle and *archê* is a kairotic principle.

21. Translated by A. L. Basham, *The Wonder That Was India,* 248.

4. Dialectical Beginnings

1. Burke is synthetic, as usual, in his understanding of dialectic. He says that all the definitions he lists are in some way variants of three broad principles of dialectic: merger and division, opposing pairs, and transcendence.

2. G. E. L. Owen describes Plato's dialectic as the "master-science" above all others, even mathematics (214). Owen says that early in Plato's career, dialectic revolved around "trapping an opponent into self-contradiction" but that later dialectic became much more a self-conscious method, focusing "on serious paradoxes of the sort developed in the *Parmenides, Theaetetus,* and *Sophist.*" This self-consciousness was a result of Plato's recognition of the problem of oversimplification, the risk of missing the true complexity of the world. Owen also observes that the reason Plato considered dialectic above all other sciences was that he believed in a connection between the dialectical method and the Forms—a matching of method and the stable realities of the world (215). In the *Topics,* Aristotle describes dialectic as "a method from which we shall be able to syllogize about every proposed problem on the basis of generally accepted opinions *[endoxa]* and while upholding an argument ourselves say nothing self-contradictory" (Kennedy 289–90). Kennedy describes Aristotelian dialectic as a process in which one student would state a thesis and another student would try to refute the thesis through questions. "If successful, the interlocutor led the respondent into a contradiction or logically undefensible position by means of definition and division of the question or by drawing analogies" (26).

3. See Kainz 14–21; Harris 157–65; Rescher 61–68.

4. See Wilkerson 3–5. Kant's solution to this problem is based on what he called his "Copernican revolution" in epistemology, a decentering of our knowing of the world. By demonstrating that knowledge depends on both *a priori* and empirical knowing, Kant shows that we are not merely passive observers of the world, knowing only through our senses, as radical skeptics like Hume argued. Our innate *a priori* knowing means that we cannot ever know the thing in itself but only its appearance. Indeed the phenomenal world depends our own cognitive apparatus (Kant 22–23).

5. There is also, as this language suggests, a strong moral dimension to Kant's critique of metaphysics. He says that he

> found it necessary to deny knowledge, in order to make room for faith. The dogmatism of metaphysics, that is, the preconception that it is possible to make headway in metaphysics without a previous criticism of pure reason, is the source of all that unbelief, always very dogmatic, which wars against morality.

He further posits that his critique is directed especially at "enquiring youth" so that they may be discouraged from taking up the wastrel's game of dogmatic metaphysics and might instead take up "the better-established sciences" of mathematics and physics (29–30).

6. Even after all the scientific advances since Kant's time, the question of a beginning in time still cannot be resolved with certainty by means of empirical

evidence, as the previous chapter argued. Perhaps this issue is destined to remain one of the antinomies of pure reason. I prefer, however, a conclusion that is not as despairing as Kant's. For me, the lack of empirical evidence gives us the freedom to choose the answer that is the most beneficial in terms of a larger worldview. Mine is that there is no beginning in time.

The other three antinomies of pure reason are *(2)* that every substance is made up of simple composite parts and that there is nothing simple in the world; *(3)* that all things act freely and that all things act according to the laws of nature; and *(4)* that there exists a necessary being as a part of the world and is its cause and that a necessary being exists nowhere in the world as its cause (396–421).

7. For the sake of convenience, my own and the reader's, I have taken most of my citations of Marx's writing from the one-volume work *Karl Marx: Selected Writings*. For citations that were not in that volume, I have used the *Collected Works* (Marx and Engels) and *Capital*.

8. Marx cites Feuerbach's critique of religion as the source for the idea of the movement from the material to the ideal and back to the material. See also the fourth of Marx's "Theses on Feuerbach" (*Karl Marx* 157).

5. Archelogical Dialectic

1. Some scholars place the real source of this vision of Marx in his friend and interpreter Friedrich Engels, who, after Marx's death, marketed a deterministic brand of Marxism based to a large degree on the teleological dialectic of the later Hegel. Terrell Carver says that Engels had a far greater impact on what we know as Marxism than Marx (96–97). Carver traces the origin of historical materialism to an 1859 review of Marx's *A Contribution to the Critique of Political Economy* that Engels wrote at Marx's request. That review, in which Engels first used the phrase *"materialist conception of history"* (98), revealed an Engels who was becoming obsessed with the idea of a methodology that would reveal what Carver describes as "an inner coherence" of history (103). Carver says that Engels's idea was based on the grave misinterpretation of both Hegel and Marx, thus emphasizing a gross historical methodology over the subtleties of substance in Marx's arguments about political economy (108; 114–15).

According to H. B. Acton, Engels set forth what later became known as dialectical materialism, the application of dialectical theories to the natural world, in works such as *Anti-Dühring, Dialectics of Nature,* and *Ludwig Feuerbach and the Outcome of Classical German Philosophy.* Engels established three natural laws that could be applied to all facets of existence, natural as well as mathematical, musical, philosophical, historical, et cetera. Acton says he was extending Hegelianism to a kind of positivism that was based in the natural sciences in the belief "that knowledge of the world can be obtained only by the methods of the special sciences" (392–94).

See also Loewenstein 125; Warren 90; and Wilde, *Marx* 2.

2. Alvin Gouldner describes a "critical Marxism" and a "scientific Marxism"; Warren a "positivist marxism" and a "dialectical marxism"; Sherover-Marcuse a "dogmatic Marxism" and "dialectical Marxism"; Loewenstein "science" and "dogmatism." Marxian theorists tend to line up according to these two camps. In the former camp are Engels, Lenin, Bukharin, Althusser, Balibar, and Godelier; in the latter camp are Korsch, Gramsci, Lukács, Merleau-Ponty, members of the Frankfurt School, Leszek, and Kolakowski. See Warren 70–89; Wilde, "Logic" 292–94.

3. This is obviously an oversimplification of the complex relationship between Kierkegaard and Hegel. For a fuller treatment of that relationship, see Hannay 19–53.

4. Desmond fits into neither the Kierkegaardian nor Marxian branch of dialectical theory. He may be described as more Hegelian, but that would overstate his

connection to Hegel. *Art and the Absolute,* Desmond's first book, may be seen as a defense of Hegel in the light of the deconstructionist portrayal of Hegel's tendency toward totalizing transcendence. Desmond says he wrote that book in reaction to what he saw as the silliness of the vastly overstated and small-minded attacks on this complex philosopher ("Being Between" 325–26). In later works, like *Desire, Dialectic, and Otherness,* which I discuss here, he offers his own respectful critique of Hegel.

5. This philosophy is explored in *Desire, Dialectic, and Other* and other books and articles. See particularly *Philosophy and Its Others, Being and the Between,* and "Being Between."
6. See, for example, Porush 58; Hayles, "Introduction" 1; Kellert ix–x.
7. Besides Gleick, I recommend two other introductions to chaos theory that nonscientists can understand, Kellert and Lorenz. About the role of weather in the making of the science of chaos, see Gleick 11–31; Lorenz 77–110. Also, Lorenz presents a copy of his original paper that spawned the concept of the butterfly effect, 181–84.
8. See also Kellert 20–22; Lorenz 25–76. A keyword search reveals how extensively bifurcation theory is used in mathematics, science, and engineering.
9. He also points out another paradox. In the classical sciences, the concept of time is literally reversible, meaning that the world is static, never changing, the same physical laws and properties of the universe holding true no matter what is the direction of time. Time, indeed, is merely a human illusion. This view is contrasted with entropy once again, which portrays a universe that is slowly running down, so that time can go in only one direction. The problem, then, is how time can be both reversible and irreversible (xxix).
10. Ruf does not explicitly use Prigogine's sense of chaos, but his understanding of chaos is quite similar to Prigogine's.
11. Indeed, certain philosophers of science and theologians have seized on chaos theory as a way to understand the interwoven relationship between contradictions. David Steenburg, for example, describes chaos theory as "the interpenetration of determinacy and randomness, order and chaos" (449). He uses chaos to argue for the interpenetration of three other oppositions that he hopes will lead to a postmodern redefinition of science: science and humanism, science and aesthetics, and science and philosophy. Also, physicist and theologian John Polkinghorne uses chaos theory to argue that the world "is open in its process, that the future is not just a tautologous spelling-out of what was already implicit in the past, but there is a genuine novelty, genuine *becoming* in the history of the universe" ("Chaos and Cosmos" 107–8). Chaos theory provides a way to understand the interrelationship between the lines from simplicity (particles) to complexity (complex biology) and vice versa (110); and between the material and the mental. Chaos theory allows us to understand the relationship between top-down intentional causality and the bottom-up free will created by an open universe (115–16). The result is an understanding of God as both being and becoming, eternal and in time (116–17).
12. Whitehead's cosmology does not allow for an absolute beginning of the universe. Because every moment of existence is constructed of previous moments of existence, there can be no point at which anything was constructed out of nothing. This is what Whitehead means when he emphasizes that God exists "not *before* all creation, but *with* all creation" (521). He is speaking both physically and theologically. For further explanation of this aspect of Whitehead's cosmology, see Cobb and Griffin 65–67; Griffin, "Creativity" 77.

6. Defining Writing

1. Among the contraries that Elbow identifies are doubting and believing, constraints and freedom, individualism and community, being creative and being critical, careful and careless thinking, and taking authority and giving authority.

2. Thomas E. Recchio makes a similar argument about what becomes of the writer's authority when we teach an uncritical acceptance of conventions. In academic writing, he says, authority lies in "a collision between the personal and the disciplinary" (132). The provisional nature of such authority "results from a disjunction between a determinate sense of convention and the indeterminate feel of writing" (132). A writer's authority, then, comes neither from a dominant sense of the self in writing nor from the conventions of the discipline but from "a contested middle ground" between the two (132). Thus he makes an archelogical argument regarding authority in academic discourse: "I came to see that the critical dimension of writing, the place where authorship can be realized, lies on the boundary between a discipline and a person, between convention and experience" (134).
3. Aristotle sets out this procedure for definition in Book 13 of *Posterior Analytics*. See particularly 97a23–97b25. Aristotle posits two movements in the act of definition. The first is the movement to kind or classification into a higher class. The second is the movement to differentiation or distinguishing what is being defined from other members of the class (66–67).
4. Davis offers a dichotomy similar to utterance and text with her critique of the myths of common-being, those foundations in communal belief systems that writers are typically encouraged to use as starting points. The effect of these myths is that "the Unthinkable remain[s] unthinkable." Davis prefers "writing that takes off from *anywhere* but 'common ground,' writing that pushes the limits of communal knowledge" (13–14). The two kinds of writing Davis describes here are tantamount to utterance and text and, in the terms I use later, scribing and writing.
5. Up to this point, I have been using *text* as a generally negative term because of the one-dimensional perspective it tends to give to writing. Dillon and Lotto's use of *text* is quite different, however, especially in the understanding of it as undermining the social and linguistic status quo signified by "utterance." In this way, I see "text" as linked to the postmodern suspicion of text. It emphasizes the complexities of writing. "Text" and "utterance" indicate two kinds of writing, capturing a distinction that is similar to the one in postmodern and modern writing.
6. I suspect that it would be possible to find a parallel set of terms for spoken discourse, such as articulating and talking. The point is that "text" and "utterance" can be applied to spoken discourse in a way that is similar to the way I am applying it to written.
7. See Onions; Barnhart.

7. Valuing Writing

1. See Boorstin 40–46.
2. Plato's long digression on madness in *Phaedrus* and his ironic portrait of the "mad rhapsodist" in *Ion* are important sources of this tradition. In the Middle Ages, the idea of the mad poet was put forward by Statius, Nemesianus, and Fulgentius, who "gave poetry special privilege as divinely inspired" (Burwick 3).
3. For contemporary studies that focus on the link between creativity and madness, see Andreasen, Becker, Ludwig, Ochse, Prentky, and Rothenberg, *Creativity*. I find the research of Hans J. Eysenck particularly interesting. He shows that there is little correlation between creativity as a personal trait, which tends to be distributed along a bell curve, and actual creative achievement, which tends to align itself along a J-shaped curve (202–11). But if you define *trait* differently, there is a high correlation between creativity and mental disorders (211). This finding does not mean that all creative people are insane but that they tend to exhibit what Eysenck calls psychoticisms, the mental disorders associated with psychosis but not quite so extreme (213–23). He especially points to the link between creativity and schizophrenic thinking (227–31). In short, creative

people may be distinguished from the rest of us because they exhibit a greater tendency toward psychoticisms and elevated ego strength.

4. Indeed, philosopher Carl R. Hausman, who has written extensively on the concept of creativity, questions whether we can actually define creativity or the creative process outside its results: "an act that is considered creative must have as its outcome something that is new with respect to the way in which it is both intelligible and valuable" (381). The act is regarded as creative and therefore valuable only insofar as its outcome is regarded as creative and therefore valuable. This idea is echoed by many others who have thought about this issue. Albert Rothenberg says that "creativity is . . . the production of something that is both new and truly valuable" (*Creativity* 5). Donna Y. Ford and John J. Harris say that creativity "is verified through the uniqueness and utility of the product created" (187). John G. Young defines creativity as "the skill of bringing about something new and valuable" (79). (In each of these quotations, I have eliminated italics, either because the entire passage was italicized or because the author's emphasis was different from mine.)

   The natural extension of this commodification of creativity has been the development of the social science of creativity, which demands the ability to quantify creativity. The drive to quantify creativity is, I think, the most extreme instance of its commodification. The focus here is not just with the creative product itself, as the object that marks a creative act. It is possible to measure, for example, the degree of divergent thinking in the process or the various cognitive styles that characterize human thought (Guilford; Kirton). The results of these tests are new objects that represent the further objectification of creativity. The radical distinction between subject and object in the unilateral concept of creativity embedded in the Creator tradition has become more extreme in the modern era as what we consider creative objects becomes further removed from creative subjects.

5. See Feyerbend and Boyers for discussions of the way creativity has been defined by our culture. Both writers focus particularly on the elevation of *individual* creativity and both recommend looking to other cultures for alternative assumptions on which to base creativity.

6. Mason refers to this as the "creative tradition," thus distinguishing it from the Creator tradition. He uses this terminology because his larger argument is that it is this other tradition that actually better represents what we call creativity. My position is somewhat different. I contend that the Creator tradition has engendered its own very powerful conception of creativity, one that has dominated modernism. Neither tradition, then, can claim to possess *the* concept of creativity; rather, each tradition is characterized by its own version of that concept.

7. Postmodern philosopher Michel Serres points out that though *De Rerum Natura* has traditionally been interpreted as a metaphysical statement of the materiality of the soul—an argument that human beings are free of the needless fear of death promoted by religion—it should also be seen as a physics, a literal description of the world. He says that this physics, long forgotten in the history of science, has been recovered in the paradigm shift to the new science of chaos.

   > This world set adrift never to return is bestrewn, here and there, at indefi-nite times and in indefinite places, with pockets, where vortices are born in pseudo-returns. . . . The Lucretian world is globally entropic, but negatively entropic in certain swirling pockets. (116)

8. In Genesis, for example, Mason identifies several places where the Creator tradition of creativity is presented as antithetical to the archelogical tradition. The story of Adam and Eve represents a deeply held suspicion of sexuality and innovation as well as of the classic trickster character of the serpent. In the mortal dispute between Cain and Abel, it is God's preference for Abel's

sacrifice over Cain's, whose name may be interpreted as "smith" or "metal worker," that leads to the murder and the casting out of Cain and all his descendants. And the Tower of Babel provoked God's wrath because the skill and daring represented in building it symbolized a dangerous disobedience to God's authority as Creator (708–9). The broader cultural message is clear: archelogical creativity, with its potential for disrupting the order, is forbidden.

9. Alfred North Whitehead was not a theologian and, though he recognized that there were theological implications in his process philosophy, had no interest in developing them. Process theology, then, may be understood as an attempt to interpret Whitehead's philosophical writings as a formal theology. This theology has been associated primarily with Christian Protestant theologians, but it has played a role in other religions as well. For an interesting discussion of process theology in Judaism, for example, see Lubarsky and Griffin, *Jewish Theology and Process Thought*. The most accessible treatment of process theology is Cobb and Griffin's *Process Theology: An Introductory Exposition*.

10. For an elaboration of this process of the creation of every moment in time, see Beardslee 31–32; Cobb and Griffin 14–24; Suchocki 12–21; Whitehead, *Process* 519–33.

11. Suchocki admits, though, that few actual occasions involve such an awareness. This rarity is due to a tendency toward habitual engagements with experience but also to the dominance of negative prehensions of the past, which do not allow much opportunity for the positive possibilities from the divine, thus generating insufficient contrast (60–61).

12. Worsham's "The Question Concerning Invention" is an extended study of Heidegger on language and the potential in writing to experience Being.

13. Desmond takes his terminology from two of the many forms of love in ancient Greek, agape and eros, one a self-giving love and the other desire. Metaphysical mindfulness is doubly mediated; it is both and between these two forms of love. Metaphysical mindfulness, then, is a form of love.

14. McKeon and Miller did not necessarily reach these similar conclusions independently. Miller refers to McKeon's essay in her own article.

15. See Otto Dieter's excellent discussion of *stasis*. Dieter argues that the rhetorical doctrine of *stasis* is directly related to *stasis* in Aristotelian physics, the "space" between two physical movements, such as the point at which a pendulum changes directions. Dieter call *stasis* "a latent stage in the process of becoming. The two opposite, or contrary, *dynameis* . . . have come into contact with one another and are now 'together.' . . . Out of the *apophasis* as the material, the *kataphasis* as the formal principle constitutes the 'fetation' out of which the [rhetorical] controversy grows" (366). I see *stasis* as archelogical, the generative power of opposing forces in the creation of discourse. See also Carter, "*Stasis* and *Kairos.*"

16. Royer takes these contrastive terms from Louise Wetherbee Phelps's phenomenological analysis of her own writing process.

8. Definition: Should Writing Be Taught?

1. In a review of articles published in *College English* and *College Composition and Communication* since the publication of Vitanza's piece, I found only two that mentioned "Three Countertheses" and then only with a quick reference (see L. Carroll and Segal et al.). There was also a review by Stephen M. North which only briefly remarked on the radical nature of the piece.

2. A word on terminology: I have chosen to shift usage at this point from *ludic* to *deconstructive* because the latter is the term that Griffin and other reconstructive postmodernists typically use and because *de*construction and *re*construction capture so well, conceptually and stylistically, both the philosophical antithesis and the mutual relationship at work in these two interpretations of the postmodern.

Also, as Griffin's series title indicates, he tends to use the term *constructive* as a label for the other postmodernism. He does mention *revisionary* and *reconstructive* as alternative labels. Indeed, he says that this type of postmodernism "perhaps should have been officially dubbed '*re*constructive' to indicate more clearly that a deconstructive moment is presupposed" ("Introduction: Constructive" 1). That's the relationship I hope to capture in these two terms.

3. See, for example, Callicott and da Rocha; Ferré, *Being and Value* and *Knowing and Value;* Grant; Prakash.
4. See Freeman for a full treatment of Gorgias's argument (128–29).
5. It is important that I distinguish my treatment of the postmodern in composition from Barbara Couture's in *Toward a Phenomenological Rhetoric: Writing, Profession, and Altruism.* Though I admire the ideals Couture brings to her work, I believe that her response to postmodern relativism, establishing a phenomenological foundation for the truth, is untenable. It represents a return to a worldview that is, while attractive in a nostalgic way, very difficult now to accept. What is phenomenology a return to? From one perspective, it is a return to high modernism, a humanistic metaphysics designed to save Western philosophy (Leitch 33). Or perhaps, as Robert Sokolowski, an advocate of phenomenology, says, it "breaks out of modernity and permits a restoration of the convictions that animated ancient and medieval philosophy." From that perspective, it is a return to premodern philosophy in that it "understands reason as ordered toward truth" (202). My own project, however, accepts the critique of deconstructive postmodernism but attempts to find a productive worldview within postmodern relativism.
6. Though Vitanza doesn't include this subsection within his third counterthesis—he sees the entire counterthesis as relevant to composition—I will do so in mine.
7. For a discussion of the rhetorical implications of this type of speech and its relevance to our own work as scholars, see my "Scholarship as Rhetoric of Display."
8. This argument for the dissolution of the subject raises two questions: If the self exists only as an isolated occasion, where does the sense of the enduring self come from? How can we know anything beyond the solipsistic perception of the single, isolated moment? The answer to both questions lies in the process understanding of memory. Because we have assumed an enduring subject, we have also assumed that memory is simply a function of that self. An alternative assumption is that memory may be considered another form of nonsensory perception. Memory, then, merely gives the impression of an enduring subject. However, it also provides a way of linking the knowledge of one occasion with others, which counters accusations of solipsism without having to resort to the modernist idea of the subject ("Introduction: Construction" 23).
9. Griffin also describes a third mode of apprehending the external world, a direct, largely unconscious knowledge of entities outside the body. He accounts for this sort of perception by what is known as extrasensory perception. I have not included this mode here because it so rarely rises to consciousness ("Introduction: Constructive" 15–17, 23).
10. One of the best treatments of the possibility for such a productive relationship is in Louise Wetherbee Phelps's "Practical Wisdom and the Geography of Knowledge in Composition."
11. Joseph Petraglia's collection of essays, *Reconceiving Writing, Rethinking Writing Instruction,* makes an argument that we cannot teach general writing skills.

9. Value: A Heretical Ethics of Teaching Writing

1. Isocrates' claim to teach virtue is based on several crucial differences between his teaching and the Sophists'. Students can gain virtue through learning not

rules but more general precepts, not disputatious forensics but character-building political discourse, and not abstract philosophy but practical philosophy. See references in "Against the Sophists" and *Antidosis.*

2. See, for example, "Counterstatement."
3. This distinction between instrumental and intrinsic value is similar to the one I used in chapter 2. Hairston's point is that the good of teaching writing is *organic* to writing. This position has played a significant role in composition history. One way of looking at the process movement in the late 1960s and the 1970s is as a recognition of the value of the process itself coupled with a rejection of the instrumental "service" mentality that had long ruled composition as current-traditional rhetoric. The various values we attached to the writing process—self-actualization, learning, meaning making, discovery, knowing—were supposedly not ends derived from outside writing but by-products of the writing process, intrinsic to it. The virtue of teaching writing was captured in the very process of writing. This is, I believe, why Hairston's article is not really about ideology as much as it is about recapturing that sense of virtue located in writing itself. From her perspective, the left ideologues' approach represents a return of composition to a "service" course—serving as a means to externalized ends—which seriously demeans the virtue of teaching writing.
4. Indeed, I would say that no one in the field of composition has addressed his or her scholarly oeuvre as thoughtfully and candidly as Bizzell has in this introduction. It is an important statement from someone who has had a major impact on composition theory and pedagogy.
5. Another example may help to clarify the distinction I am drawing. Alan W. France describes the goal for his composition class as one in "which writing might become an active means to transform the existing social inequities of commodity capitalism" (593). In a telling passage, France spells out his assumptions about the *means* of achieving that end:

   > As teachers of introductory composition courses, we must of course give students the rhetorical means to achieve politically regressive as well as progressive aims. It's been my experience, however, that once a student understands the dialectics of argument, she or he has a hard time arguing in bad faith (i.e., for policies sustaining oppression, misery, hatred, etc.) *in public.* Bad faith is easier to maintain in theory than in praxis. (607)

   As Thomas G. O'Donnell observes, though, France's assumptions represent a clear instance of confusing ends and means. The seemingly value-neutral goal of providing students "the rhetorical means" hides his implicit political end, which is what is really driving the course (O'Donnell 427). I would also point out, following Bizzell, that keeping those political ends implicit and simply hoping to achieve them by putting students in a position in which they learn about and use rhetoric does *not* create a writing classroom based on instrumental ideological values. It is, indeed, very close to Hairston's faith in the process.
6. Carroll takes the term *Pomo Blues* from a presentation by Lester Faigley at the 1993 Conference on College Composition and Communication, San Diego.
7. Friend's pedagogy does seem to have a larger goal. At the end of the article, she points out that "postmodernism does not shield us from our responsibility to take part in, and engage our students in, conversations about justice and how to achieve it. On the contrary, Young extends to us an invitation to become agents of positive change—not just within our classrooms, but in the larger social world" (566). Clearly there is an agenda here that Vitanza would say was counter to postmodernism, just another foundationalism. The problem, of course, is how to define positive change without an end-state ethic and "right" answers to ethical problems.

8. Trimbur's accusation of antifoundationalist "text-based determinism" in this review stands in direct contrast to his description of a rehabilitated Marxism without its old economic determinism in another review, "The Politics of Radical Pedagogy: A Plea for 'A Dose of Vulgar Marxism.'"—an implicit contrast between postmodernist foundationalism and neo-Marxist antifoundationalism. In that latter review, Trimbur takes both postmodernism and post-Marxism to task for their tendency to slip easily into the thematization of discursive disjunctures of subjectivity while ignoring Marxist historicism and anticapitalist politics. One of the key problems with these approaches is that they tend to celebrate a "presentism," the belief that the postmodern has supplanted the old order while ignoring the continued woes of the dominance of capitalism (197). Vulgar Marxism, he says, is an attempt to rehabilitate a Marxist political agenda without tying it to economic determinism.
9. See also Hartshorne, "Creativity" 10.
10. Hartshorne points out that this sense of an ethical good as secondary to and derived from an aesthetic good means that the former is rather difficult to describe in detail ("Creativity" 10). The problem is to define an ethics that promotes the aesthetic good. Griffin says that the primacy of the aesthetic represents a shift from a morality of obedience to a morality of the creative experience ("Creativity" 80–81). This morality of creativity suggests an ethics that promotes the enjoyment associated with creativity. He offers such an ethics based on some of the principles of process theology. Panexperientialism suggests the intimate interconnectedness of all things, as contrasted to the modernist sense of the world as composed of objects. Action that is ethical reflects this interconnectedness in its desire to treat all entities of the world as beings that can experience the aesthetic good (82–83). Second, the dispersal of the isolated, independent, enduring self means that action that is ethical seeks an enjoyment of self and others that goes beyond the gratification of the ego. And third, the heretical God suggests that ethical action seeks not to dominate the world but to magnify the creativity and enjoyment of the world and itself (84–85). It is in this way that God embodies the good and thus provides a moral center for the universe. The aesthetic good that God embodies has moral implications insofar as action promotes an intensity and harmony of experience.
11. As I detailed it earlier, each occasion of self-creation consists of three forces: *(1)* the initial aim, the projection of God's ideal outcome for that occasion; *(2)* the objective content, the weight of all the preceding creative events that have an influence on the formation of the occasion; and *(3)* the subjective aim, the power exerted by the individual entity in that moment to create itself freely by finding its own balance between what has come before and the potential for newness vested in the initial aim.
12. Without God, process thought would represent existence as a series of distinct occurrences each of whose self-creation would be a product only of its objective aim, a negotiation among the collection of past occurrences. There would be no direction for positive growth and change. There would be no opportunity for the new, no sense of openness, of possibility, of hope. In other words, without God, the ethics of process thought would look much like the ethics of ludic postmodernism.
13. See Cobb and Griffin 52–54; L. Ford, "Divine Persuasion"; L. Ford, *Lure;* Hartshorne, *Whitehead's* 92; Lowe 25.
14. See Carter, "Ritual Functions"; Consigny; Rosenfield; Sullivan, "Closer," "Epideictic," *"Ethos," "Kairos"*; Walker.
15. For example, Perelman and Olbrechts-Tyteca say that the purpose of epideictic "is to increase the intensity of adherence to values held in common by the audience and speaker" (52). Bernard K. Duffy describes epideictic as "an instrument for reexamination and renewal of values" (82). Brian Vickers characterizes the role of epideictic as "reinforcing the norms of public morality" (55).

16. For a discussion of how this blend of fiction and truth works to create such a powerful vision, see my treatment of the funeral oration in Plato's *Menexenus,* "The Ritual Functions of Epideictic Rhetoric: The Case of Socrates' Funeral Oration."
17. I have explored the role of *stasis* and *kairos* in the rhetorical tradition elsewhere (see "*Stasis* and *Kairos*"). I first encountered this pedagogy in Lauer et al., *Four Worlds of Writing.* Another interesting approach may be found in Anderson.
18. There is an interesting parallel here to Plato's discussion of true rhetoric in *Phaedrus.* Plato dismissed as mere "niceties of the art" all those supposedly superficial elements of language that larded the rhetorical handbooks of his day, the proper arrangement and composition of the parts of a speech, the persuasive use of probabilities, the fine points of style, et cetera (135–36). But these "niceties" take on ethical import in the context of making the good desirable.
19. Helping students to achieve this respect for the good intrinsic to language is, of course, a tall order. I try to sensitize my students to this good by asking them to bring samples of language that they feel is coercive (which are not hard to find) and discussing how these samples make them feel and why. We also try to spot such abuses of language in our own speaking and writing, including mine.
20. As I discussed in chapter 7, the good that I portray is a reflection of a radically nondeterministic universe, encouraging students to see themselves as cocreators of knowledge, along with their professors and other students. This vision runs counter to the dominant model of students as passive consumers of predefined and predigested knowledge. The larger objective of this course, then, is to better enable them for this active participation and, in both the short and long term, to enable them to amplify their enjoyment of the experience of learning and thus to influence future moments for the good, increasing the intensity and harmony of future occasions.
21. Robert Connors documents the long, cyclical history of objections to composition over the last hundred or so years. A recent movement among composition theorists, informally known as the new abolitionists, represents only the latest challenge to the requirement, based primarily on the theoretical and empirical evidence that disputes the assumption that it is possible to teach general writing skills, the main assumption on which the requirement rests (Petraglia). This argument from impossibility takes on ethical implications as well: if the assumption on which the requirement is based is false, how is it ethically defensible for us to continue to require students to take composition?

    Another important contributor to this debate is Sharon Crowley, whose argument against composition is based on the unethical political and social impact of the course. More recently, an article by Roemer et al. offers a refutation to the major arguments for abolition, claiming that they have tended to be elitist and have undervalued the service potential of freshman composition. However, Roemer et al. make a crucial mistake that undermines their position. They begin by referring to contemporary abolitionists' argument as "against requiring first-year students to study composition" (377) but end up describing it as "simply doing away with that course" (390). I don't believe that doing away with the requirement necessarily means dismissing the course.

Works Cited

Acton, H. B. "Dialectical Materialism." *The Encyclopedia of Philosophy.* 1967.

Addison, Joanne, and Susan Hilligoss. "Technological Fronts: Lesbian Lives 'On-the-Line.'" *Feminist Cyberscapes: Mapping Gendered Academic Spaces.* Ed. Kristine Blair and Pamela Takayoshi. Stamford, CT: Ablex, 1999. 21–40.

Albright, John R. "God and the Pattern of Nature: A Physicist Considers Cosmology." *Christian Century* 109 (29 July–5 Aug. 1992): 711–14.

Alter, Robert. *Genesis: Translation and Commentary.* New York: Norton, 1996.

Anderson, Virginia. "Confrontational Teaching and Rhetorical Practice." *College Composition and Communication* 48 (May 1997): 197–214.

Andreasen, Nancy C. "Creativity and Mental Illness: Prevalence Rates in Writers and the First-Degree Relations." *American Journal of Psychiatry* 144 (1987): 88–92.

Aquinas, Thomas. *On the Eternity of the World and Selected Miscellaneous Texts.* Trans. Cyril Vollert. Milwaukee: Marquette UP, 1964. 19–73.

Aristotle. From *Rhetoric.* Bizzell and Herzberg 151–94.

———. *The Physics.* Vol. 2. Trans. Philip H. Wicksteed and Francis M. Cornford. London: Heinemann, 1952.

———. *Posterior Analytics.* Trans. Jonathon Barnes. Oxford: Clarendon, 1994.

Armstrong, Karen. *In the Beginning: A New Interpretation of Genesis.* New York: Knopf, 1996.

Arp, H. C., G. Burbidge, F. Hoyle, J. V. Narlikar, and N. C. Wickramasinghe. "The Extragalactic Universe: An Alternative View." *Nature* 346 (30 Aug. 1990): 807–12.

Arp, Halton. "Galaxy Creation in a Non-Big-Bang Universe." *Philosophy, Mathematics, and Modern Physics.* Ed. Enno Rudolph. New York: Springer, 1994.

Arthur, Chris. "Dialectic and Labour." *Dialectics and Method.* Vol. 1. Ed. John Mephram and David-Hillel Ruben. Atlantic Heights, NJ: Humanities, 1979. 87–116.

Bakhtin, Mikhail. From *Marxism and the Philosophy of Language.* Bizzell and Herzberg 928–44.

Balashov, Yuri. "Uniformitarianism in Cosmology: Background and Philosophical Implications of the Steady-State Theory." *Studies in Philosophy and the History of Philosophy* 25 (Dec. 1995): 933–58.

Barclay, William. *The Gospel of John*. Vol. 1. Edinburgh: Saint Andrew's, 1961.
Barnhart, Robert K., ed. *The Barnhart Dictionary of Etymology*. New York: Wilson, 1988.
Barrow, John D., and Frank J. Tipler. *The Anthropic Cosmological Principle*. Oxford: Clarendon, 1986.
Barth, Karl. *Church Dogmatics*. Edinburgh: Clark, 1960.
Bartholomae, David. "Inventing the University." *When a Writer Can't Write: Studies in Writer's Block and Other Composing Process*. Ed. Mike Rose. New York: Guilford, 1985.
———. "Writing Assignments: Where Writing Begins." *Fforum: Essays on Theory and Practice in the Teaching of Writing*. Upper Montclair, NJ: Boynton, 1983.
Basham, A. L. *The Wonder That Was India*. Calcutta: Rupa, 1967.
Beardslee, William A. *A House for Hope: A Study of Process and Biblical Thought*. Philadelphia: Westminster, 1972.
Becker, George. *The Mad Genius Controversy: A Study in the Sociology of Deviance*. Beverly Hills, CA: Sage, 1978.
Berlin, James A. "Composition and Cultural Studies." *Composition and Resistance*. Ed. C. Mark Hurlbert and Michael Blitz. Portsmouth, NH: Boynton, 1991. 47–55.
———. "Contemporary Composition: The Major Pedagogical Theories." *College English* 44 (Dec. 1982): 765–77.
———. "Poststructuralism, Cultural Studies, and the Composition Classroom: Postmodern Theory in Practice." *Rhetoric Review* 11 (Fall 1992): 16–33.
———. "Rhetoric and Ideology in the Writing Class." *College English* 50 (Sept. 1988): 477–94.
Bertans, Hans. *The Idea of the Postmodern: A History*. London: Routledge, 1995.
Berthoff, Ann E. *The Making of Meaning: Metaphors, Models and Maxims for Writing Teachers*. Upper Montclair, NJ: Boynton, 1981.
Bitzer, Lloyd. "Rhetorical Situations." *Philosophy and Rhetoric* 1 (1968): 1–14.
Bizzell, Patricia. *Academic Discourse and Critical Consciousness*. Pittsburgh: U of Pittsburgh P, 1992.
———. "Beyond Anti-Foundationalism to Rhetorical Authority: Problems Defining 'Cultural Literacy.'" Bizzell, *Academic* 256–76.
———. "Cognition, Convention, and Certainty: What We Need to Know about Writing." *PRE/TEXT* 3 (1982): 213–44.
Bizzell, Patricia, and Bruce Herzberg, eds. *The Rhetorical Tradition: Readings from Classical Times to the Present*. Boston: Bedford, 1990.
Boden, Margaret A. Introd. Boden, *Dimensions* 1–11.
———, ed. *Dimensions of Creativity*. Cambridge: MIT P, 1994.
Boorstin, Daniel J. *The Creators*. New York: Random, 1992.
Borg, Marcus J. *Reading the Bible Again for the First Time: Taking the Bible Seriously But Not Literally*. San Francisco: Harper, 2001.
Bowers, C. A. "Educational Implications of an Ecologically Centered View of Creativity." *Education Theory* 44 (Spring 1994): 159–71.
Brown, Richard Harvey. "Reconstructing Social Theory after the Postmodern Critique." *After Postmodernism: Reconstructing Ideology Critique*. Ed. Herbert W. Simons and Michael Billig. London: Sage, 1994. 12–37.
Brueggemann, Walter. *Genesis. Interpretation: A Bible Commentary for Teaching and Preaching*. Atlanta: Knox, 1982.
Bruffee, Kenneth. "Getting Starting." *The Territory of Language: Linguistics, Stylistics, and the Teaching of Composition*. McQuade 103–13.
———. "Social Construction, Language, and the Authority of Knowledge: A Bibliographical Essay." *College English* 48 (Dec. 1986): 773–90.

Brush, Stephen G. "How Cosmology Became a Science." *Scientific American* 267.2 (Aug. 1992): 62–70.

Burke, Kenneth. "De Beginnibus." *Reclaiming the Imagination: Philosophical Perspectives for Writers and Teachers of Writing.* Ed. Ann E. Berthoff. Upper Montclair, NJ: Boynton, 1984. 29–37.

———. *A Grammar of Motives* [published together with *A Rhetoric of Motives*]. Cleveland: Meridian, 1962.

———. *The Rhetoric of Religion: Studies in Logology.* Berkeley: U of California P, 1970.

Burwick, Frederick. *Poetic Madness and the Romantic Imagination.* University Park: Pennsylvania State UP, 1996.

Callicott, J. Baird, and Fernando J. R. da Rocha, eds. *Earth Summit Ethics: Toward a Reconstructive Postmodern Philosophy of Environmental Education.* Albany: State U of New York P, 1996.

Carroll, Lee Ann. "Pomo Blues: Stories from First-Year Composition." *College English* 59 (Dec. 1997): 916–33.

Carroll, William E. "Big Bang Cosmology, Quantum Tunneling from Nothing, and Creation." *Laval Théologique et Philosophique* 44 (Fall 1988): 59–75.

Carter, Michael. "Problem Solving Reconsidered: A Pluralistic Theory of Problems." *College English* 50 (1988): 551–65.

———. "The Ritual Functions of Epideictic Rhetoric: The Case of Socrates' Funeral Oration." *Rhetorica* 9 (Summer 1991): 209–32.

———. "Scholarship as Rhetoric of Display: Or, Why Is Everybody Saying All Those Terrible Things about Us?" *College English* 54 (Mar. 1992): 303–13.

———. "*Stasis* and *Kairos:* Principles of Social Construction in Classical Rhetoric." *Rhetoric Review* 7 (Fall 1988): 97–112.

Carver, Terrell. *Marx and Engels: The Intellectual Relationship.* Brighton: Wheatsheaf, 1983.

Cobb, John B., Jr. "Process Theology and the Present Church Struggle." *Introduction to Christian Theology: Contemporary North American Perspectives.* Ed. Roger A. Badham. Louisville: Westminster, 1998. 154–65.

Cobb, John B., Jr., and David Ray Griffin. *Process Theology: An Introductory Exposition.* Philadelphia: Westminster, 1976.

Coe, Richard M. "If Not to Narrow, Then How to Focus: Two Techniques for Focusing." *College Composition and Communication* 32 (Oct. 1981): 272–77.

Coleridge, Samuel Taylor. From *Biographia Literaria. The Norton Anthology of Literature.* Ed. M. H. Abrams. 4th ed. Vol. 2. New York: Norton, 1979.

Colletti, Lucio. "Marxism and the Dialectic." *New Left Review* 93 (1975): 3–29.

Connors, Robert J. "The New Abolitionism: Toward a Historical Background." Petraglia 3–26.

———. "The Rise and Fall of the Modes of Discourse." *College Composition and Communication* 32 (Dec. 1981): 444–63.

Consigny, Scot. "Gorgias's Use of the Epideictic." *Philosophy and Rhetoric* 25 (1992): 281–97.

Cooper, Marilyn M. "The Ecology of Writing." *College English* 48 (Apr. 1986): 364–75.

"Counterstatement." *College Composition and Communication* 44 (May 1993): 248–55.

Couture, Barbara. *Toward a Phenomenological Rhetoric: Writing, Profession, and Altruism.* Carbondale: Southern Illinois UP, 1998.

Craig, William Lane. "What Place, Then, for a Creator: Hawking on God and Creation." *British Journal for the Philosophy of Science* 41 (Dec. 1990): 473–91.

"Creation Account." *Encyclopedic Dictionary of Religion.* 1979.
"Creation Epic." *Encyclopedic Dictionary of Religion.* 1979.
Criss, R. E., and A. M. Hofmeister. "Thermodynamic Cosmology." *Geochimica et Cosmochimica Acta* 65 (1 Nov. 2001): 4077–85.
Cross, Geoffrey A. "A Bakhtinian Exploration of Factors Affecting the Collaborative Writing of an Executive Letter of an Annual Report." *Research in the Teaching of English* 24 (May 1990): 173–203.
Crowley, Sharon. "A Personal Essay on Freshman English." *PRE/TEXT* 12 (1991): 155–76.
Cumming, Robert Denoon. *Starting Point: An Introduction to the Dialectic of Existence.* Chicago: U of Chicago P, 1979.
Davis, D. Diane. *Breaking Up [at] Totality: A Rhetoric of Laughter.* Carbondale: Southern Illinois UP, 2000.
Dennett, Daniel C. *Darwin's Dangerous Idea: Evolution and the Meanings of Life.* New York: Simon, 1995.
Desmond, William. *Art and the Absolute: A Study of Hegel's Aesthetics.* Albany: State U of New York P, 1986.
———. *Being and the Between.* Albany: State U of New York P, 1995.
———. "Being Between." *Clio* 20 (1991): 305–31.
———. *Desire, Dialectic, and Otherness: An Essay on Origins.* New Haven: Yale UP, 1987.
———. *Philosophy and Its Others: Ways of Being and Mind.* Albany: State U of New York P, 1990.
Dewey, John. "Some Questions about Value." Lepley 4–12.
Dieter, Otto Alvin Loeb. "Stasis." *Speech Monographs* [now *Communication Monographs*] 17 (1950): 345–69.
Dillon, George L. *Constructing Texts: Elements of a Theory of Composition and Style.* Bloomington: Indiana UP, 1981.
Dobrin, Sidney I. "From Writing Processes to Cultural (Re)production: Composition's Theoretical Shift." Conference on College Composition and Communication. Chicago. 22 Mar. 2002.
Drees, Willem B. *Beyond the Big Bang.* La Salle, IL: Open Court, 1990.
Duffy, Bernard K. "The Platonic Functions of Epideictic Rhetoric." *Philosophy and Rhetoric* 16 (1983): 79–93.
Ebert, Theresa L. "The 'Difference' of Postmodern Feminism." *College English* 53 (Dec. 1991): 886–904.
———. "For a Red Pedagogy: Feminism, Desire, and Need." *College English* 58 (Nov. 1996): 795–819.
———. *Ludic Feminism and After: Postmodernism, Desire, and Labor in Late Capitalism.* Ann Arbor: U of Michigan P, 1996.
———. "Ludic Feminism, the Body, Performance, and Labor: Bringing *Materialism* Back into Feminist Cultural Studies." *Cultural Critique* 38 (Winter 1992–93): 5–50.
Ehrhardt, Arnold. *The Beginning.* New York: Barnes, 1968.
Elbow, Peter. *Embracing Contraries: Explorations in Learning and Teaching.* New York: Oxford UP, 1986.
———. *Writing Without Teachers.* London: Oxford UP, 1973.
Emig, Janet. "Writing as a Mode of Learning." *College Composition and Communication* 28 (May 1977): 122–28.
Eysenck, Hans J. "The Measurement of Creativity." Boden 199–242.
Faigley, Lester. "Competing Theories of Process: A Critique and a Proposal." *College English* 48 (Oct. 1986): 527–41.
———. *Fragments of Rationality: Postmodernity and the Subject of Composition.* Pittsburgh: U of Pittsburgh P, 1992.

Ferré, Frederick. *Being and Value: Toward a Constructive Postmodern Metaphysics.* Albany: State U of New York P, 1996.

———. *Knowing and Value: Toward a Constructive Postmodern Epistemology.* Albany: State U of New York P, 1998.

Fetz, Reto Luzius. "Creativity: A New Transcendental?" Rapp and Wiehl 189–207.

Feyerabend, Paul. "Creativity—A Dangerous Myth." *Critical Inquiry* 13 (1987): 700–11.

Filson, Floyd V. *The Layman's Bible Commentary.* Vol. 19. Richmond: Knox, 1963.

Flower, Linda. *Problem-Solving Strategies for Writing.* 3rd ed. San Diego: Harcourt, 1989.

Flower, Linda, and John R. Hayes. "The Cognition of Discovery: Defining a Rhetorical Problem." *College Composition and Communication* 31 (Feb. 1980): 21–32.

Flynn, Elizabeth A. "Rescuing Postmodernism." *College Composition and Communication* 48 (Dec. 1997): 540–55.

Ford, Donna Y., and J. John Harris III. "The Elusive Definition of Creativity." *Journal of Creative Behavior* 26 (Third Quarter 1992): 186–98.

Ford, Lewis S. "Contrasting Conceptions of Creation." *Review of Metaphysics* 45 (Spring 1991): 89–109.

———. "Creativity in a Future Key." *New Essays in Metaphysics.* Ed. Robert C. Neville. Albany: State U of New York P, 1987. 179–97.

———. "Divine Persuasion and the Triumph of Good." *Process Philosophy and Christian Thought.* Ed. Delwin Brown, Ralph E. James Jr., and Gene Reeves. Indianapolis: Bobbs, 1971. 287–304.

———. *The Lure of God: A Biblical Background for Process Theism.* Philadelphia: Fortress, 1978.

Foucault, Michel. "The Order of Discourse." *Untying the Text: A Poststructuralist Reader.* Ed. Robert Young. Boston: Routledge, 1981.

France, Alan W. "Assigning Places: The Function of Introductory Composition as a Cultural Discourse." *College English* 55 (Oct. 1993): 593–609.

Frankena, William K. "Value and Valuation." *The Encyclopedia of Philosophy.* 1967.

Freeman, Kathleen. *Ancilla to the Pre-Socratics: A Complete Translation of the Fragments in Diels,* Fragmente der Vorsokratiker. Cambridge: Harvard UP, 1948.

Friend, Christy. "Ethics in the Writing Classroom: A Nondistributive Approach." *College English* 56 (Sept. 1994): 548–67.

Garnett, A. Campbell. "Intrinsic Good: Its Definition and Referent." Lepley 78–92.

Gelpi, Donald L. *Varieties of Transcendental Experience: A Study in Constructive Postmodernism.* Collegeville, MN: Liturgical, 2000.

Gier, Nicholas F. *Spiritual Titanism: Indian, Chinese, and Western Perceptions.* Albany: State U of New York P, 2000.

Gilboa, R. *Intercourses in the Book of Genesis: Mythic Motifs in Creator-Created Relationships.* Sussex, Eng.: Book Guild, 1998.

Gleick, James. *Chaos: Making a New Science.* New York: Viking, 1987.

Gouldner, Alvin W. *The Two Marxisms: Contradictions and Anomalies in the Development of Theory.* New York: Seabury, 1980.

Grant, Don Sherman. "Religion and the Left: The Prospects of a Green Coalition." *Environmental Ethics* 19 (1997): 115–34.

Griffin, David Ray. "Creativity in Post-Modern Religion." Mitias 64–85.

———. "Introduction: Constructive Postmodern Philosophy." Griffin et al. 1–31.

———. Introd. to SUNY Series in Constructive Postmodern Thought. Griffin et al. vii–x.

———. "Postmodern Theology and A/Theology: A Response to Mark C. Taylor." *Varieties of Postmodern Theology.* Ed. David Ray Griffin. Albany: State U of New York P, 1989. 25–56.

Griffin, David Ray, John B. Cobb Jr., Marcus P. Ford, Pete A. Y. Gunter, and Peter Ochs, eds. *Founders of Constructive Postmodern Philosophy: Peirce, James, Bergson, Whitehead, and Hartshorne.* Albany: State U of New York P, 1993.

Guilford, J. P. "Varieties of Divergent Production." *Journal of Creative Behavior* 18 (1984): 1–10.

Guthrie, W. K. C. *A History of Greek Philosophy.* 6 vols. Cambridge: Cambridge UP, 1962.

Hairston, Maxine. "Diversity, Ideology, and Teaching Writing." *College Composition and Communication* 43 (May 1992): 179–93.

———. "The Winds of Change: Thomas Kuhn and the Revolution in the Teaching of Writing." *College Composition and Communication* 33 (Feb. 1982): 76–88.

Hall, Ronald. "Dialectic." *The Encyclopedia of Philosophy.* 1967.

Hannay, Alastair. *Kierkegaard.* London: Routledge, 1982.

Harkin, Patricia, and John Schilb, eds. *Contending with Words: Composition and Rhetoric in a Postmodern Age.* New York: MLA, 1991.

Harper's Bible Commentary. San Francisco: Harper, 1988.

Harris, Errol E. *Formal, Transcendental, and Dialectical Thinking: Logic and Reality.* Albany: State U of New York P, 1987.

Hartshorne, Charles. "Creativity as a Value and Creativity as a Transcendental Category." Mitias 3–11.

———. *Whitehead's Philosophy: Selected Essays 1935–1970.* Lincoln: U of Nebraska P, 1972.

Hausman, Carl R. "Philosophical Perspectives on the Study of Creativity." Isaksen 380–89.

Hawking, Stephen W. *A Brief History of Time: From the Big Bang to Black Holes.* Toronto: Bantam, 1988.

Hayles, N. Katherine. "Introduction: Complex Dynamics in Literature and Science." Hayles, *Chaos* 1–33.

———, ed. *Chaos and Disorder: Complex Dynamics in Literature and Science.* Chicago: U of Chicago P, 1991.

Hegel, Georg Wilhelm Friedrich. *Encyclopedia of Philosophy.* Trans. Gustav Emil Mueller. New York: Philosophical Library, 1959.

———. *Hegel's Philosophy of Right.* Trans. T. M. Knox. Oxford: Clarendon, 1942.

———. *Hegel's Science of Logic.* Trans. A. V. Miller. London: Allen, 1964.

———. *The Philosophy of History.* Trans. J. Sibree. New York: Co-operative Pub. Soc., 1900.

Hepburn, Ronald W. "The Religious Doctrine of Creation." *The Encyclopedia of Philosophy.* 1967.

Hilbert, Betsy S. "It Was a Dark and Nasty Night It Was a Dark and You Would Not Believe How Dark It Was a Hard Beginning." *College Composition and Communication* 43 (Feb. 1992): 75–80.

Humphreys, W. Lee. *Crisis and Story: An Introduction to the Old Testament.* 2nd ed. Mountain View, CA: Mayfield, 1990.

Hunt, Ian. *Analytical and Dialectical Marxism.* Aldershot, Eng.: Avebury, 1993.

Hurlbutt, Robert H., III. *Hume, Newton, and the Design Argument.* Lincoln: U of Nebraska P, 1963.

Hyers, M. Conrad. *The Meaning of Creation: Genesis and Modern Science.* Atlanta: Knox, 1984.

The Interpreter's Bible. Vol. 8. New York: Abington, 1952. 12 vols.
Isaksen, Scott G., *Frontiers of Creativity Research: Beyond the Basics*. Buffalo, NY: Bearly Limited, 1987.
Isocrates. "Against the Sophists." Bizzell and Herzberg 46–49.
———. From *Antidosis*. Bizzell and Herzberg 50–54.
Jaki, Stanley L. *Cosmos and Creator*. Edinburgh: Scottish Academic, 1980.
"Janus." *Encyclopedia Britannica*. 15th ed. 1978.
Juncker, Clara. "Writing (with) Cixous." *College English* 50 (Apr. 1988): 424–36.
Kainz, Howard P. *Paradox, Dialectic, and System: A Contemporary Reconstruction of the Hegelian Problematic*. University Park: Pennsylvania State UP, 1988.
Kant, Immanuel. *Immanuel Kant's Critique of Pure Reason*. Trans. Norman Kemp Smith. New York: St. Martin's, 1965.
Kellert, Stephen H. *In the Wake of Chaos: Unpredictable Order in Dynamical Systems*. Chicago: U of Chicago P, 1993.
Kennedy, George A. *Aristotle on Rhetoric: A Theory of Civic Discourse*. New York: Oxford UP, 1991.
Kent, Thomas. Introd. *Post-Process Theory: Beyond the Writing-Process Paradigm*. Ed. Thomas Kent. Carbondale: Southern Illinois UP, 1999. 1–6.
———. *Paralogic Rhetoric: A Theory of Communicative Interaction*. Lewisburg: Bucknell UP, 1993.
Kirton, Michael J. "Adaptors and Innovators: Cognitive Style and Personality." Isaksen 282–304.
Koestler, Arthur. *The Act of Creation*. New York: Macmillan, 1964.
———. *Janus: A Summing Up*. New York: Random, 1978.
Laib, Nevin K. *Rhetoric and Style*. Englewood Cliffs, NJ: Prentice, 1993.
Laszlo, Ervin. *The Age of Bifurcation: Understanding the Changing World*. Philadelphia: Gordon, 1991.
Lauer, Janice M. "Writing as Inquiry: Some Questions for Teachers." *College Composition and Communication* 33 (Feb. 1982): 89–93.
Lauer, Janice M., Gene Montague, Andrea Lunsford, and Janet Emig. *Four Worlds of Writing*. 2nd ed. Cambridge, MA: Harper, 1985.
Leggo, Carl. "Questions I Need to Ask Before I Advise My Students to Write in Their Own Voices." *Rhetoric Review* 10 (Feb. 1991): 143–52.
Leitch, Vincent B. *Postmodernism—Local Effects, Global Flows*. Albany: State U of New York P, 1996.
Lepley, Ray, ed. *Value: A Cooperative Inquiry*. New York: Columbia UP, 1949.
Lerner, Eric J. *The Big Bang Never Happened*. New York: Times, 1991.
Linde, Andrei D. "Particle Physics and Inflationary Cosmology." *Physics Today* 40.9 (Sept. 1987): 61–68.
Liu, Hongya, and Paul S. Wesson. "Universe Models with a Variable Cosmological 'Constant' and a 'Big Bounce.'" *Astrophysical Journal* 562 (20 Nov. 2001): 1–2.
Loewenstein, Julius I. *Marx Against Marxism*. Trans. Harry Drost. London: Routledge, 1980.
Lombroso, Cesare. *The Man of Genius*. London: Scott, 1891.
Long, Charles H. "Cosmogony." *The Encyclopedia of Religion*. 1987.
Lorenz, Edward N. *The Essence of Chaos*. Seattle: U of Washington P, 1993.
Lotto, Edward. "Utterance and Text in Freshman English." *College English* 51 (Nov. 1989): 677–87.
Lowe, Victor. *Understanding Whitehead*. Baltimore: Johns Hopkins UP, 1962.
Lu, Min-zhan. "Conflict and Struggle: The Enemies or Precondition of Basic Writing?" *College English* 54 (Dec. 1992): 887–913.
———. "From Silence to Words: Writing as Struggle." *College English* 49 (Apr. 1987): 437–47.

Lubarsky, Sandra B., and David Ray Griffin. *Jewish Theology and Process Thought*. Albany: State U of New York P, 1996.

Lucretius. *The Way Things Are: The* De Rerum Natura *of Titus Lucretius Carus*. Trans. Rolfe Humphries. Bloomington: Indiana UP, 1968.

Ludwig, Arnold M. "Reflections on Creativity and Madness." *American Journal of Psychotherapy* 43 (Jan. 1989): 4–14.

Macrorie, Ken. *Telling Writing*. 3rd ed. Rochelle Park, NJ: Hayden, 1980.

Maddox, John. "Down with the Big Bang." *Nature* 340 (10 Aug. 1989): 425.

Markov, M. A. "Some Remarks on the Problem of the Very Early Universe." *The Very Early Universe*. Ed. G. W. Gibbons, S. W. Hawking, and S. T. C. Siklos. Cambridge: Cambridge UP, 1983.

Marx, Karl. *Capital: A Critique of Political Economy*. Trans. Samuel Moore and Edward Aveling. New York: Modern Library, 1906.

———. *Karl Marx: Selected Writings*. Ed. David McLellan. Oxford: Oxford UP, 1977.

Marx, Karl, and Frederick Engels. *Collected Works*. Vol. 3. New York: International, 1975.

Mason, John Hope. "The Character of Creativity: Two Traditions." *History of European Ideas* 9 (1988): 697–715.

McCrimmon, James M. *Writing with a Purpose*. 3rd ed. New York: Houghton, 1963.

McKelway, Alexander J. *The Systematic Theology of Paul Tillich: A Review and Analysis*. Richmond: Knox, 1964.

McKeon, Richard. "Creativity and the Commonplace." *Rhetoric: Essays in Invention and Discovery*. Ed. Mark Backman. Woodbridge, CT: Oxbow, 1987. 25–36.

McQuade, Donald A., ed. *The Territory of Language: Linguistics, Stylistics, and the Teaching of Composition*. Carbondale: Southern Illinois UP, 1986.

Miller, Carolyn R. "The Aristotelian Topos: Hunting for Novelty." *Rereading Aristotle's Rhetoric*. Ed. Alan G. Gross and Arthur E. Walzer. Carbondale: Southern Illinois UP, 2000. 130–46.

Miller, David Lee. *Philosophy of Creativity*. New York: Lang, 1989.

Mitchell, William C. *The Cult of the Big Bang: Was There a Bang?* Carson City, NV: Cosmic Sense, 1995.

Mitias, Michael H., ed. *Creativity in Art, Religion, and Culture*. Amsterdam: Rodopi, 1985.

Monsma, John Clover, ed. *The Evidence of God in an Expanding Universe*. New York: Putnam, 1958.

Murphy, Nancey. *Anglo-American Postmodernity: Philosophical Perspectives on Science, Religion, and Ethics*. Boulder, CO: Westview, 1997.

Murray, Donald M. "Write Before Writing." *College Composition and Communication* 29 (Dec. 1978): 375–82.

———. *Writing to Learn*. New York: Holt, 1984.

Narlikar, Jayant V. "The Concepts of 'Beginning' and 'Creation' in Cosmology." *Philosophy of Science* 59 (Sept. 1992): 361–71.

Neel, Jasper. Rev. of *Fragments of Rationality: Postmodernity and the Subject of Composition*, ed. Patricia Harkin and John Schilb. *Rhetoric Review* 12 (Fall 1993): 198–204.

Neville, Robert C. *God the Creator: On the Transcendence and Presence of God*. Chicago: U of Chicago P, 1968.

———. *Reconstruction of Thinking*. Albany: State U of New York P, 1981.

North, Stephen M. Rev. of *Contending with Words: Composition and Rhetoric in a Postmodern Age*, ed. Patricia Harkin and John Schilb. *College Composition and Communication* 43 (Dec. 1992): 532–34.

———. *The Making of Knowledge in Composition: Portrait of an Emerging Field.* Upper Montclair, NJ: Boynton, 1987.

Nozick, Robert. *Philosophical Explanations.* Cambridge, MA: Harvard UP, 1981.

Ochse, R. "The Relation Between Creative Genius and Psychopathology: A Historical Perspective and a New Explanation." *South African Journal of Psychology* 21 (1991): 45–53.

Odenwald, Sten F. "A Modern Look at the Origin of the Universe." *Zygon* 25 (Mar. 1990): 25–45.

O'Donnell, Thomas G. "Politics and Ordinary Language: A Defense of Expressivist Rhetorics." *College English* 58 (Apr. 1996): 423–39.

Olson, David R. "From Utterance to Text: The Bias of Language in Speech and Writing." *Harvard Educational Review* 47 (1977): 257–81.

Olsson, Robert G. "Teleological Ethics." *The Encyclopedia of Philosophy.* 1967.

Onions, C. T. *The Oxford Dictionary of English Etymology.* Oxford: Clarendon, 1966.

Owen, G. E. L. *Logic, Science, and Dialectic.* Ithaca, NY: Cornell UP, 1986.

Pannenberg, Wolfhart. "Theology and Science." *Princeton Seminary Bulletin* 13 (1992): 299–310.

Parker, Dewitt H. *The Philosophy of Value.* New York: Greenwood, 1968.

Partridge, Eric. *Origins: A Short Etymological Dictionary of Modern English.* New York: Macmillan, 1966.

Paull, Michael, and Jack Klingerman. *Invention: A Course in Pre-Writing and Composition.* Cambridge, MA: Winthrop, 1973.

Pepper, Stephen C. *The Sources of Value.* Berkeley: U of California P, 1958.

Perelman, Chaim, and Lucie Olbrechts-Tyteca. *The New Rhetoric.* Trans. John Wilkinson and Purcell Weaver. Notre Dame: U of Notre Dame P, 1969.

Perl, Sondra. "Understanding Composing." *College Composition and Communication* 31 (Dec. 1980): 363–69.

Perl, Sondra, and Arthur Egendorf. "The Process of Creative Discovery: Theory, Research, and Implications for Teaching." McQuade 251–68.

Petraglia, Joseph, ed. *Reconceiving Writing, Rethinking Writing Instruction.* Mahwah, NJ: Erlbaum, 1995.

Phelps, Louise Wetherbee. "Practical Wisdom and the Geography of Knowledge in Composition." *College English* 53 (Dec. 1991): 863–85.

Pinkard, Terry. *Hegel's Dialectic.* Philadelphia: Temple UP, 1988.

Plato. *Gorgias.* Bizzell and Herzberg 61–112.

———. *Ion.* Phaedrus, Ion, Gorgias, *and* Symposium, *with Passages from* The Republic *and* Laws. Oxford: Oxford UP, 1938.

———. *Phaedrus.* Bizzell and Herzberg 113–43.

Polkinghorne, John. *Belief in God in an Age of Science.* New Haven: Yale UP, 1998.

———. "Chaos and Cosmos: A Theological Approach." *Chaos: The New Science.* Lanham, MD: UP of America, 1993. 105–17.

———. *Science and Creation: The Search for Understanding.* London: SCM, 1988.

Porter, James E. "Developing a Postmodern Ethics of Rhetoric and Composition." *Defining the New Rhetorics.* Ed. Theresa Enos and Stuart C. Brown. Newbury Park, CA: Sage, 1993. 207–26.

———. "Intertextuality and the Discourse Community." *Rhetoric Review* 5 (Fall 1995): 34–45.

Porush, David. "Fiction as Dissipative Structures: Prigogine's Theory and Postmodernism's Roadshow." Hayles, *Chaos* 54–84.

Powell, Corey S. "The Golden Age of Cosmology." *Scientific American* 267.1 (July 1992): 17–22.

Prakash, Madhu Suri. "The Beginning of Justice: Ending Global Education and the Assumption of Scarcity." *Philosophy of Education* 49 (1994): 404–8.

Prentky, R. A. *Creativity and Psychopathology: A Neurocognitive Perspective.* New York: Praeger, 1980.

Prigogine, Ilya, and Isabelle Stengers. *Order out of Chaos: Man's New Dialogue with Nature.* Toronto: Bantam, 1984.

———. "Postface: Dynamics from Leibnez to Lucretius." *Hermes: Literature, Science, Philosophy.* Ed. Josué V. Harari and David F. Bell. Baltimore: Johns Hopkins UP, 1982.

Puccio, Gerrard J. "William Duff's Eighteenth Century Examination of Original Genius and Its Relationship to Contemporary Creativity Research." *Journal of Creative Behavior* 25 (First Quarter 1991): 1–10.

Ramban: Commentary on the Torah. Trans. Charles B. Chavel. New York: Shilo, 1971.

Rapp, Friedrich, and Reiner Wiehl, eds. *Whitehead's Metaphysics of Creativity.* Albany: State U of New York P, 1990.

Recchio, Thomas E. "On Composing Ethnographically: Strategies for Enacting Authority in Writing." *Rhetoric Review* 10 (Fall 1991): 131–42.

Reese, William L. "Creation." *Dictionary of Philosophy and Religion.* Atlantic Highlands, NJ: Humanities, 1980.

Reither, James A. "Writing and Knowing: Toward Redefining the Writing Process." *College English* 47 (Oct. 1985): 620–28.

Rescher, Nicholas. *Dialectics: A Controversy-Oriented Approach to the Theory of Knowledge.* Albany: State U of New York P, 1977.

Reynolds, Nedra. "Interrupting Our Way to Agency: Feminist Cultural Studies and Composition." *Feminism and Composition Studies.* Ed. Susan C. Jarratt and Lynn Worsham. New York: MLA, 1998. 58–73.

Rhook, Greame, and Mark Zangari. "Should We Believe the Big Bang? A Critique of the Integrity of Modern Cosmology." *Proceedings of the Biennial Meetings of the Philosophy of Science Association* 1 (1994): 228–37.

Ritchie, Joy S. "Beginning Writers: Diverse Voices and Individual Identity." *College Composition and Communication* 40 (May 1989): 855–67.

Roemer, Marjorie, Lucille M. Schultz, and Russel K. Durst. "Reframing the Great Debate on First-Year Writing." *College Composition and Communication* 50 (Feb. 1999): 377–92.

Rohman, D. Gordon. "Pre-Writing: The Stage of Discovery in the Writing Process." *College Composition and Communication* 16 (May 1965): 106–12.

Rosen, Menahem. *Problems of the Hegelian Dialectic: Dialectic Reconstructed as a Logic of Human Reality.* Dordrecht, Neth.: Kluwer, 1992.

Rosenfield, Lawrence W. "The Practical Celebration of Epideictic." *Rhetoric in Transition.* University Park: Pennsylvania State UP, 1980. 31–55.

Rothenberg, Albert. "Creative Contradictions." *Psychology Today* 17 (June 1979): 54–62.

———. *Creativity and Madness: New Findings and Old Stereotypes.* Baltimore: Johns Hopkins UP, 1989.

Rouzie, Albert. "Beyond the Dialectic of Work and Play: A Serio-Ludic Rhetoric for Composition Studies." *Journal of Advanced Composition* 20 (Summer 2000): 627–58.

Royer, Daniel J. "Creative Experience and the Problem with Invention on Demand." Petraglia 161–78.

Rozental, I. L. *Big Bang Big Bounce: How Particles and Fields Drive Cosmic Evolution.* Trans. Juri Estrin. Berlin: Springer, 1988.

Ruf, Frederick J. *The Creation of Chaos: William James and the Stylistic Making of a Disorderly World.* Albany: State U of New York P, 1991.

Russell, Robert John. "Contingency in Physics and Cosmology: A Critique of the Theology of Wolfhart Pannenberg." *Zygon* 23 (Mar. 1988): 23–43.

Saa, A., E. Gunzig, L. Brenig, V. Faraoni, T. M. Rocha Filho, and A. Figueiredo. "Superinflation, Quintessence, and the Avoidance of the Initial Singularity." *International Journal of Theoretical Physics* 40 (Dec. 2001): 2295–307.

Said, Edward W. *Beginnings: Intention and Method*. New York: Basic, 1975.

Schiralli, Martin. *Constructive Postmodernism: Toward a Renewal in Cultural and Literary Studies*. Westport, CT: Bergin, 1999.

Schroeder, Gerald L. *Genesis and the Big Bang: The Discovery of Harmony Between Modern Science and the Bible*. New York: Bantam, 1990.

Segal, Judy, Anthony Paré, Doug Brent, and Douglas Vipond. "The Researcher as Missionary: Problems with Rhetoric and Reform in the Disciplines." *College Composition and Communication* 50 (Sept. 1998): 71–90.

Seitz, James. "Composition's Misunderstanding of Metaphor." *College Composition and Communication* 42 (Oct. 1991): 288–98.

———. "Roland Barthes, Reading, and Roleplay." *College English* 53 (Nov. 1991): 815–25.

Serres, Michel. "Lucretius: Science and Religion." *Hermes: Literature, Science, Philosophy*. Ed. Josué V. Harari and David F. Bell. Baltimore: Johns Hopkins UP, 1982. 98–124.

Sheard, Cynthia Miecznikowski. "The Public Value of Epideictic Rhetoric." *College English* 58 (Nov. 1996): 765–94.

Sherover-Marcuse, Erica. *Emancipation and Consciousness: Dogmatic and Dialectical Perspectives in the Early Marx*. Oxford: Blackwell, 1986.

Singer, Peter. *Hegel*. Oxford: Oxford UP, 1983.

Slevin, James F. "Interpreting and Composing: The Many Resources of Kind." *The Writer's Mind: Writing as a Mode of Thinking*. Ed. Janice N. Hays, Phyllis A. Roth, Jon R. Ramsey, and Robert D. Foulke. Urbana, IL: NCTE, 1983. 197–210.

Sloyan, Gerard S. *Interpretation: A Bible Commentary for Teaching and Preaching—John*. Atlanta: Knox, 1973.

Smith, Jeff. "Students' Goals, Gatekeeping, and Some Questions of Ethics." *College English* 59 (Mar. 1997): 299–320.

Smith, Norman Kemp. *A Commentary to Kant's Critique of Pure Reason*. New York: Humanities, 1950.

Smith, Paul. *Discerning the Subject*. Minneapolis: U of Minnesota P, 1988.

Smith, Quentin. "A Big Bang Cosmological Argument for God's Nonexistence." *Faith and Philosophy* 9 (Apr. 1992): 217–37.

Sokolowski, Robert. *Introduction to Phenomenology*. Cambridge: Cambridge UP, 2000.

Sommers, Nancy. "Between the Drafts." *College Composition and Communication* 43 (Feb. 1992): 23–31.

———. "Revision Strategies of Student Writers and Experienced Adult Writers." *College Composition and Communication* 31 (Dec. 1980): 378–88.

Spellmeyer, Kurt. "Foucault and the Freshman Writer: Considering the Self in Discourse." *College English* 51 (Nov. 1989): 715–24.

Steenburg, David. "Chaos at the Marriage of Heaven and Hell." *Harvard Theological Review* 84 (1991): 447–66.

Suchocki, Marjorie Hewitt. *God Christ Church: A Practical Guide to Process Theology*. New York: Crossroad, 1982.

Sullivan, Dale L. "A Closer Look at Education as Epideictic Rhetoric." *Rhetoric Society Quarterly* 23 (1993): 70–89.

———. "The Epideictic Character of Rhetorical Criticism." *Rhetoric Review* 11 (1993): 339–49.

———. "The *Ethos* of Epideictic Encounter." *Philosophy and Rhetoric* 26 (1993): 113–33.

———. "*Kairos* and the Rhetoric of Belief." *Quarterly Journal of Speech* 78 (1992): 317–32.
Taylor, Mark C. *Erring: A Postmodern A/Theology.* Chicago: U of Chicago P, 1986.
Tilley, Terrence W., and Craig Westman. "David Ray Griffin and Constructive Postmodern Communalism." *Postmodern Theologies: The Challenge of Religious Diversity.* Ed. Terrence W. Tilley. Maryknoll, NY: Orbis, 1995. 17–27.
Tillich, Paul. *Systematic Theology.* Vol. 2. Chicago: U of Chicago P, 1957.
The Torah: A Modern Commentary. New York: Union of Amer. Hebrew Congregations, 1981.
Toulmin, Stephen. *The Uses of Argument.* Cambridge: Cambridge UP, 1958.
Towner, W. Sibley. *Genesis.* Louisville: Westminster, 2001.
Trimbur, John. "The Politics of Radical Pedagogy: A Plea for 'A Dose of Vulgar Marxism.'" *College English* 56 (Feb. 1994): 194–206.
———. "Taking the Social Turn: Teaching Writing Post-Process." *College Composition and Communication* 45 (Feb. 1994): 108–18.
Vickers, Brian. *In Defense of Rhetoric.* Oxford: Clarendon, 1988.
Vitanza, Victor J. "Three Countertheses: Or, A Critical In(ter)vention into Composition Theories and Pedagogies." Harkin and Schilb 139–72.
Vollert, Cyril. Translator's introd. *On the Eternity of the World and Selected Miscellaneous Texts.* By Thomas Aquinas. Milwaukee: Marquette UP, 1964. 2–18.
Von Rad, Gerhard. *Genesis: A Commentary.* Trans. John H. Marks. London: SCM, 1961.
Walker, Jeffrey: "Aristotle's Lyric: Re-Imagining the Rhetoric of Epideictic." *College English* 51 (1989): 5–28.
Ward, Graham. *The Postmodern God: A Theological Reader.* Malden, MA: Blackwell, 1997.
———. "Postmodern Theology." *The Modern Theologians: An Introduction to Christian Theology in the Twentieth Century.* 2nd ed. Ed. David F. Ford. Cambridge, MA: Blackwell, 1997. 585–601.
Warren, Scott. *The Emergence of Dialectical Theory: Philosophy and Political Inquiry.* Chicago: U of Chicago P, 1984.
Weekley, Ernest. *An Etymological Dictionary of Modern English.* Vol. 1. New York: Dover, 1967.
Welch, Kathleen E. "Dialectic/Rhetoric/Writing." *Learning from the Histories of Rhetoric.* Ed. Theresa Enos. Carbondale: Southern Illinois UP, 1993. 133–43.
Welch, Nancy. "Resisting the Faith: Conversion, Resistance, and the Training of Teachers." *College English* 55 (Apr. 1993): 387–401.
Westermann, Claus. *Creation.* Trans. John H. Scullion. Philadelphia: Fortress, 1974.
Whitehead, Alfred North. *Adventures of Ideas.* New York: Macmillan, 1933.
———. *Process and Reality: An Essay in Cosmology.* New York: Macmillan, 1929.
Wilde, Lawrence. "Logic: Dialectic and Contradiction." *The Cambridge Companion to Marx.* Ed. Terrell Carver. Cambridge: Cambridge UP, 1991. 275–95.
———. *Marx and Contradiction.* Aldershot, Eng.: Avebury, 1989.
Wilkerson, T. E. *Kant's Critique of Pure Reason: A Commentary for Students.* Oxford: Clarendon, 1976.
Wilson, Matthew. "Writing History: Textbooks, Heuristics, and the Eastern European Revolutions of '89." *College English* 54 (Oct. 1992): 662–80.
Worsham, Lynn. "The Question Concerning Invention: Hermeneutics and the Genesis of Writing." *PRE/TEXT* 8 (1987): 197–244.

———. "Writing Against Writing: The Predicament of *Ecriture Féminine* in Composition Studies." Harkin and Schilb 82–104.

Yorke, James A., and Tien-Yien Li. "Period Three Implies Chaos." *American Mathematical Monthly* 82 (1975): 985–92.

Young, John G. "What Is Creativity?" *Journal of Creative Behavior* 19 (Second Quarter 1985): 77–87.

Young, Norman. *Creator, Creation, and Faith*. Philadelphia: Westminster, 1976.

Young, Richard E. "Invention." *Encyclopedia of Rhetoric and Composition*. Ed. Theresa Enos. New York: Garland, 1996. 349–55.

Young, Richard E., Alton L. Becker, and Kenneth L. Pike. *Rhetoric: Discovery and Change*. New York: Harcourt, 1970.

Index

Michael Carter teaches writing and rhetoric at North Carolina State University where he founded and is now the associate director of the Campus Writing and Speaking Program. His scholarship in writing theory and rhetorical history has appeared in *College English, College Composition and Communication, Rhetorica,* and *Rhetoric Review.* He teaches a wide variety of courses, including first-year composition on a regular basis, the analysis of style, the essay, composition theory, and science writing on both undergraduate and graduate levels. His recent work has focused on an exploration of classroom genres, including a National Science Foundation–funded project on teaching the laboratory report in science classes.